Swedish Design

A History

Lasse Brunnström

BLOOMSBURY VISUAL ARTS

LONDON · NEW YORK · OXFORD · NEW DELHI · SYDNEY

BLOOMSBURY VISUAL ARTS
Bloomsbury Publishing Plc
50 Bedford Square, London, WC1B 3DP, UK
1385 Broadway, New York, NY 10018, USA

BLOOMSBURY, BLOOMSBURY VISUAL ARTS and the Diana logo are trademarks of
Bloomsbury Publishing Plc

First published in Great Britain 2019

A catalogue record for this book is available from the British Library.

A catalog record for this book is available from the Library of Congress.

ISBN: HB: 978-1-3500-0011-7
        PB: 978-1-3500-0015-5
        ePDF: 978-1-3500-0013-1
        ePub: 978-1-3500-0014-8

Typeset by Integra Software Services Pvt. Ltd.
Printed and bound in Great Britain

To find out ~~more~~ ... ~~books visit www.~~ ... ~~bloomsb~~ury.com and ~~sign up for our newsletters.~~

Swedish Design

Contents

List of Plates

1 The rapid urbanization associated with the rise of industrialization gave the large joineries the opportunity to supply all kinds of prefabricated buildings. Ekmans Snickerifabrik's 1890 catalogue presented, among other things, a simple church in the then-popular Gothic Revival style. The church was sold to several locations in the upper part of Norrland.

2 The early twentieth century was the golden era for the building of the large bank palaces. The picture shows a detail of the lavish entrance to the Skåne enskilda bank (Skåne individual bank) on the corner of Fredsgatan and Drottningatan in Stockholm. The bank was erected in the year 1900 and was designed by the architect Gustaf Wickman and the ornaments that were intended to take visitors' breath away depicted the rich farming communities in Skåne.

3 The textile artist Märta Måås-Fjetterström was the head of the Malmöhus läns hemslöjdsförening (Malmö county handicrafts association) and had there learned of the treasure-trove of patterns in the traditional peasant textiles from Skåne. Her breakthrough came in 1909 with the tapestry 'Staffan Stalledräng', which was an independent interpretation of an old Swedish religious motif. Ten years later she started her own textile workshop in Båstad, which is still in operation, specializing in rug weaving.

4 The architect Gunnar Asplund was given the opportunity to decorate an office in his refined style at the 1925 Paris Exhibition. The room's most elegant piece of furniture was the leather-clad Senna chair with a relaxed curvature and armrests adorned with antique ivory medallions. The copy in the picture was made by the Italian Cassina S.p.a in the 1980s.

5 One of the Swedish items that was highlighted at the Paris Exhibition was a park bench, or garden bench, which had been designed by the architect Folke Bensow. It was cast at Näfveqvarns bruk and had already been shown at the Gothenburg Exhibition in 1923.

6 Inspired by the Swedish success at the Paris Exhibition and influenced by French Art Deco the phone manufacturer Ericsson in 1929 redesigned its twenty-year-old sheet metal telephone. This occurred during a period of expansion when Ivar Kreuger had a majority share and the desk phone was launched with the help of a couple of posters that refer to modern urban life. The skyscraper in the background (Södra Kungstornet in Stockholm) was Sweden's first and housed, among other things, Ericsson's headquarters.

7 The Atlantic cruiser M/S *Kungsholmen* was from 1928 until the Second World War used as a floating travelling exhibition of the finest Swedish interior design in Art Deco style. The interior design work was led by Carl Bergsten, who was assisted by a number of the architects, artisans and artists who had participated in the exhibitions in Gothenburg and Paris. The image shows the luxurious, bordering on vulgar entrance to first class, 'Grand Entrance', which was designed by the architect Rolf Engströmer.

8 The springy steel tube chairs, so popular in Central Europe, did not, due to their streamlined coldness, prove popular in the Swedish interior design of the 1930s. However, a customized outdoor chair made of solid spring steel was shown at the Stockholm Exhibition, which would become a big seller. Designed by the smith Artur Lindqvist at Grythyttans verkstad, the chair originally had a dark red frame and later became known as the A2.

9 The Austrian architect Josef Frank had an extensive production behind him when he came to Sweden in 1934. He added vegetative motifs and fresh colours in the spirit of William Morris to the Swedish pattern flora. Aralia from the 1920s is a good example of this.

10 The Pia-chair is a pretty, white-lacquered tubular steel chair for outdoor use from 1942. It was designed by Tore Ahlsén for KF and has a practical foldable seat that makes it easy to stow away. The chair is still in production as are other products in the Pia-series, for example, the airy, delicate Pia-lamp.

11 Washing by hand was one of the hardest aspects of housework. The first washing machines arrived at the end of the 1940s, after inspiration from the USA and some common brands were Calor, Alfa-Laval and Bohus. The latter machine was of the recommended cylinder type. Brochure photo from 1955.

12 Passenger flights developed in parallel with the professionalization of the designer corps, which is one of the reasons that so many designers have been given commissions from airlines. ABA, which from 1946 was included in SAS, employed Anders Beckman to market the company with the help of striking posters.

13 The large Helsingborg Exhibition in 1955 was the definitive breakthrough of the beautiful Swedish everyday product and a manifestation of the Swedish Society of Crafts and Design's half-century-long effort to bring together artists with industry. Anders Beckman was in charge of the graphic design and in the theme of H55 he had in chemical formula managed to merge the city and exhibition year into a powerful slogan.

14 Few had the ability to market their projects with the help of striking visionary sketches as Ralph Erskine could. Here he excels in an advertising brochure from 1954 showing a future 'Europe's first Shopping Centre ... a complete miniature city with a controlled climate, which would give comfort and enjoyment ... with streets, alleys and squares, where the trees flourish and diverse flowers shine all year round ... even if the thermometer "outside" shows severe freezing

temperatures'. Even though the supply of electricity appeared to be assured by all the hydropower in northern Sweden that was under development, the reality never lived up to the expectations. Luleå in the north of Sweden did get its shopping centre, but a considerably more modest one.

15 The cooperative idea was concerned with minimizing costs for households. It was therefore logical that KF was at the forefront in terms of a standardized generic low-price range where you only paid for what you got. KF's so-called Blåvitt (Blue-white) range of staple commodities that spoke for themselves in simple packaging and uniform decoration was introduced in 1979. Blåvitt was an immediate success and the range was extended several times.

16 Geometric patterns, preferably in grey scale, dominate Ingrid Dessau's textile work. At her debut exhibition at Galerie Moderne in 1953, she showed among other things the drapery Manhattan, where she skilfully interprets the big city's regular city plan with the cars hurrying down the straight streets or, if you like, the light shining from the windows in the equally straight rectilinear skyscrapers.

17 The artist Sture Johannesson's provocative poster, popularly known as 'Haschflickan' (The Hash-girl), was made for the exhibition Underground at Lunds Konsthall in 1969. It was a paraphrase of Eugène Delacroix's painting Liberty Leading the People in the spirit of drugs and liberalism. The poster was seized by police, the exhibition was closed before it opened and the art gallery manager was forced to resign.

18 The establishment of the Umeå Institute of Design in 1989 came to be very significant for the establishment of design awareness in northern Sweden. Some of the first graduated design students started the consultancy Struktur Design, which got off to a flying start with the innovative design of a conference phone, Konftel 100 from 1994.

19 The concept car Saab EV1, which was developed in 1985 under the leadership of the chief designer Björn Envall, was one of the decade's most interesting car projects. It was made fully drivable and was in many respects ahead of its time. Based on the popular Saab 900 Turbo platform, a red four-seater sports coupe was created with deformation resistant front and rear sections of plastic, black panel-type dashboard, extremely light and ergonomic seats, and last but not least a spectacular solar cell-fitted glass roof where the solar cells powered a fan that ventilated the coupe when the car was parked.

20 Källemo's furniture producer Sven Lundh took on a whole team of designers with strong personal styles. One of these was the innovative Mats Theselius who made this cabinet congenially suited to twenty-five years of the magazine National Geographic.

21 BD1 for David Design from 1996 appears almost to be a graphic character. Björn Dahlström's background as a graphic designer is evident in much of his wider production.

22 Lei by Officeline might be the world's first ergonomic office chair for women. The chair is a result of a lengthy study on female sitting posture. Designed by Monica Förster Design Studio 2009.

23 Ecolean is a super-light packaging material: a one-litre beverage package weighs just less than half what a gable top or pet bottle weighs. The material consists of 40% degradable calcium carbonate (chalk). The image shows Ecolean in practical use.

24 The design process and exploration are at the heart of the internationally acclaimed design group Front, founded by Sofia Lagerkvist (b. 1976), Anna Lindgren (b. 1977), Charlotte von der Lancken (b. 1978) and Katja Sävström (b. 1976). Furia Rocking Horse for Gebrüder Thonet Vienna was launched in 2016, when Front only consisted of the first two designers. The project stemmed from a thorough study of the company's long tradition of working with bent wood.

List of Figures

Foreword

There is an element of dissatisfaction in writing a historical overview and I imagine that it resembles a work of design. In particular, one has the creeping feeling of having forgotten something crucial. At some point, however, you have to decide to move on. This is, after all, only the beginning of a history; a history which, in addition, is interpreted by my temperament and my experiences. It is based to a certain extent on my lectures, which began tentatively at the Umeå Institute of Design in 1989 and eventually continued at my former workplace, the School of Design and Crafts (HDK) at the University of Gothenburg.

The past is always present, at certain times more than at others. It is in my opinion important for prospective designers to train themselves to take a historical-critical approach. A new design is ultimately a small step in a larger context. Studies of older design solutions often yield ideas, demonstrate exemplary role models or by contrast, reveal approaches to distance oneself from. Outdated technology, unsuitable material or another age's aesthetic principles may have formed a temporary dead end. Ensuring that one has critically evaluated previous design efforts becomes, in other words, part of the quality assurance in the design process.

Even my contribution to the history of design rests largely on earlier knowledge. It should be noted that this is just one of many possible and equally valid interpretations of Swedish design history. Other angles and explanations are perfectly legitimate. Design history is a burgeoning subject, which is why the need for analysis and review is considerable, not only in Sweden. I have noted with interest the national design histories written by art historians in several other European countries; for example, in the Netherlands, Finland and Norway (Simon Thomas 2008, Korvenmaa 2009, Fallan 2017).

This book is primarily meant to be used by different design educations as an overview. All the examples of designers' work may hopefully also inspire future generations to become interested in both this creative subject and the profession. The book is structured chronologically and shows design's most important tasks; that is to appeal to our senses, to describe the product or service, and to adapt it to people's needs.

Now when it is published in an English version the text has been slightly revised and updated with some new images. I have received valuable comments on the manuscript from several Swedish colleagues, not mentioned here but none forgotten. However, I would like to take this opportunity to thank my editor Rebecca Barden at Bloomsbury Publishing and her assistant Claire Constable. Special thanks go to my life partner Lisa Brunnström for her support. The translation is performed by Jon Buscall and has been reviewed by Åsa Moberg-Grout. The work has been carried out with a travel grant from the Estrid Ericson Foundation and the Royal Society of Arts and Sciences in Gothenburg. Contributions to the book's English version have been provided by the Torsten Söderberg Foundation. Thank you all.

Lasse Brunnström
Gothenburg January 2018

Design, Design History, Swedish Design History

Design is a concept-based activity practised in close collaboration with other professions, usually resulting in a product or service. Ideas are normally visualized in the form of sketches, drawings and models, but can in principle be communicated through oral instructions or more or less finished solutions (prototypes). With the help of design, a holistic approach is undertaken in order to increase the value of the experience and create a sense of satisfaction; in other words, to make life easier and reduce the friction between people and artefacts, or between people. This clear focus on the consumer differs from the engineer's focus on verifiable partial solutions and a functional end product. The term 'design' originated in the USA, the home of industrial design, and has only been in use in Sweden for about seventy years. Before that the narrower, German-influenced term *formgivning*, meaning 'to give shape to something', dominated.

A fundamental idea of the design concept concerns conscious creation, an ancient phenomenon linked to the artisanal production of objects. 'Crafts' is the most common term for this activity in today's terminology. In connection with the nineteenth-century's mechanization and industrialization of the Western world, entirely different conditions for mass production were created. But mass production required mass consumption at the other end of the chain. In order to sell products, they must be adapted to the consumer, the users. Limited requirements are made in terms of colour, shape and user-adaptability for new inventions and immature product categories, but once a product has reached a certain maturity, and the competition has stiffened, higher and more sophisticated demands are made on its actual execution. The more numerous and complex artefacts we surround ourselves with, in other words, the more important the design is and the greater potential scope is given to the designer.

In parts of the textile, ceramic and glass industries, certain elements of craft have persisted within manufacturing due to lower product development requirements and a tradition of appealing directly to affluent consumer groups. Because of the strong artistic elements of this type of production it has often been thought of as 'art industry'. The term is still used today, especially in Sweden's neighbouring Nordic countries to describe the focus of art industry museums that collect and display select objects. In Swedish there is also the older, comprehensive term *konstslöjd* for design and craft.

But it is the word 'design' that has gained an increasingly strong foothold in the Swedish language, now replacing virtually all older terms with the exception of craft. The widespread use of the concept of design and all its creative definitions have at the same time rendered it somewhat watered down and meaningless where it is not complemented by an accompanying clarification. A common sweeping division, which is used in design education at university level and elsewhere, is between industrial design/product design, interior design/furniture design and graphic design/visual communication. It is these areas that will mainly be addressed in this overview; however, since the topics are not dependent on material this does not preclude traditional disciplines such as textiles, ceramics and glass also being covered, albeit briefly.

Design is above all a practical activity but it can also be explored from a variety of perspectives. Traditionally, it was scholars in the humanities and social sciences who studied questions of form, design processes and the development of the profession. It is only in recent years that artistic or IT-oriented research has emerged where designers themselves apply their proven experience and methods. The results are reported both in the shape of design solutions, so-called artefacts, and critical textual analysis. In this context, research through design is being referred to, as opposed to previous research about design or for design, in accordance with a concept that originated in the UK (Frayling 1993). Even though the problem of critically approaching one's own creation, the link between empiricism and theory, as well as the usefulness of this practice-based art research, is still being debated, there is much to suggest that this research should provide exciting new approaches and solutions in the long term.

One might ask oneself whether it is at all relevant to speak about a specifically Swedish design when nowadays we live in a globalized world, where the manufacturing industry has moved abroad, international design companies work in the Swedish market and where even Swedish design consultancy companies open local offices in Japan and Hong Kong. I would like to argue that it is. Although expressions of design less and less represent any form of national specificity, design has always been a practice with strong national overtones. International design venues such as museums and design centres, located throughout the world are now, as before, largely pawns in a larger game that is about gaining global share. Much of the design literature operates in the same way on a smaller scale, but with the same zeal to highlight its own excellence. This is something that is difficult to avoid and I am aware that even this book could be accused of presenting excessively idealized national images. What is easily forgotten is that even failures, or perhaps above all failures, move development forward.

Placing one's own performance in a wider context, preferably framed by a good story, is a marketing strategy employed by both authorities and companies. Within the design field the good story has, in the last fifty years, been about positioning Swedish design within the Scandinavian Design tradition, with visual language that has been characterized by both sculptural elegance as well as a simplicity of materials and lack of decoration. This particular combination has proven to be a financially successful export concept that was well adapted to the brand of the Swedish Welfare State – and a rational Swedish production apparatus. It is a concept that is still viable and that has, over the years, been incorporated into the official image of Swedish design. It is marketed by our ministers and embassies abroad, especially in the USA and Japan, and it is something that IKEA and many Swedish design-intensive firms continue to capitalize on. The focus has been on the household goods sector, with products associated with a number of recurring designers who have an almost iconic status. But as we know the good story is not always the completely true story. In striving to emphasize a marketable national character homogeneity is often exaggerated. In other words, I want to demonstrate that Swedish design has a far more diverse history than is usually depicted.

Design history research first developed in Britain and the USA where, during the 1970s, it had developed out of the closely related fields of art history and architecture. The subject has since undergone a rapid development, as material culture has become an increasingly important part of our lives. Today, there are scientific journals, associations, societies and conferences in the field of design history. Professorships and courses have been established at several universities, particularly those offering practical design and arts and craft courses.

The focus of design history is the designer, the design process and the designed object. A recurring theme in this and other similar overviews of design history is the designer's ever-increasing field of work with more and increasingly complex tasks. The profession (with various professional designations) had, with few exceptions, a subordinate role during the 1800s and up until the Second World War and was usually focused on creating additional aesthetic value to ready-made products or messages. Today the situation is completely different. Now designers work in several parallel ways and are often in executive positions. At the same time one has to understand that there are, and have been, major differences between designing, for example, a chair and a complex industrial product.

The British art historian John A. Walker (1989), who wrote an excellent survey of this field of research, believes that the design historian cannot avoid delving deeper into issues of style, taste, the role of the commissioner, management, marketing and consumers. And it does not end there as these elements cannot be studied in isolation but are part of a larger social and historical context. The design historian must therefore always be prepared to widen the framework of their investigations. In this regard, design history is an interdisciplinary subject in the fullest sense and I hope that will be apparent in this study as well.

Swedish design history, unlike, for example, the history of Swedish architecture, has primarily been a research field dominated by women. Despite four of the real pioneers in the field being male art historians – Gregor Paulsson, Arthur Hald, Ulf Hård af Segerstad and Dag Widman – the dominance of female design historians (see Bibliography) has in recent years been overwhelming. The vast majority have, or had in some way or another, been working out of one of the country's art history institutions and many are active design critics. But there are also examples of design-oriented historical studies on subjects such as the history of ideas, business administration and the history of architecture. Research has for some time also been carried out at the country's larger museums with design-history oriented collections; for example, Nationalmuseum and the Nordic Museum in Stockholm, the Röhsska Museum in Gothenburg and Kulturen in Lund. Here, the gender distribution has been slightly more even. The most influential design historian of the last few decades has been Kerstin Wickman, who in the anthology *Under Ytan* (Under the Surface) gives an insightful overview of Swedish design history research (Wickman 2007).

Nineteenth- and twentieth-century Swedish designs have their obvious highlights that are almost always referred to and that serve as confirmation of the development of a particular Swedish or Nordic interpretation of international Modernism. The simple, unadorned and functional, the pure, and even the blonde have been spoken of as fixed and typical features of form creation. It is an image that has been maintained by museum employees, art experts and the association Svensk Form (the Swedish Society of Crafts and Design), enthusiastically cheered on by the auction houses' well-read curators. Only in recent years has this image, somewhat simplified and often without context, started to be questioned and even criticized for being a consciously, commercially driven construction. This argument can certainly be accused of including rhetorical exaggerations but has still served as a wake-up call in what has long been a relatively closed and self-contemplative design world.

The fact remains, however, that today the history of Swedish design all too often consists of the repetition of relatively well-known facts and phenomena. At the same time there are significant gaps in the knowledge concerning development in areas such as graphic design, packaging design, service design and industrial design in connection with the production of small and medium-sized businesses. More research is also needed on material development in a design context, as well as design and manufacturing processes. Overall one is struck by how little broad, everyday production has been studied and written about in relation to all the energy that has been devoted to examining and understanding already established names, major exhibitions and glamorous products. This somewhat one-sided product and person selection, which has long existed in English-language studies, has led to the conventional image of Swedish design being firmly rooted in handicrafts in the writing of international history (Sparke 1983, Woodham 1997: 177 and Simon Thomas 2008: 210), which is not entirely true.

Hopefully, this book will broaden the understanding of Swedish design. It takes as its starting point the middle of the nineteenth century when everyday design was actualized and depicts the period leading up to the present day. In the early sections there is, due to necessity, a conscious drift between design and craft. Like design, the history condenses and is complicated the closer we get to our own time. The chapters are thematic while chronology holds the presentation together. This approach, of course, is pluralistic. The selection is mainly done on the basis that the designs and design-related phenomenon should mean something to us today, but I also try to break with the trend that according to Werner (2008) exists in the history of aesthetic arts, that is to describe what should have been rather than what actually was.

Several earlier overviews of Swedish design have been written. The most closely related are Dag Widman's *Konsthantverk, konstindustri, design 1895–1975* (Crafts, art industry, design) (1975), Kerstin Wickman's (ed.) *Formens rörelse: Svensk Form genom 150 år* (The movement of form: Swedish Design through 150 years) (1995) and Hedvig Hedqvist's *Svensk form, internationell design* (Swedish design, international design) (2002) as well as the last four volumes of *Signums svenska konsthistoria* (Signum's Swedish art history) (2000–2005). Denise Hagströmer's *Swedish Design* (2001) for the Swedish Institute is also worth mentioning in this context. What possibly distinguishes this account from the others, all excellent in their genre, is the contemplation of design history as part of material cultural history as well as art history. Finally, it must be noted that although the book has become extensive, there are weak areas and even gaps that need to be filled such as web design, game design, newspaper and magazine design.

1 Art to Industry, 1840s to 1910s

The Nations Struggle for Product Dominance

Considering the technical, artistic and ultimately commercial significance of design, it is no coincidence that many design historians use the first World's Fair, the Great Exhibition, which took place in London in 1851, as a starting point. This exhibition represents the breakthrough of mass production and globalized trade. At the same time it also stands as a symbol for the many new technical advances and, indeed, also for the artistic shortcomings in the design of new industrial products. As a world power and leading industrial nation, it was considered important in Victorian England that the Empire also held a world-leading position in design and

Fig. 1.1 A very diverse range of goods was on display at the first World's Fair in London in 1851, almost everything was overloaded with ornaments. Around forty nations participated with over a million objects. According to Elias Cornell (1952) detailed pictures of the Swedish-Norwegian section, which is said to have been organized by the German architectural theorist Gottfried Semper, do not exist. However, this synoptic and only known colour lithography provides some idea of the modest efforts from the industrially underdeveloped Scandinavian countries.

construction. An important incentive was probably to try to outshine the series of successful French industrial and craft exhibitions, which had taken place in previous decades.

The World's Fairs became an important part of the economic warfare between the industrialized Western nations with exhibition floors as the battlefields. The *Edinburgh Review* wrote in a retrospective of the Great Exhibition that: 'All of Europe's trading cities had been turned into camps for armed forces' (Gårdlund 1942). The exhibition, which was originally conceived as a purely British project, eventually attracted exhibitors from more than forty nations. They shared the world's hitherto largest and brightest glass building, which had been erected for the purpose in less than a year using prefabricated parts. The exhibition building most closely resembled a giant greenhouse and was named the Crystal Palace. It was as simple and undecorated as the construction was ingenious. The building had, unusually, not been designed by an architect but by an experienced and practical gardener, Joseph Paxton, and therefore lacked the magnificent facades that were common in similar constructions. In order to allow the giant glass building to function as a showroom, sunlight was blocked with white cloth while the glass was cooled with water, which was funnelled away through hollow loadbearing iron columns. In addition, there was also mechanical ventilation.

By the time the exhibition closed after about five months, some six million visitors had marvelled at all the innovations. A large number of medals had been awarded by the jury whose criteria were strikingly modern, resembling the demands that are made in association with today's design awards. It took into account the product's relative usefulness, the level of professionalism in the execution, the material's novelty, the low price as well as 'beauty of form or colour' (Wollin 1951: 12). So what did the nearly 14,000 exhibitors show? France's structurally sound, quality, and above all rococo products were much in evidence and this is also where most of the medals ended up. The British demonstrated their skill for designing machines for textile, iron and steel processing. They exhibited lathes, planing machines, standard systems for screws and special tools and machine parts. Not to be outdone, the Americans were able to boast a number of remarkable inventions that were both practical and comfortable, like Isaac Singer's mass-produced sewing machines, McCormick's revolutionary harvester, Charles Goodyear's vulcanized rubber pontoons, buoys and boats, prosthetic legs and the first modern office chair with a swivel and tilt function. Samuel Colt's revolver assembled from standardized parts was also displayed, and which according to a contemporary senate report was seen as the only weapon that could subdue the federation's wild and fearless Indian tribes.

The exhibition undoubtedly contained many curiosities, but it also revealed a lot of problems. At this crossroads between craft and industry the finishing was not of the highest quality and the traditional aesthetic framework had been eliminated. Forms were standardized and adapted for mechanical manufacturing and decorations were usually added after, without apparent context. The British products, not to mention the American, appeared aesthetically inferior and immature in comparison with the craftsmanship of the luxury furniture in the French and Austrian sections. The subsequent criticism and debate was in many respects quite ruthless. Exhibits were considered vulgar and tasteless, almost disastrous from an artistic point of view. Practically every single everyday object was overloaded with ornaments, or as a later observer wrote: 'Candelabras sagged under fruit and flower garlands, mythological figures coiled around handles, brackets and candlesticks, fat putti danced on the edge of plates' (Tempelman 1943).

The American products were considered to lack finish and have poor durability. The forms were simplified and reduced, and the decor was repeatable and cheapened. The response was reminiscent of the slightly stingy and suspicious attitude that greeted Italian and Japanese goods after the Second World War, and that later also affected South Korea and now also China and Vietnam. It has never been easy for new industrial nations to break into the international market. The American manufacturers had a considerably more rational and down-to-earth approach to production than was common in Europe. The London Exhibition's official catalogue entry for the American section provided an explanation, which in many respects also encapsulated the idea of early mass production. It stressed that, unlike some European manufacturers, it was uncommon in the USA to spend months or years on a product only to increase the price or the product's artistic value. Instead the goal was to satisfy a large homogeneous internal market with a desperate need for innovative, standardized and affordable products that make life easier for ordinary people (Official Descriptive 1851: 1431).

It was precisely this difference of opinion about the subservient role of aesthetics which was so evident in the design of the first telephones a few decades later. The telephone began to be widely marketed by the American Bell Company in the late 1870s, but several manufacturers were quick to follow, not least the Swedish Ericsson. The best seller was a solid three-piece wooden wall-mounted phone with space for an inductor with a bell and hook switch, fixed microphone and battery box. The American version was actually designed as three boxes mounted rationally one above the other on a simple wall board, while Ericsson using skilled carpenters developed the concept into a balanced whole, with a great deal of finish and attention to detail. The telephone also became a cheap everyday product significantly faster in America than in Sweden, where for a long time it was restricted to the business world and the upper classes (Brunnström 2006).

Sweden's efforts at the London Exhibition showed no evidence of this design skill, but were described as generally weak by Torsten Gårdlund (1942). The Swedish-Norwegian union section, which was dominated by raw materials and relatively rough-hewn cottage industry production, attracted little attention. There were different samples of ore, pig iron, bar iron, flax, wool, birch bark and the like. The Swedish novelist and feminist Frederika Bremer, who visited the exhibition, enjoyed seeing a porphyritic vase from Älvdalen and a large Bofors cannon, but other than that she felt ashamed of the poor and inexperienced Swedes. Otherwise, the high-quality iron ore and steel attracted the most appreciation as well as a smaller so-called flatiron stove made by Bolinder; heating is something that Swedes have always mastered. Swedish industrialization was still in its infancy, which may explain the meagre showing at the exhibition. In Stockholm in 1866, the first Swedish, as well as the first Nordic, industrial manifestation, *Allmänna Industri- och Konstutställningen* (The General Industry and Art Exhibition), took place but it would take until the turn of the twentieth century before the Swedish manufacturing industry could seriously begin to assert itself in a global market.

Education for Increased Industrial Competitiveness

It was difficult to live up to any high artistic aspirations during the birth of industrialism. The simple production methods available in the eighteenth and nineteenth centuries were inherently unable to compete with traditional craft production in this area. There also existed a fundamental difference between traditional craftsmanship and industry, insightfully described by Karl Marx in the first volume of his work *Das Kapital* (Capital) in 1867: 'In manufacture and handicrafts the worker uses a tool; in the factory he serves a machine. In the former case the movements of the instrument of labour proceed from the worker; but in the latter the movements of the worker are subordinate to those of the machine'. In other words, there was, in addition to the subordination itself, an interface problem causing difficulty in transferring the dexterity and quality assurance of the craftsmen to the machines. Another peculiarity that emerged was that the hand's imprint in the form of distinguishing irregularities and flaws was now replaced by mechanically produced, similar and by necessity highly simplified forms.

Within the crafts and in the manufactories, which were a conglomerate of craft workshops, ideas and experiences were transferred from master to apprentice. There was also usually close contact with both clients and artists, who could provide models. Even though old models and patterns could be copied in an emergency, art and craft skills were in short supply in connection with the division of labour of industrialization. As a result of the abolition of the guild system in 1846 and the introduction of freedom of trade in 1864, professional knowledge was no longer required to start a business, workshop or factory. With factory owners who possibly lacked expertise, machines that needed instructions and more or less unskilled workers, another professional group was required. It was a profession that could provide sketches and models, that is to say good design models. Today they are called designers whereas in the past they were usually referred to as pattern draughtsmen, artists and architects; furthermore, in the manufacturing industry one can also add many engineers and constructors to this group. The shift from craft production to the mass production of industrialization was therefore in itself an innovation, but at the same time entailed obvious problems that had to be solved (Danielson 1991: 44).

In the aftermath of the London Exhibition a general mobilization followed in the defence of art and discussion of industrial society's lack of a culture of form, colour and pattern intensified over the years. It did not matter, it was said, whether the nation was in the possession of the most amazing natural resources. These needed to be refined and if the artistic skills did not thrive in the industry, or *(konst)* *slöjderna*, which was the nineteenth- and early twentieth-century term, then there did not exist any grounds for domestic industrial development either. The art industry mobilization movement reacted against the anonymity, imitations and lack of quality in early industrial production. It originated in the UK but quickly spread to the rest of northern Europe and eventually came to include a comprehensive action plan. Initial efforts were made as early as the first half of the nineteenth century through encouragement in the form of scholarships and prizes, soon followed by state subsidies for the establishment of schools, museums and, as in London, major exhibitions.

Particular emphasis was placed on the issue of education. In 1837 the Government School of Design, now the Royal College of Art, was established in London. This was vocational training with the ambition of raising the artistic level of the burgeoning industry. A private drawing school, primarily for craftsmen, had been started a few years earlier in Denmark. This was something that also took place in Stockholm in 1844 and Gothenburg in 1848.

The Swedish schools still exist, although they have long since become state funded and have taken new names: respectively Konstfack (University College of Arts, Crafts and Design) and HDK (School of Design and Crafts). They each had their own support organization whose financial and pedagogical support was, from the beginning, crucial for the continuity of operations. In Stockholm this was the Swedish Society of Crafts and Design (Svenska Slöjdföreningen), which had been formed in 1845 to support the then Söndagsritskolan (Sunday Drawing School), renamed the Swedish Society of Crafts and Design School the following year. The motive was highly protectionist, or patriotic as it was called at the time; to raise the quality of Swedish industry and oppose 'the corrosive and disgraceful predilection for all things foreign' (Wollin 1951: 31).

In the country's second-biggest city this was the Society of Crafts and Design in Gothenburg (Göteborgs Slöjdförening), which set up its own craft and design school and here also the nationalist motives were undisguised. As outlined in the first paragraph of the association's statutes:

> The association's purpose is to try to promote the Swedish arts and industries, as well as the so-called home industries advancement, so that the domestic production may, through quality and price, make the foreign less necessary and desirable, and that Swedish handicraft products thereby might gain increased consumption and circulation. (Ericson 1948: 18)

From the perspective of today's free-trade-friendly climate such statements might seem somewhat distasteful, but compared to their competing countries the situation was precarious at this time. The need for education was extensive. Although state schools did impart Christian knowledge, the supply of other knowledge was exceedingly meagre. Tens of thousands of journeymen and apprentices, who were about to start work in the growing industrial sector, needed some basic knowledge about material properties and to be able to measure, draw and design in the context of the execution of design work. There was no adequate training for them. Nor was there any for the many painters, lacquerers, carpenters, turners, mechanics, machinery and metal workers, masons, construction workers, blacksmiths, sheet-metal workers, goldsmiths, jewellers, sculptors, modellers, lithographers, chasers, engravers, gilders, etc., who were in need of qualified training. The so-called craft schools met a giant collection of educational needs and were also pioneers with regard to giving women the right to further education. The justification given at the time was that it benefited society: women could better manage their positions as housewives and also serve as assistants to the men (Wollin 1951: 68).

As early as the nineteenth century, an important aim of the two courses in Stockholm and Gothenburg was to train pattern draughtsmen as they were called at the time, for the emerging industries, particularly the arts industry. It is also the more artistic approach that has persisted through the years and been made increasingly scholarly. Both schools grew rapidly and were initially divided into departments for men and women, but lessons were soon given to mixed classes divided into different categories and levels. Although several technical and constructive subjects were included in the male curriculum, from the outset the schools invested considerable resources in developing the student's artistic sensibilities by means of freehand drawing and modelling. Such skills were considered, as a promoter of the Swedish Society of Crafts and Design School in Stockholm so intricately put it, to both mitigate 'the Nordic hardness of temper' and provide 'the taste in drawing, shape and colour that a variety of products must have to be viable in countries, where taste holds a higher standing than it currently does with us' (Wollin 1951: 60).

One has to keep in mind that the crafts schools' freehand drawing lessons at the time were based on copying. The models were spheres, gypsums and posters with landscapes and ornaments. The focus was on simple geometric figures and the point was to learn how to draw carefully and with precision. 'Accurate-drawing' was a term used in the literature and it concerned everything from how the hands should be held to the depiction itself. At the same time the subject involved more than one might imagine. At the Society of Crafts and Design School in Gothenburg students first had to learn line drawing and contour drawing for posters, then shading for posters, sphere drawing and contour drawing for ornaments and plaster figurines. This was followed by clay and wax modelling and shaded plaster drawings (Ericson 1948). Artistic freedom was not encouraged, but rather the education's purpose was to stick to a given style. 'It was considered that only by sticking to one fixed historical style or another could the conditions be created to restore the form's balance and the general public's tastes, which were lost during the earlier part of the century', writes the art historian Nils G. Wollin, in his comprehensive history of Konstfack (Wollin 1951: 227). The subject of art history was included in these contexts as a taste-propagating correlative.

Around the turn of the twentieth century the focus of freehand drawing changed with the introduction of the drawing of natural objects and exercises in stylization, something that would be of great significance to the development of pattern drawing. The architect Sigfrid Ericson writes in his history of HDK that these impulses primarily came from the USA where it was argued that accurate-drawing inhibited the imagination and independent artistic development. Now, instead of slavish copying, a more personal interpretation could be expressed in the drawings. The printer Waldemar Zachrisson and the artist Axel Goës were among the main proponents of this reorganization of the Gothenburg school. Under the influence of the Arts & Crafts and Art Nouveau movements the teaching was brought up to date and given a more arts and craft orientation. The object was for students to regain a connection to their own time (Ericson 1948: 56–62).

Fig. 1.2 Life drawing and model sculpting quickly became major subjects in the craft schools' curriculum. The picture is from Konstfack, the University College of Arts, Crafts and Design, around 1900 and also illustrates the open atmosphere that existed at these schools with mixed classes for male and female students.

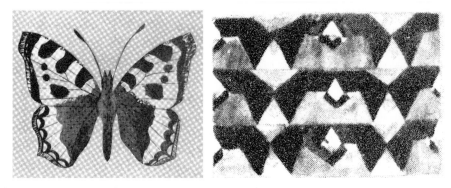

Fig. 1.3a and b In the early 1900s freer exercises in stylization had been introduced in the drawing lessons. In this student's work from HDK the butterfly's pattern design has been translated into a surface pattern.

Fig. 1.4 Students at the Society of Crafts and Design School in Gothenburg, today called HDK, have always been attracted to the graphic arts. At the beginning of the twentieth century a lot of time was devoted to exercises in decorative painting and calligraphy as a knowledge base for, for example, hand-painted advertisements on walls and billboards.

On a Mission to Improve Taste and Morality

The building of museums constituted a third important link in the nineteenth century art industry mobilization pedagogy, alongside schools and international exhibitions. In these permanent venues the battle for good taste would be fought and the objects would serve as patterns for the craft school students. They would receive guidance from object lessons instead of just settling for reproductions of illustrated works. During the nineteenth century, there existed a notion of a necessarily close relationship between art, business and morality, according to the Norwegian art historian Ingeborg Glambek (1997). And to promote good taste was precisely the fundamental action needed to improve morals and achieve a better society. The museum of crafts and design was the place where the fight for good taste would be fought.

The first in a series of similar museums was the Victoria & Albert Museum in London (from 1852 the Museum of Manufacturers, 1853 the Museum of Ornamental Art, 1857 the South Kensington Museum and after 1899 the Victoria & Albert Museum, the V&A). Some of the exhibits from the recently finished Great Exhibition were brought there: high quality objects from throughout the vast British Empire. In the fight for good taste, a department was immediately opened which they named in their educational zeal *Examples of False Principles in Decoration*, or the 'Chamber of Horrors' as it was commonly called. In general the Victorian era was appalled by disorder and particularly reacted when three-dimensional naturalistic patterns were applied to two-dimensional surfaces. The gallery was, however, closed down fairly soon after as it endured intense criticism from the producers whose products had been on display. There was talk of censorship and, among other things, it was claimed, 'manufacturers needed to apply complex rather than simple decoration in order to sell products with added values, and what sold was "true" to them' (Yasuko 2004: 54).

The V&A became a sort of parent museum for the crafts and design movement, with collections that today are the world's largest in the field: over four and a half million objects spread over 145 galleries. The movement spread like wildfire across Europe. The many international exhibitions that succeeded each other in quick succession after the Great Exhibition demonstrated the importance of building collections of exemplars to raise artistic skill and thereby enhance the welfare and power of a nation. New museums were built in Vienna in 1864, Berlin in 1868, Helsinki in 1874, Oslo in 1876, Frankfurt in 1877, Bergen in 1886, Trondheim in 1894, Copenhagen in 1895 (1890) and Paris in 1905. In Sweden, the foundation was laid for a museum in Stockholm by the Swedish Society of Crafts and Design as early as 1872, but the lack of a separate building for the museum led to the collections passing to the National Museum in 1884 in a special section for crafts and design.

The only Swedish museum of crafts and design was instead founded in Gothenburg in 1904 on the initiative of the Society of Crafts and Design. Aided primarily by donations from the wholesale brothers Wilhelm and August Röhss, the Röhsska Museum of Crafts and Design was built following the designs of the architect Carl Westman. The museum was opened in 1916 and had from the outset large collections of Chinese and Japanese material. Interest in exotic China was then, as now, high and during the anarchy that characterized the country about a century ago, many European countries took advantage of the opportunity to fill their museums with easily obtainable rarities. The Röhsska Museum was no different and had a few years earlier been sent some 700 Chinese items which had been obtained through a daring, and by today's collection ethics, despicable expedition led by the botany scholar Thorild Wulff. Detailed descriptions of

Fig. 1.5 The Röhsska Museum is still today Sweden's only museum specializing in crafts and design. It was inaugurated in 1917 and lies in the traditional style next to the School of Design and Crafts (HDK), together occupying a whole block of Göteborg (Gothenburg) city centre. The entrance to the severe building is guarded by two so-called Chinese Fu dogs.

the adventurous collecting of Buddha statues and temple bells, of dummy purchases, bribes and what most closely resembles outright tours of thievery are found in Wulff's diaries, which have been compiled and published by the museum. As an aside, copies of a pair from the collected objects, the lion-like so-called Fu dogs, flank and guard the museum's grand entrance to this day.

The objective that the crafts and design museums should work towards improving tastes had come to epitomize their collections. Traditionally, they have collected a selective range of objects just like art museums and therefore differ from the museums of cultural history, which do not have the same dogmatic collection policy. The collectable would have to pass the so-called measure of good taste and was dependent on the preferences of museum managers and the collective preferences of curators. As early as 1926, Gustaf Munthe summed up the modernist norm for these arbitrators of good taste in a way that has remained valid almost to this day: efficiency, material honesty and good form. Therefore, it followed that 'an iron garden urn should be heavy, fairly rugged, massive, it cannot be slender. In contrast, a silver cream bowl should be light, with soft lines, thin and graceful'. The status of the late nineteenth-century's new styles and blending of styles was low and was considered by Munthe as 'the greatest decline in domestic culture witnessed so far', an opinion he was far from alone in holding. In 1917, the Swedish Society of Crafts and Design's secretary Gregor Paulsson had dismissed 'the greater part of the crafts and design objects from the 1860s–1890s' as being directly detrimental to good taste if displayed (Waldén 1995: 26). It is only recently that these objects have attracted renewed interest.

Many museums adopted the British model of co-locating the museum with a crafts and design school so as to create a more hard-hitting entity. This also happened in Gothenburg where the Röhsska Museum had to share quarters with HDK's recently completed and custom-built school building. Education and propaganda, as in the cultivation of taste and the bringing of awareness of good design to 'the younger generations' and 'the men of crafts and industry', as stated by earlier historians, have from the outset been regarded as this particular museum's main tasks.

Teaching took the form of lectures and courses in, for example, the history of textile arts, furniture and bookbinding, with accompanying demonstrations of the collections. Practical courses such as weaving and engraving were also offered, while the earlier workshops for carpentry and bookbinding in the museum's basement were allotted to artisans who wished to base their work on pieces in the museum. The well-stocked library, previously with an attached reading-room, is still an attractive venue.

In addition to the East Asian material, the Röhsska Museum's collections focused initially on older textiles, book bindings and various examples of eighteenth-century Sweden. A separate exhibition hall for contemporary design was built in 1936 which connected the museum to HDK. The hall was named after the architect Melchior Wernstedt, who gave the building a modernist touch with a fully glazed street-facing facade. The contrast with the closed older building was particularly striking at night, when the exhibitions were exposed in the brightly lit room almost like in a supermarket.

Right from its inception, the immediate proximity to the museum made HDK's students into frequent visitors. It is evident that the excellent textile collection long constituted an important source of inspiration. Unfortunately these light-sensitive textiles have since gradually been relegated to darkened warehouses. Instead, the Röhsska Museum has in recent decades largely concentrated on a historical survey of Swedish and international design development. Nowadays both Röhsska Museum and Nationalmuseum have large design collections from the 1800s to the present that constitute excellent overviews of Swedish design history.

The municipally administered Röhsska Museum is to this day the country's only museum specializing in craft and design, and as such receives government support as well as municipal and regional grants and donations. The nineteenth-century's rhetoric about engendering good taste has been toned down. Over the years, interest has shifted somewhat from arts and crafts to design and fashion, which in practice has meant a move towards the sphere of cultural history. A more contemporary goal for today's craft and design museums was elegantly formulated by Anniken Thue, the former head of the Norwegian Museum of Decorative Arts and Design in Oslo (1998), to 'make the eye think and the objects speak'. This pedagogical ambition is still a high priority, and the most important target group today is children and young people. Several design educators skilfully make design and decorative art history come alive with specially decorated designer bags, dramatizations and hands-on teaching.

The Promised Land of Windsor Chairs and Iron Stoves

Iron stoves, and to some extent also simple Windsor chairs, both excellent symbols of the simple, self-sustaining country household, have now almost played out their roles. During the second half of the nineteenth century, however, they appeared to be two of the most visible representatives of Sweden's primary industries: iron and wood. In actuality, it was quite natural that Sweden had not achieved a prominent position at the first World's Fair as Sweden's development as an industrial country was, from a Western European perspective, late. Less than a hundred years ago about half of Sweden's population was still considered to be farmers. Many did not own more than the clothes on their backs and the dwelling of a smallholder could not accommodate more than a handful of interior objects. The plainness of most households was therefore very palpable, but as long as you had a roof over your head, there was usually an iron stove to heat food on and a Windsor chair to sit on, perhaps also a dining table, sofa bed, clothes chest, washstand with a water jug and a basin to wash in.

Sweden was still one of Europe's poorest countries as late as the end of the nineteenth century. A small proportion of the country's population lived in urban apartments or in barracks and workers' tenement blocks. This was just at the beginning of the big export of the lumber mills' wood processing, before the large-scale exploitation of Sweden's rich supply of iron ore, before the development of the many waterfalls and the establishment of all the export-oriented creative industries. This was at a time when the vast majority of people lived in cottages in the countryside, in small spaces and in poor conditions. This is why many people left the promised land of Windsor chairs and iron stoves to seek a brighter future in North America.

Poor soil or, perhaps even more commonly, seasonal underemployment made people supplement farm work with various types of handicrafts to cover household needs. As a rule, the simple furniture that was used by many did not call for more craftsmanship experience than making an axe handle or a hay rake. For some this production developed into an important ancillary enterprise, with sales held in squares and markets, or through a distributor. When these so-called commercial crafts were sold in an anonymous and remote market the production took on an almost industrial character. It can be seen as a proto-industry and was in some regions, not just in Sweden, an alternative to factories and mass production but also an important prerequisite for continued industrial expansion (Magnusson and Isacson 1988).

In Sweden the commercial crafts dominated in three main regions: southern Västra Götaland, the border regions of Småland and Skåne and Dalarna. Perhaps the most famous and initially important for Sweden's industrialization was the proto-industrial textile distribution system that supplemented the agricultural incomes of the farmers of Västra Götaland. In Linnaeus's travels through Västra Götaland in 1747 there are vivid quotes from the town of Borås and its surrounding district of Sjuhäradsbygden:

> the women spun, wove, knitted hats and other items, more than elsewhere, they made fabrics and walmar, which often compared favourably with a passably good broadcloth. The habitants also bought most of their goods from Marks county and Halland, where all people spin and weave, so that often the men have to sit at the spinning wheel, but the women rarely leave the weaving stool, but instead leave the man mostly to take care of the barn. (A:son Palmqvist 1988: 66)

The distributors who controlled the Sjuhäradsbygden production were landed farmers, sometimes called factory-owning farmers. The largest distributor in the 1850s employed close to 2,000 weavers working in their homes. For this typically female work the weavers often had to walk to the distributing farm to fetch the cotton yarn and sometimes the patterns and then return with the finished weave. The pay could be similar to that of a farm hand (A:son Palmqvist 1988).

The production was primarily sold by hawkers, so-called *knallar*. Many of these were small-scale farmers from the seven districts of Bollebygd, Veden, Gäsene, Ås, Redväg, Mark and Kind, who by a royal decree in 1776 had been given trading privileges to sell local products throughout the country. Only after the freedom of trade reform in 1864 were others permitted to engage in hawking. Recent research has shown that hawking reached almost every household and played an important role in industrialization and the emergence of consumer society during a period of time when Sweden lacked other effective distribution channels such as mail order and department stores. It was the hawkers who, through their range of attractive cotton fabrics, were responsible for the Swedish starting to wear clothes made from something other than linen and wool. The product range also included, for example, headscarves, shawls and scarves in various colours and designs, which attracted a large female clientele. At the same time, this possibility to consume more than the bare necessities led to many critical voices being raised against what was considered a growing desire for luxury items; the hawkers were spreading vanity and luxury in the communities (Lundqvist 2008).

In Småland and the north of Skåne the manufacture of furniture and construction carpentry, and also for example wooden toys, acted as active measures against the emigration flow westward. Larger-scale production started at Gemla Leksaksfabriks AB in Diö in 1861. The range included pull toys, alphabet boxes, rocking horses, boxes of building blocks, construction kits in a variety of designs, wooden boats, bocce sets, croquet sets, animal collections, as well as sleds, slingshots, crossbows and a variety of games. Another toy company from the city of Osby in Skåne would become even bigger and longer lasting. It was Ivar Bengtsson, who in 1884 together with his wife and sons, started the company that soon would be known as Bröderna Ivarsson, Osby or abbreviated as BRIO. Their pull toys and building blocks of solid wood became popular and sought-after export items. At the time, many toys contained more or less clear educational and gender-loaded messages in which boys were encouraged to help themselves while girls were expected to be passive and subservient (Isacson 1988 and Designarkivet).

Swedish timber management had long been focused on the production of rough, unprocessed wood. Further processing was done mainly by rural farmers in the form of commercial crafts production or the manufacture of household furniture, domestic wares and utensils. The wood used came from hardwoods, which before the days

Fig. 1.6 Painted wooden toys were a typical Swedish phenomenon. BRIO's Osby-horse from 1907, which could be placed on a cart and used as a pull toy, was among the most popular.

of the pulp industry was of no great economic value. The gradual mechanization of steam sawmills and joineries, however, led to the previously handmade houses, interiors and furniture being mass-produced at an ever-faster pace. This affected the popular Windsor chairs, which by the end of the nineteenth century were being produced in almost every small carpenter's workshop in Småland. In 1881, at least 70,000 Windsor chairs were supposedly produced in the Jönköping area alone and it was precisely along the Jönköping-Kalmar line that the Windsor chair factories were concentrated. 'Just as Austria has its bentwood chairs, Italy its Chiavari chairs, Paris its chaises articulées … so does Sweden has its Jönköping Windsor chairs of birch or beech', as Gårdlund (1941: 322) quotes a German visitor in the 1870s. The bentwood chairs referred to were the popular Thonet brothers' so-called Vienna chairs, whose fourteenth model from 1859 was supposedly manufactured in over 50 million copies until 1930. In contrast to these, the first demountable café chairs, the Swedish Windsor chairs were above all sold in neighbouring areas and never became a major export article.

According to tradition the production of the first Swedish Windsor chairs followed American models. The originator of the idea is supposed to have been Mrs. Henriette Killander, of the Hook manor house in Svenarum parish, who in the 1850s, had some chairs made to follow a model she had brought home from a trip. A characteristic feature of the Windsor chair are the lathed legs and back pins which are embedded slantingly into a curved upper frame and a massive, often anatomically designed, so-called saddle seat. The upper frame and the outer back pins were generally given a richer profile. The Swedish-American model of Windsor chair may, in turn, have had many influences, especially from the traditional British Windsor armchairs but also from graceful Chinese bamboo furniture.

The Windsor chairs had for a long time been manufactured in farms for home consumption and as an ancillary enterprise during winter. The large domestic demand, however, created the conditions for a burgeoning cottage industry and later also for a true furniture industry. And there are many indications that it was precisely a mass production of Windsor chairs using foot lathes in the 1850–1860s that laid the foundation for the Swedish furniture industry. One example is the founding of the Nässjö chair factory, where the son of a farmer, Per Johan Andersson, who had started his enterprise together with his wife had to treadle a lathe for the first six years. They had no workers to assist them but instead the farmers and crofters in the area delivered semi-finished products in the form of pin materials, which were then processed on the lathe. The lathed parts were then sold to carpenters and painters for assembly in Jönköping. In 1876 the workshop moved to a low, turf-covered cottage and a year or so later the married couple purchased a used mobile steam boiler with a three-horsepower engine. This small portable steam engine could, through the use of belts, be used to power a band saw, a rotary saw and a lathe, which was set up in an easily assembled wooden shed on the side of the house. The workshop soon became a factory where the Anderssons employed seven workers, who, specializing in different tasks, mass-produced a single type of simple Windsor chair. The material

Fig. 1.7 During the second half of the nineteenth century, production at minor carpentries in the south of Sweden was focused on the Windsor chair. The picture shows a '7-pin chair' with a saddle seat from the late nineteenth century, manufactured at the Nässjö chair factory.

for the pins was delivered in the same way as before while the roundwood for the upper frame and seats was purchased and sawed on the premises. Soon a small number of carriages with finished chairs were being driven every week to Jönköping or continuing on by steamer to Stockholm. After yet another move, and many years later, the company had grown to become Scandinavia's largest Windsor chair factory (Lagerquist 1943).

In the more artisanal production of Windsor chairs the pins had been cleaved from birch logs with an axe. After the materials had been dried they were placed in the hand- or foot-powered lathe. The upper frame and seats were, in turn, hand-sawn from birch planks and then the seat was hollowed out with an axe. Finding the right angles when hand-drilling diagonally into the seat to attach the legs required a great deal of skill. The industrial manufacturing process could be significantly facilitated by the setting up of a power-driven drilling rig with fixed angles that drilled all four holes at the same time. Belt-driven lathes, saws, planers and slot mortisers also speeded up the production (Gårdlund 1941 and Stavenow-Hidemark 2000). Two other important machines were the grinding machine and polishing machine. At the Windsor chair factory in Nässjö, an American sander was bought in 1912, which was operated by one man instead of the twenty to twenty-five people who had previously taken care of the unpleasant, fingertip-wearing hand-sanding with sandpaper. The polishing machine came in the 1930s and, in turn, replaced about fifteen men. But already in 1888 they had, inspired by the Thonet café chairs, made another simplification to the Windsor chair by replacing, in some models, the massive seats with perforated veneer sheets inserted in round or square frames (Lagerquist 1943).

Dalarna had the greatest diversity in its commercial craft production. Everything from knives and scythes to watches and leather goods were manufactured here. Several of the objects had through their names a direct link to the town of Mora. The Mora clock, the Mora knife and the Mora horse are lasting conceptual objects, although the latter is usually called a Dala horse nowadays. It was carved and whittled from late-maturing, knot-free pine and a skilled craftsman could make a dozen a day.

But commercial craft production was practised even outside these areas, sometimes even reaching international fame, such as the so-called Lindome furniture from northern Halland. This production had its origins in the seventeenth century but was during the nineteenth century, and all the way up to the Second World War, the main source of income for many local farmers. The comfortable yet still stylishly designed Gothenburg chair became particularly popular. The idea behind the model, which was notable for its gently curved and backward-leaning open-work back, had probably reached the Lindome carpenters via returning émigrés from America. During the late nineteenth century, the Lindome carpentry employed about 800 people in approximately 300 carpentry workshops (Tärby 1977 and Martinius 2012).

A lot of wrought or cast iron factory-made furniture was shown at the 1851 London exhibition, including rocking chairs, beds and garden furniture, the latter shaped in natural forms that imitated gnarled branches and large leaves. With cast iron technology it was easy to reproduce identical copies with relatively advanced ornamentation, which led to imitations and the use of standardized motifs. It also required less labour and fuel than the older form of smithery. Bolinder's mechanical workshop in Stockholm was one of the Swedish manufacturers that, early on, focused on cast iron furniture following British models, alongside an extensive production of machines, engines, cooking utensils and iron stoves (Stavenow-Hidemark 2000).

The manufacture of general cargo items in cast iron included various architectural pieces such as spiral staircases, balconies, fountains, park benches, handrails, gratings, urns, umbrella stands and also, for those who eventually would be able to afford it, a great number of objects that facilitated housework. Husqvarna Vapenfabrik (Husqvarna Weapons Factory) for example, aside from iron stoves, also manufactured meat tenderizers, coffee roasters, coffee grinders, pots, mortars, frying pans, griddles, spittoons, juicers, bread mills, mustard seed grinders, fruit cutters, spice mills, cherry de-stoners, various flat and smoothing irons; and for more professional purposes, sausage stuffers as well as dough kneaders and mills for the preparation of marzipan for pastry shops. The most successful product on the domestic side was the meat grinder that came in nine different sizes, which sold a total of 12 million items, making it Husqvarna's best-selling product in all categories. Like the company's other cast iron production during the nineteenth century, it was given a rich and somewhat complicated form (Bergenblad and Hallerstig 1989).

Iron stoves quickly gained a strong and rapidly growing sales position in the domestic market. When they appeared in the second half of the nineteenth century, they became symbols of the transformation from the old agrarian Sweden to a more modern and urbanized country with escalating house building. The iron stove replaced and complemented the open hearth, which was still an important light source in many Swedish homes. Although there existed, in certain contexts, lavish cast iron, so-called illumination stoves, well into the twentieth century, it is a reasonable assumption that the sealed, heat-saving iron stove was a catalyst for the introduction of supplementary kerosene lighting. The one room with fireplace, which was a combined kitchen and living quarters, was until the early twentieth century standard in the typical worker's house.

Cast iron ovens and stoves as well as tiled stoves did exist previously in a few wealthy homes. However, the mass-produced iron stoves would revolutionize both domestic heating and housework for ordinary people. They may have originally been black and wood-burning but, nevertheless, retained the heat better and resulted in much cleaner and smoke-free interiors compared to the old open fireplaces. It had a proper baking oven and cooking was made easier by hot plates that could be expanded or reduced by means of removable rings. The hearth was fitted with an underlying ash-collecting compartment and hanging on at least one side was usually

Fig. 1.8 The practical, wood-burning and heat-saving iron stove soon became mandatory in every domestic kitchen, both in the country and city. Husqvarna's standard model No. 107, which had its origins in the nineteenth century, has here been given an Art Nouveau-inspired decoration and is included in the 1910 catalogue.

a small valve-fitted water heater usually made of copper. Lots of variations existed: about fifty different types were presented in the 1902 Husqvarna casting catalogue. The slightly larger ovens were fitted with both warming ovens and appendant plate cabinets connected to the chimney (Husqvarna 2005). Most mills and the country's major mechanical workshops manufactured their own models. Apart from Bolinders, who started manufacturing stoves as early as the 1840s, and Husqvarna, the better known brands include Norrahammar, Näfveqvarn, Brevens bruk, Åkers styckebruk, Kockums, Ankarsum and Skoglund & Olsson.

Like many casting products, the iron stoves' fronts and many hatches in particular were decorated. The relief-like motifs consisted partly of the brand name and partly of stylized flower and leaf scrollwork and classicist architectural motifs in the shape of columns and capitals, which were considered to convey a universal beauty. The work was carried out by draughtsmen and design artists, often craftsmen who had acquired skills in ornamental drawing in one of the craft schools. The surviving notes from a draughtsman at Bolinders in Kungsholmen demonstrate clearly how informally things could be done in the 1870s:

> Then one day the factory director Bolinder came down and asked me if I wanted to come and help him with the planning of the iron stoves. Of course I was interested as I had a great deal of inclination for, and had also practised, ornamental design, modelling and embossing. Director Bolinder also wished for me to continue taking lessons in the different styles as well as the distribution of different surfaces. Now I was designing stoves, ornamental castings, stable fittings, chandeliers, water features. (Rosell 1997: 66)

Design at this time was subordinate work that was supposed to deliver traditional and saleable surface decoration, preferably in the form of copies in different historical styles.

The Product Range Grows and Is Differentiated

Even though agriculture, particularly in winter, was supplemented by small-scale distribution and cottage industries, it was only with the help of steam and waterpower that industrialization and mass production began to take off. Railways and factories were built, brand new industrial centres were constructed and people left cottages and farms for rapidly growing urban areas. In 1870, 35,000 factory workers were registered, a number that had increased eightfold by the year 1900. A uniform and robust definition of what distinguishes industry from craft has proved difficult to find, and there are far too many intermediate forms. An example of this is the rich tradition of the art industry, which, despite having an extensive production of primarily glassware and ceramics, has retained a large element of craftsmanship. For the same reason, but also because of the many small production units and the large range of period furniture which was difficult to standardize, part of the furniture industry can be qualified as a handicraft industry despite an increased degree of mechanization.

The economic historian Maths Isacson (2007) has described the process of Swedish industrial revolution in a few important steps. It began with the construction of mechanical textile mills and mechanical paper mills as early as the 1830s, continued with the construction of all the steam sawmills along the coast of northern Sweden ('Norrland') from the 1850s, as well as the mechanical workshops and iron and steel mills in the 1870s. The definitive breakthrough came during the economic boom in the 1890s with pulp factories and a new manufacturing industry with a range of new commodities. Faced with this new competition, rural craft practitioners could no longer compete. Competition was further increased by the additional imports associated with the introduction of steam-powered ships and the growth in railway construction.

Urban migration initially created a larger market for both crafts and design. A large number of new city apartments needed to be filled with all sorts of artefacts. Much was factory-made but there were also some unique handcrafted items in the homes of the more wealthy. The flagships of the art industry, the porcelain factories in Rörstrand (1726) and Gustavsberg (1825) as well as the glassworks in Kosta (1742), grew in size and increased their sales. Gustavsberg, for example, doubled its workforce to 600 during a ten-year period in the 1870s, and at Rörstrand the number of workers increased from around a hundred in the 1850s to about 1,100 at the turn of the twentieth century. Similarly, Rörstrand's mechanical equipment increased from a steam engine and fifteen furnaces in 1863 to ten steam engines and thirty-six furnaces in about 1890, when they also had about 100 pottery wheels, fifteen wood turning lathes, 265 *formskivor* and eighteen presses. Kosta installed its first steam engine in 1861 to power a grinding mill with twenty seats. At the turn of the twentieth century a new grinding mill was built with ninety seats. About 500 people were working at the glassworks at the time (Nyström and Brunius 2007 and Artéus 1992).

One distinguishing feature was the differentiation that occurred in the production range, first in the area of household dining goods and then in an increasing number of collections. Gregor Paulsson's collective works from over sixty years ago; *Svensk stad*, which contains many sharp analyses, discusses how decorative refinement became more pronounced when a host of new elements were incorporated into tableware and glassware sets, not always to satisfy a practical function but to serve as purely decorative objects. While the fish-knife and lobster fork were functionally serviceable for their purposes, possibly the champagne jug also, many people could probably do without the asparagus holder.

It was above all improved living standards along with new eating and drinking habits that led to the manufacturers extending their ranges. At Gustavsberg the tableware goods were increased from about twenty pieces in the 1860s to approximately fifty a decade later. Those large dinner services were the principal production of the porcelain factories, at the time usually produced from the cheaper porcelain-like flintware. They were decorated with patterns that were possible to mass-produce with new printing techniques (intaglio printing), often with flower patterns that were transferred from originals of well-known flora. The domestic production soon became very fashionable and in Swedish castles and manor houses imported East Indian tableware was replaced with fashionable tableware services from the two competitors Rörstrand and Gustavsberg. Stove tiles were also included in the product range, these being the visible tiles that covered the sophisticated tile ovens with heat-retaining channel systems. The tiles were decorated with patterns in various colours and reliefs by famous artists and architects such as castle architect Jean-Eric Rehn during the eighteenth century and Ferdinand Boberg and Magnus Isaeus during the late nineteenth century.

A wide range of prestige and status items for exhibitions, shelves and pedestals were also produced. The strangest and seemingly most impractical from a modern perspective are the showpieces: the man-high, decorated urns, vases and candelabras that were cast using different ceramic techniques (see Figure 1.13). These could certainly be discussed but above all they were visible evidence of the manufacturers' technical skill and aesthetic creativity. This was particularly important when the pieces were displayed at the major exhibitions. Then they were usually hand-painted with magnificent scenery by skilled artists who were inspired by the landscapes and genre motifs of salon painting. The models were often reused, however, as the casting moulds were expensive to manufacture (Kåberg 2007).

Not just porcelain but also glass now became an everyday item. A large number of new glassworks were built in the late nineteenth century, mostly in Småland but also as far up as Norrland. Potash produced from the ashes of birch or beech together with quartz-rich sand and red lead were among the most common raw materials in the smelting works. The proximity to the necessary wood resources controlled the localization and the railways facilitated both the transportation of the heavy materials for the glass and the resulting fragile product; glass from Kosta was exported as far away as Russia and India. Gas-fired glass furnaces as well as new techniques simplified and cut the cost of production.

The rational way of thermoforming glass in every possible shape now became more common after already having been introduced in the 1830s. This technology could also imitate the complex patterns of the expensive polished crystal glass. Windows, beer and wine bottles, glasses, inkhorns, pharmacy jars, kerosene lamps, hip flasks, chamber pots, and, in fact, most things could now be manufactured in large quantities and relatively cheaply in glass. The number of pieces in the glassworks' dinner services increased significantly, not only with carafes, glasses and bowls, but also with matching dishes, vases, candlesticks and other essentials. Different glasses for each function became more common; alcohol consumption was widespread and around the turn of the twentieth century there were about 240 breweries, well over a hundred distilleries and in Stockholm alone around fifty vintners. The standardization of glass production was not yet developed, so the quality was not particularly high, particularly when compared with what was being achieved at the French and Italian glassworks at the same time. Much of this was due to the fact that the different owners, as so often in a glassworks context, prioritized the wooden raw material over the management of the glass production itself.

Differentiation and variability were likewise typical of the production of furniture and other furnishings. From the 1830s, furniture in all the art historical styles was produced. At the end of the century these styles could be used side by side in elegant settings, but distributed in different rooms. The dining room was usually furnished in a simultaneously austere and pompous, blackened neo-renaissance furniture, while the smoking room preferably went with a colourful Moorish style. The lady's cabinet or the salon, on the other hand, were decorated with large quantities of textiles and perhaps stuffed, plush Emma armchairs, all in an easy and light rococo. The abundance of varieties in these new styles has often, from the point of view of later Art Nouveau and functionalism, been condemned and ridiculed for being an unoriginal cavalcade of styles. But Elisabet Stavenow-Hidemark (2000) has come to the defence of historicism and claimed that such style choices were not primarily about aesthetics but about creating historical relevance. It was not a question of copying but more of reinterpretations, or rather dramatizations, based on a detailed knowledge of the various styles' artistic expressions. This historicism, according to her, stood for an educational ideal that required knowledge from designers and manufacturers as well as their audience.

Fig. 1.9 An extravagance of expression, colours and shapes characterized the late nineteenth century's grander residential interiors. The salon in Sven R. Högberg's floor at Kungsportsavenyn 6 in Gothenburg had wallpaper, curtains, carpets, furniture and even the flowerpots on their little pedestals done in the same matching floral pattern. The picture was taken in about 1900.

During the second half of the nineteenth century many innovations were introduced that would make urban living considerably more tolerable in general. Storage systems for drinking water, intricate water and sewage systems, gas works and electrical works were built. All of this created a need for new products and tools and thereby altered living accommodation. These innovations first gained a foothold in the manor houses and luxury apartments, then with the growing middle classes and lastly in the workers' dwellings. These developments put the focus on hygiene. Composting toilets in yards or passageways dominated well into the twentieth century but indoor toilets and water closets started to appear as early as the 1880s in newly developed urban apartments. Some installed zinc bathtubs, while others used portable, curtain-fitted so-called closet showers, reminiscent of today's shower cubicles. These conserved water and the pumping system for the shower hose was powered by pedals on the floor above the water reservoir (Paulsson 1950).

On the lighting side the real revolution came with the introduction of electricity in the 1880s. Although gas had already been introduced in a number of cities by the middle of the century, the earliest in Gothenburg in 1846, its main purpose was street lighting. Indoor gas never became a common commodity even though some iron stoves were replaced or supplemented with the more convenient gas cookers. Instead, it was the flammable and difficult to manage candles, oil lamps and above all kerosene lamps that dominated before electric lighting. It was no coincidence that electric light was first introduced in industry, according to ethnologist Jan Garnert (1993), because workplaces were vast and they could thereby turn more of the day's hours into work hours. For artisanal production the light from oil lamps and candles had been enough, but to illuminate the sawmills' timber yards and the huge spinning halls the new powerful electric arc lights were welcomed. By the end of the century there were also many light bulbs installed in the old chandeliers of upper-class homes.

Inventions Pave the Way for the Manufacturing Industry

The introduction of steam power meant that industry was no longer dependent on location. When it became unnecessary for production to be located near a running watercourse, the factories made their way to the cities, especially to good port locations in order to facilitate the comprehensive management of coal and ash in the firing of the steam boilers. The woodworking industry is an early example of the emergence of urban industry, centred in Gothenburg and Stockholm. The first mechanical joinery was founded in Gothenburg in 1851, at the same time as the London Exhibition was in progress. It was steam-powered and had both veneer saws (for the cutting of millimetre-thin layers) and circular saws, planing machines and lathes as well as various specialized machines, such as a so-called ornament machine. Production was focused on such diverse products as windows and cigar boxes. The refinement of Swedish wood resources was an important factor in the process of industrialization, demonstrated by, among other things, the growth in the number of factories in the joinery industry being twice as high as in other industries around the turn of the twentieth century (Gårdlund 1941).

Urbanization in connection with early industrialization in Britain, as well as on the continent, provided an outlet for the increasing export of Swedish iron and timber. Several of the larger joineries invested in the production of prefabricated wooden buildings and standardized fittings. The most well known is Ekmans Mekaniska Snickerifabrik (Ekman's Mechanical Joinery) in Stockholm, which started operations in 1858 under the direction of the architect Pehr Johan Ekman. He had left an established career as a city architect and creator of, for example, the Gothenburg Stock Exchange building, for the joinery business. The company won numerous awards for their hospitals, military barracks, churches and summer villas at the many international exhibitions during the 1870s–1890s (Plate 1). The houses were pictured with cosy smoking chimneys in lavish, colour catalogues. Around the turn of the twentieth century the factory employed nearly 500 workers.

Much of the production from the Ekman joinery was exported to emigrants and settlers in, for example, Brazil and Argentina but also to early industrialized Britain. The prefabricated houses had an obvious advantage in their transportability; they were also quick to build: about four to five weeks for a detached house with an attending fitter and carpenters on site. They were therefore well adapted to industrial society's increasing mobility and changeable way of life. The catalogue houses' walls were made of planed tongue-and-groove boards with cardboard spacers, which were knocked together to form large boards. The method is reminiscent of Swedish industrial wooden house building today, which is also based on prefabricated wall modules and quick installation. To be able to move into a completed catalogue house within a month of starting production, as Swedish companies offered, was still in 2007 something 'completely unique from an international perspective' (DI 23/8 2007), according to the Swedish Federation of Wood and Furniture Industry. Building styles varied, not between different functional styles like today, but from an American-inspired panel architecture and English cottage style to an old Nordic style, often with almost overwhelming gingerbread work. The factories also supplied doors, windows, frames, mouldings and painted or varnished pine furniture, sometimes supplemented with iron stoves from one of the ironworks (Arnshav 1997).

In terms of furniture, there was also some experimentation with prefabricated standardized designs that were presented and sold through richly illustrated catalogues. It was the accelerating urban migration of the late nineteenth century that led to a rapidly increasing demand for ready-made furniture. The Austrian company Firma Gebrüder Thonet, which in 1841 had received a patent for a method that made it possible to bend solid and laminated wood using heat on an industrial scale, dominated this area. The principle, which in itself was not new but had long since been used in areas such as shipbuilding, conserved timber and resulted in strong constructions. Because the furniture was sold unassembled and could therefore be delivered in flat packages, their work spread all over the world.

The bentwood method inspired many furniture designers to come up with new design ideas. It became a successful concept in the Nordic countries, which loved natural materials, particularly in the 1930s and 1940s. However, as early as 1901 a Swedish joinery was ready to take up production, namely the toy factory Gemla (in 1910 reformed as Gemla Fabrikers AB) in Diö, Småland. The range was called Wiener furniture and included in addition to the famous café chairs, other chair types in a similar style as well as armchairs, tables, bookshelves, flower stands, wash basins, stools and coat racks with or without umbrella stands, all according to the Gemla catalogue from 1921 (Designarkivet, Pukeberg). The catalogue notes in particular the much stronger seat ring of the chairs, which was bent out of one piece instead of joined together in several parts as tradition stipulated. Even the under rings were completely bent and there were special arched connectors and reinforcements between the back and seat available as extras. Plain or perforated seats were made of triple veneer and were available in light or dark mahogany or walnut. The furniture was delivered amply packed in paper wrapping and transported in separate returnable cages.

Bending wood (at this time mainly beech) in moulds using hot steam was difficult and also time-consuming because the assembly had to dry in the moulds for up to fourteen days. In an attempt to improve quality some experienced woodbenders from

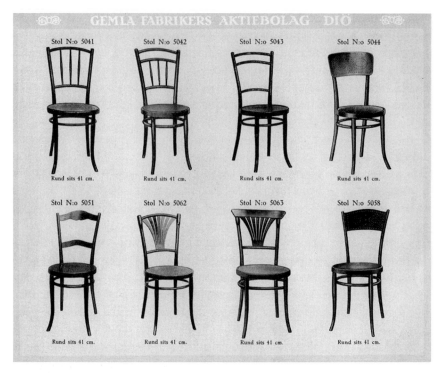

Fig. 1.10 Thonet's bentwood furniture was not just a popular import item, but also inspired many furniture factories. Gemla Fabrikers AB from Småland built a whole product line around the café chair with standardized bases and variable backrests.

Bohemia were hastily recruited to the factory in Småland. Some letters of recommendation from large furniture dealers in January 1909 also indicate that Gemla's Vienna furniture was cheaper and 'in every way as solid and comparable to the products from the finest Austrian firms'. In addition, the Swedish factory was punctual when it came to deliveries, which was also an advantage compared to the cumbersome furniture shipments from Vienna (Artéus 2006). Compression moulding was also used by other companies, not only for furniture, but also, for example, for tray manufacturing by Åry Fanérprodukter AB later in the 1900s.

Development in the textile industry began in the early nineteenth century, despite strong competition from all the spinning wheels and looms within the arts and crafts. An interesting division occurred when wool production was concentrated in the important industrial city of Norrköping, while western Sweden and Borås in particular with the surrounding Sjuhäradsbygden became a centre for cotton textiles, and eventually also for design-intensive ready-to-wear clothes. With the help of several well-known inventions, mainly developed in Britain, mechanized spinning and weaving mills were built following British designs with hundreds of predominantly female workers. They were usually water powered and the spinning mills were housed in massive brick buildings adjacent to watercourses. The heavy, vibrating mechanical looms were, however, not readily placed in tall multi-storey buildings, but instead a new type of structure was developed in the form of extensive single-storey buildings covered with glass ceilings. The glass panes, which were supposed to provide the desired lighting inside the factory, were arranged in a serrated so-called saw-tooth roof, which was supported by a forest of cast iron pillars. The oldest and best-known example is the sail- and tent-weaving mill in Jonsered, which was set up by Scottish immigrants as early as the mid-1830s.

The sewing machine, invented in the 1840s and shown by Singer as one of the flagship products in the American section of the London Exhibition, became a prerequisite for the establishment of a ready-to-wear clothes industry. In Sweden, a country where even up to the turn of the twentieth century 90 per cent of all clothes were sewn at home or by seamstresses or tailors, it supplemented or replaced the loom in many homes. Husqvarna Vapenfabrik, originally a rifle factory started in 1689, was the first to begin large-scale Swedish sewing machine manufacturing. However, initially it was a struggle. Only 500 units of the very first design from 1872, Nordstjernan (The North Star), or 'cat back' as it was called because of its special hunched shape, were produced. It turned out that the slender and heavily curved cast iron arm that was meant to give the user plenty of workspace was far too weak in its dimensions and twisted when sewing thick fabrics. The company's engineers were sent over to the USA to study production on site. Two main models were subsequently produced, one for home use (Freja) and a more robust one for professional use (Triumf); both remained in production relatively unchanged for several decades. The foundry also had a large woodworking shop with the important task of producing wooden supports for the machines and even entire sewing machine furniture. After the uncertain start, sewing machine production increased rapidly and by the turn of the nineteenth century Husqvarna had supplied over 200,000 sewing machines and the new product category quickly began to dominate the company's production (Husqvarna Fabriksmuseum).

During the nineteenth century the manufacture of iron products in the Swedish ironworks and machine shops was strongly influenced by British and subsequently American models. At the same time the manufacture of sewing machines and larger pieces, such as steam engines, boilers, saw frames, motors, planing machines, locomotives and ships, was largely focused on the domestic market. While household artefacts were usually provided with a narrative decoration, designers put a lot of effort into giving the machines, machine parts and other practical objects an attractive architectural design, in which the material's character, but also the classical ideals of symmetry, harmony and balance were leading expressions. The architecture and design historian Björn Linn (2002) called this production engineering culture.

The situation changed drastically in the decades around the turn of the twentieth century particularly as a result of new Swedish inventions. Several new industrial companies were formed that successfully invested in the worldwide export of mass-produced goods. They learned how to make new steel grades and embraced

Fig. 1.11 A prerequisite for the achievement of a streamlined standardized mass production was the ability to calibrate instruments and measure with sufficient precision. C. E. Johansson's gauge block set was, in this context, an invaluable tool that spread across the whole world.

new organizational principles. These so-called smart-industries, among whom Alfa-Laval (the separator), ASEA (generators and motors), Bahco (the wrench and plumber wrench), AGA (lighthouse illumination), Electrolux (vacuum cleaners, refrigerators), Ericsson (telephones) and SKF (bearings) are among the more well known, have been the backbone of Swedish business and still survive, in one way or another, to this day. These companies established Sweden as a leading technological nation.

Many of the products from these companies were primarily intended for use in the workplace, and were related to manufacturing. They in turn helped facilitate the production of goods that were intended to reach consumers. An excellent but lesser-known example of so-called 'producer goods design' was Carl Edvard Johansson's invention of a gauge block (known as 'Jo Blocks') for use in the mechanical industry. Johansson was granted a patent in 1901 for a gauge block consisting of over a hundred precisely polished pieces. This turned out to be an indispensable tool for calibrations and making precision measurements down to a few thousandths of a millimetre. Johansson's gauge blocks were used, for example, early on in the automotive industry by Ford, among others. It laid the foundation for a common industrial measurement standard which facilitated the accuracy of standardization and mass production. On an intellectual level, they also came to symbolize the rational twentieth century where precision and measurability were encouraged, often at the expense of emotional values.

A characteristic feature of these new inventions was that the originators themselves had usually been responsible for the products' basic design. Gustaf Rosell (1997) argues that it is possible to discern some common traits in the great minds behind these turn of the century inventions. They were trying to solve problems that were related to needs that were well known to them. They were more interested in totalities than detailed solutions. They were obsessed by their ideas and saw no obstacle to their execution. They often thought in metaphors and were often messy or downright sloppy. They were practically minded and experimented rather than theorizing or analysing problems. Their approach to work had more in common with art and craft rather than science, although several had scientific training. They sketched, designed and built prototypes, all supported by very simple calculations. In this way they resembled modern-day designers more than modern-day engineers.

The New Industrial Products Are Aestheticized but Criticized

The essential feature of these new products was the simple, bare structures where component was added to component, preferably in symmetrical, balanced compositions. All the product's components were revealed openly, honestly and clearly. A holistic approach with the intention of achieving a specific, coherent design for the particular product category was rare. This engineering aesthetic contained, of course, a measure of pride in showing off new achievements; nevertheless, it should not be forgotten that they were untested which is why it was necessary to arrange things so that it was easy to reach all the components for service and repair. At the same time, there had rarely been a greater need, at least for sales-related reasons, to devote further work to aesthetic refinement. Many of the new products sold themselves and demand usually exceeded the potential rate of production.

A typical example of this was the Ericsson telephones, especially the so-called 'skeleton type', which was personally designed by Lars Magnus Ericsson. At the turn of the twentieth century, 95 per cent of Ericsson's production was exported; Britain was the largest market and customers had to wait for up to fifteen months for delivery. With its stark, symmetrical shape and curved framework of magnetic steel the skeleton type was magnificent in its appearance and resembled Paris's Eiffel Tower. But even though it was meant to adorn the writing desks and tables of directors around the world, and therefore had been nickel-plated and decorated

Fig. 1.12 The skeleton type, which was designed by the founder of the telephone company Ericsson, Lars Magnus Ericsson, in 1884, is a typical example of an engineering product in which component has been added to component to create a functional whole with visible and easily accessible components. This model with handset from 1892 is, like sewing machines and other early consumer products, decorated with pre-printed transfer images, so-called decalcomanias.

with attractive, gold coloured ornamentation, the shape was fundamentally construc-tive. The double-curved framework was an ingenious way to integrate two inductor magnets, which were necessary for the apparatus to be able to make calls. The skel-eton type with the epochal handset soon became an icon for Ericsson and served for many years as the company logo (Brunnström 2006).

Tools and machine components with low levels of exposure were designed practi-cally and functionally without unnecessary decoration; the purpose should speak for itself. SKF's spherical, self-aligning ball bearing is perhaps the most extreme exam-ple. It was in production from 1907 and was soon an integral component in moving machine parts such as the drive shafts of various power units. The then newly estab-lished company made a remarkable breakthrough in Swedish business. After about a decade, SKF was Sweden's largest company and a major player in world industry. The bearings with their precise, hardened balls of polished stainless steel, which could move almost without any friction in all directions, fascinated the public. The outer bearing ring's spherical shape made it possible even for axles that were some-what lopsided and skewed from, for example, uneven ground to now be attuned and start spinning thanks to the balls. SKF's spherical, self-adjusting ball bearings were the embodiment of Swedish manufacturing quality. But with its stripped aesthetic and high finish, the ball bearing was soon to symbolize something bigger; namely, the mechanized modern society that was moving at an ever-faster rate. In the 1930s the ball bearing had been elevated to an art and culture object and was even exhibited at the Museum of Modern Art in New York.

The newly invented machines and devices were arranged practically and acces-sibly on carts, foundations, tripods, slabs and boards that could be rolled on the ground, or alternatively bolted, placed on tables or hung on the wall. The relationship between the position and the expected surface was, in other words, an important aspect to take into consideration, quite different from the small, mobile objects of today where considering a lying or standing design is less interesting. Wood and metal, above all iron and steel, were the key materials. The joineries received new assignments when sewing machine manufacturers began to demand cabinets and stands, and telephone manufacturers were in need of carved boards and boxes. The carpentry was simple and not too detailed, which facilitated mass production, while striving for furniture-like qualities.

Many products appeared to come straight from the factory floor and were not adapted for offices or homes. Black was the usual metallic paint, it being both the cheapest and most practical considering soot, oil spills and the like. What decoration there was, was simple and repeatable. Decoration was used to domesticate the products, that is to say adapt them to a life outside the factory. But decorative orna-ments were also used at this time, as they are today, to raise the product's status or to conceal various defects in the coating. The technique of pre-printed trans-fer images – so-called decalcomanias – was common. The motifs were preferably rendered in gold print on a black background and the subject of motifs was taught at craft schools.

The criticism of many of these early industrially manufactured products was at times very harsh even during the nineteenth century. Many such comments can be found in the Swedish Society of Crafts and Design's notices, which in 1905 changed its name to Svenska Slöjdföreningens Tidskrift (today known as the design magazine *Form*). A representative example is the cultural historian Bernard Salin's assertion in 1892 that the ornamentation on industrial products lacked originality; they were just imitations of the past and the works of other cultures. Ornamentation was a controversial topic among nineteenth century design critics. Many of the new items shown at the 1851 London Exhibition were almost grotesque in their over-decorated appearance. They did not give much consideration to practical issues such as handling, storing and maintenance.

But the debate concerning taste, which gained momentum during the second half of the nineteenth century, was not only about the excessive decoration and the lack of consideration of practical issues. It was also about all the borrowed, tired and archaic forms, just as Salin had expressed. The motifs were usually taken from published ornament collections, so-called pattern books, and were primarily of two main types: picturesque genre or still-life motifs or architectural and organically formed ornaments, the latter usually in the shape of classicist columns and stylized plant motifs with ancient models. Popular motifs were long, slender lotus flowers, round rosettes, sprawling palmettes and lushly growing acanthuses, often separated by zigzag bands.

Counter-movements like the Arts and Crafts Movement in Britain and the international Art Nouveau movement offered alternative ornamentation that was very much inspired by the design language of immediate nature. Art Nouveau ornamentation was lighter, more resplendent and vibrant. It could manifest itself in the form of ornamental carrier pigeons on the Postverket (Post Office) building in Stockholm or dragonflies and Swedish summer flowers on porcelain from Rörstrand and Gustavsberg. In Sundborn, Karin and Carl Larsson's innovative home interiors were inspiring; particularly after their book *Ett Hem* (A Home) was published in 1899.

The Sundborn style's colourful and slightly contradictory sober rusticity became an ideal for Ellen Key, one of Sweden's great propagandists for simplicity and elegance in home furnishings. In an essay from 1897, which two years later was expanded into the book *Skönhet i hemmen* (Beauty in the home), she focused on the Swedish woman in particular who she said could and should exert an influence over the layout of the home. Everyone could learn to have good taste regardless of material circumstances. There was no need to start decorating and crafting in an excessive way but rather the simple was beautiful. Functionality and satisfaction in everyday life was created through the use of bright, airy textiles and light, comfortable furniture arranged against harmonious wall and wallpaper backgrounds. The advice was well intentioned but it also gave Key's writing an air of the authoritarian cultivation of aesthetic tastes that the functionalists later took on and developed further.

There was an inherent problematic dualism in industrial art production at the beginning of the new century. On the one hand, simplicity and naturalness were advocated, yet on the other, there was deadly serious competition for awards at the recurring exhibitions, which encouraged the prestigious and grandiose. In order to be recognized in competition with high-quality French and Japanese manufacturing, one had to target the elite, that is to say ceramic art and art glass with signed works by, for example, Alf Wallander from Rörstrand, Gunnar G:son Wennerberg from Gustavsberg or Anna and Ferdinand Boberg. It was also here that artistic efforts were made and observed, which led to the simpler manufacturing being neglected and the quality products only reaching out to the intellectual and wealthy groups in society; that the so-called *Allkonstnärer* (All-Artists) usually received their commissions from industrial society's emerging bourgeoisie reinforced the skewed focus of production.

After the 1914 Baltic Exhibition in Malmö these insights were formulated into a scathing criticism that affected the entire Swedish industry. The Swedish Society of Crafts and Design's new secretary Erik Wettergren set the tone together with the architect Torsten Stubelius and art historian Gregor Paulsson. The exhibition appeared to be stuck in a rut and lacked courage in dealing with the new tasks of the day, claimed Wettergren, and he highlighted several possible sources of inspiration such as mechanized German society and Danish craftsmanship. Stubelius attacked the exhibited furniture, which he felt should be less extraordinary and more adapted to people. He also took the opportunity to have a dig at the largely anonymous body of pattern constructors that the furniture industry had employed, and wanted to see younger, academically trained architects in these positions who 'should focus on simple and cheap furniture for the industrial worker and farmer' (Ivanov 2004: 145). For his part, Paulsson fuelled the more technocratic critique with the article 'Anarki eller tidsstil (Anarchy or style of the time)' in which he lamented the train's similarity to coaches on rails, the car's similarity to horse-drawn carriages with engines and the electric fixture's imitation of gas fixtures and kerosene lamps. According to Paulsson (1915) the risk of imitation was obvious in the transition from craft to industry, with its reduced, simplified parts and repeated, cheapened decoration.

These criticisms led to the reorganization of the Swedish Society of Crafts and Design in 1915 and a young, radical generation to take over the educational work. Inspired by developments in Germany where, among others, the world-famous Deutscher Werkbund movement worked to unite art with industry, they decided to try to strengthen the contact between artists and industrial companies organizationally. An intermediary agency was established, which from spring 1917 was led by the forceful textile artist Elsa Gullberg. In a short space of time, she managed to provide artistic labour to twenty-two companies in diverse industries, not just in the arts industry. Some of her unions came to be lifelong and significant such as Wilhelm Kåge with Gustavsberg and Simon Gate and Edward Hald with Orrefors (Hald 1989).

An intensive propaganda campaign continued in the Swedish Society of Crafts and Design's name. Gregor Paulsson followed up his article with manifestos in book form: *Den nya arkitekturen* (The new architecture) (1916) and *Vackrare vardagsvara* (More beautiful everyday items) (1919). The main message was that you had to embrace the new technology's opportunities and strive for new product categories as demanded by the new product forms. Elsa Gullberg successfully continued her placement enterprise in design until 1924. She managed to provide all the leading porcelain factories, half a dozen furniture makers, wallpaper and textile factories, glassworks, ironworks, watchmakers and goldsmiths, and companies in the electrical industry and packaging industry with artistically trained employees. She helped household stores with their selection, organized competitions for new types of furniture, ceramics and cast iron objects, helped KF (The Swedish Co-operative Union) with standardized fittings and furnished, together with a large number of architects and artistic consultants, some twenty hospitals, and much more. Gullberg also wrote nuanced critical articles and gave lectures. The following lines are taken from a speech she gave during an 'industry week' in 1919:

> The artist should replace the convention which is based on outdated forms, he should replace the shameless or stupid plagiarism, he should against the influence of the vulgar, popular tastes set a sound and educated judgment and, finally, he should give the public exactly what it needs and can appreciate ... It will not do to restrain the artist in the same way that one restrains an accountant or official who daily has to do the same work in the same limited business area. It will not do to place him in a small closet far away from the factory and ask him to produce a pattern when you stick an order sheet through the door, in the same way that a vending machine discharges something when you put a coin in it ... The industrial man and the artist must unite in the creation of economic and cultural values. (Hald 1989: 21)

Elsa Gullberg's forward-thinking argument could be used as a summary of the debate about design throughout the twentieth century.

Attempts at Artistic Renewal

Gregory Paulsson's talk about a necessary standardization of industrial products was derived from German models, most consistently realized by the electro-technical company AEG with the help of the artist Peter Behrens. They were, in turn, based on American ideas of standardization and rationalization. During the years 1907–1914 Behrens developed a carefully thought-out company profile that included everything from factory architecture, logo and advertising campaigns to a large series of electric kettles, lighting fixtures and other manufacturing. No Swedish company was able to manage anything similar, although ASEA (now ABB) which had started a similar production in the town of Västerås was strongly influenced by its German rival. Parallel to Behrens's work in Germany, ASEA also consulted the art school educated architect Erik Hahr to design the facade of ASEA's new factory buildings and the architectural partners Sigurd Lewerentz & Torsten Stubelius for the design of the more consumer-adapted part of the company's production. Stubelius, who had contacts in the Deutscher Werkbund movement and was a keen debater, asserted the close link between product design and factory architecture: 'when an industry gains an understanding of the importance of the artistic for industrial production, then it is also transferred to the workplace' (Stubelius 1914: 85).

That it could also be the other way round is shown by an early example from the manufacture of telephones. In the 1890s, Kungliga Telegrafverket (Royal Telegraph Agency, now Telia Company AB) had engaged the architect Isak Gustaf Clason to provide advice on building issues, which in practice meant that he designed their offices, telegraph stations, workshops, telephone booths and eventually also their first telephones. In particular, the table version from 1894, which was enclosed in a sturdy metal casing like a little house with a flat roof, became standard equipment in many countries for years to come. A decade or so later, Ericsson also brought in an architect, Torben Grut, to successfully design some of their export models (Brunnström 2006).

To conclude from these examples that the arts played a significant role in the design of Swedish everyday goods at the time, however, is something of an exaggeration. Furthermore, these efforts were too isolated. The telephone was a consumer product with high demands on appearance and usability. That global mass production had already started in the late 1880s was unique and was of course due to the prerequisite that it had to exist in a lot of places at once. That requirement did not exist in the art industry, which instead skilfully developed its luxury segment with the assistance of artists; this is something of a paradox given the Swedish Society of Crafts and Design's official rhetoric about the importance of more beautiful everyday products for the masses.

Together Rörstrand and Gustavsberg completely dominated the country's ceramic production. They both had experience of artists who put their personal signatures on their prestigious model ranges, mostly ornamental ceramics but also some exclusive services, from the late nineteenth century. Alf Wallander's (1862–1914) delicate naturalistic Art Nouveau pieces for Rörstrand were inspired by the indigenous fauna and flora: dragonflies, red clover and flowering thistles. His contemporary and colleague at Gustavsberg, Gunnar G:son Wennerberg (1863–1914), stayed within the same realm of motifs with primroses and lilies of the valley where as much care was devoted to the stems and foliage as to the flowers themselves. The latter was also attached to the Kosta glassworks in order to raise the level of the unique art glass for the major world exhibitions in the early 1900s; Wennerberg had, like his great role model Émile Gallé, developed a very particular feeling for the anatomy of flowers and foliage. In contrast, they were content to keep copying foreign models for their glass dinnerware (Widman 1975).

Not only an interest in Swedish nature and culture but also a sense of national pride grew increasingly strong during the early 1900s. It was noticeable in architecture where the old method of constructing timber houses came back into use as well as using natural stone. In the centre of Stockholm, the new Skånebanken building's entrance facade was decorated with, among other things, cabbage, turnips and beets carved out of sandstone from Övedskloster in Skåne. In Gothenburg the entrance to

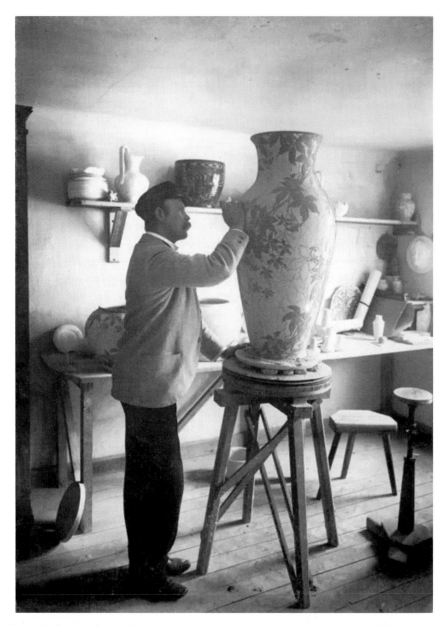

Fig. 1.13 Gunnar G:son Wennerberg, artistic leader at Gustavsberg between 1895 and 1908, decorating a sumptuous urn with sgraffito technique. Photo from 1900, Gustavsbergs Porslinsmuseum

the monumental headquarters of Telegrafverket (the Telegraph Agency) was decorated with both swallows and bears. Cottages all over Sweden were painted red with paint from the copper mines in Falun and in Kiruna, 'the nation's own treasure chest', a church that borrowed its forms from Sami huts was built. In many cases the cream of Sweden's artists was hired to do the ornamentation. It was important to strengthen the belief in one's own heritage and one's own possibilities at a time when emigration was completely draining the country of able people of working age (Plate 2). It was also noticeable in the art industry's motifs, which generally began to shift from the stylized antique to the naturalistic national. Swedish people generally began to wake up and cultivate their own garden, even in a literal sense; it was no coincidence that Swedish landscape gardening was in bloom around the turn of the twentieth century and that the organization Föreningen Svensk trädgård (The Swedish Garden Society) was formed in 1907.

On the initiative of Lilli Zickerman the organization Föreningen för Svensk Hemslöjd (Swedish Handicraft Society) was founded in 1899, which quickly developed into a popular movement. The object was to save artistic handicraft traditions, while at the same time it was also about providing employment and encouraging women to stay in the countryside. The focus was on textiles, a traditionally female domain. At the time, textiles played a very different role from today and middle-class homes were completely overloaded with all sorts of practical and decorative textiles, both for decoration but also to create cosiness and comfort. Since 1874 Handarbetets Vänner (the Association of Friends of Textile Art), a government-supported organization that was founded by Sophie Adlersparre and nineteen other women, had, like the craft associations and schools, worked towards propagating a taste for domestic products, to combat what was considered inferior imported embroidery. Nevertheless, it took a couple of decades before, above all, gloomy German renaissance patterns were replaced with lighter and brighter compositions. The association had a studio in Stockholm, which employed weavers and seamstresses who worked on original patterns under the direction of an artistically responsible manageress, and several more or less firmly attached pattern constructors. In addition, there was a network of textile workers in the provinces, who were paid and taught. Production was focused on soft furnishings and decorative textiles; everything from rugs, quilts, sheets, pillows, bedding, upholstery, curtains and tapestries to ecclesiastical textiles like altar cloths, antependia and vestments (Danielson 1991).

Led by Agnes Branting and Carin Wästberg and inspired by Swedish motifs Handarbetets Vänner's (Association of Friends of Textile Art) production developed radically in the 1900s. They took on a staff of Konstfack-educated pattern draughtsmen and the day's leading artists. Dag Widman (1975: 22) argues that they consequently laid the foundation 'for the free tapestry art that became an essential feature of 20th century Swedish art'. Also fundamental was the production of rugs using the flat-woven rolakan and flossa techniques that Märta Måås-Fjetterström began in her weaving studio in Båstad. Her exclusive production signed AB MMF spread all over the world and quickly became synonymous with artistic quality regardless of whether she herself made it or one of her many colleagues and successors (Plate 3).

Artistic renewal was less evident in the wider everyday production of furniture; instead it was mostly associated with specific expensive objects, often for private environments. Those involved were typically architects who were at the same time usually designing the building themselves and it was therefore more like furniture craft than furniture industry. Famous examples are Elis Benckert's simple and austere dining room furniture for Villa Lagercrantz in Djursholm, Carl Bergsten's Vienna Secessionist inspired chairs and cupboards and Carl Westman's white-glazed furniture for the Pressens villa in Saltsjöbaden. The latter also designed simpler furniture in green-stained aspen, labelled worker's furniture, but which instead proved to attract the intellectual circles. The so-called *Allkonstnärer* (all-artists) of the time often, like the great European role models Hoffman, Mackintosh, Horta, Gaudí, produced congenial work for their benefactors in the newly rich middle class but had considerably more difficulty understanding and interpreting the preferences of the people; you often get the feeling that their social aesthetic ideals were largely about silencing their bad consciences and justifying themselves before their colleagues.

In an attempt to shift the focus from crafts and luxury production to a simpler ideal based on typification and cheaper mass production, the Swedish Society of Crafts and Design organized the so-called Hemutställningen (Home Exhibition) in 1917. It took place in the newly built Liljevalchs konsthall (Liljevalchs art gallery) in Stockholm and contained twenty-three small apartments with related equipment. Now was the time for the Swedish Society of Crafts and Design's new generation of social aesthetes to try to convince the poorer sections of society that their version of taste was the right one. Also in the back of their minds was of course the hope of launching industrial production again after a few lean years of war. The objectives were ambitious; too ambitious as it would turn out. Many interpretations have been made of the exhibits' results, both at the time and later, and opinion has swung recently in favour of a more critical approach. There were not many tangible results from new designs based on successful collaborations between art and industry to exhibit, instead it was more about ambition; this despite the fact that in particular Elsa Gullberg had put in a massive effort to match artists with manufacturers. But as so often happens in an exhibition context a great deal was quickly produced and handmade. In addition, the working class proved not to be so easy to convince, either to attend the exhibition or buy the items being exhibited. But the exhibition was well attended and one of the more memorable items was the residential kitchen arranged by the promising architect Gunnar Asplund with rag rugs and pale wallpaper together with a gateleg table, chairs, cabinets and the obligatory kitchen sofa, all in Swedish pine.

Edward Hald's Turbinservis (Turbine service) also received deserved attention at the exhibition. In 1947, his son, the art historian Arthur Hald, interviewed Elsa

Gullberg who described her intermediary work and touched on the groundbreaking decoration:

His first dinner service was based entirely on a residual craft technique, for which the factory had a staff of dedicated female workers, namely using a brush to paint stripes on a plate spinning on a potter's wheel. Between the stripes Hald painted staccato-like brush strokes and the first modern decoration, which was built on a within the industry well-recognised method and an acceptance of its existing workforce, was born. 'That way of working was quite sensible' people said at the factory. That plate has been 'the soaped plank' that brought many colleagues into the industry. (Hald 1947: 176 and 1989: 16–17)

2 On the Industry's Terms, 1910s to 1940s

Serial Production Enables the Breakthrough of Consumer Goods

Among the radical wing of the Swedish Society of Crafts and Design there was a strong belief in what artists and architects could achieve if they were only given the opportunity to work in industry. When Gregor Paulsson in his book *Vackrare vardagsvara* (More beautiful everyday items) described the modern design of the time it was created by engineers and constructors who were guided by technology and regarded form as secondary. But now was the time, said Paulsson, for 'the artist to step in and give the goods a shape, which in part matches their method of production, and in part is contemporary and ultimately beautiful because of these and their other properties'. He should also be able to step in and 'in the industries, where the design is not obvious, introduce modern beauty' (Paulsson 1919: 15). His ideas are, despite the archaic rhetoric, strikingly prophetic and correspond well to how design work has developed in the twentieth century. The ball bearing had a given technical shape, something that did not apply to Hoovers, furniture and tableware, so-called consumer goods.

The art industry had a long experience of creating a machine-adapted decoration that was simplified and repeatable, but when it came to the design of more complicated products the machines could not yet compete with the manual dexterity of the individual. Design work stopped at the shell and never went into the core, as Björn Linn (2002) so aptly put it. If one was to reach the broad masses, it became increasingly clear that design work had to submit to the terms of serial production.

The experience of being able to manufacture complicated products quickly and cheaply existed in the USA, even if design had not caught up. The car manufacturer Henry Ford showed more than anyone else what the possibilities were for making production more effective using the engineer Fredrick Winslow Taylor's streamlining methods. Taylor's innovation meant that each worker should be highly specialized and bound to a one-sided task. The workers thus became cogs in the machinery, which could be replaced if needed, something that was later skilfully illustrated and caricatured by Charlie Chaplin in the film *Modern Times*. But at the same time Taylor argued that the working environment and tools had to be improved and adapted to the worker. This would not only reduce occupational injuries but also make better use of the workers' capacity and increase the production rate, which ultimately gave the owner a better economic return. It is this that has come to be known as Taylorism, which came to be of great significance and was widely applied in the Western world's manufacturing industries; Swedish pioneers were AB Separator, Ericsson and ASEA (Brunnström 1990).

Henry Ford achieved amazing results by making use of the new work discipline together with an innovative factory design. In addition, he included something new in the mechanical industry, the assembly line, an idea that was taken from Chicago's large slaughterhouses. There the pig carcasses first travelled down a conveyor belt in the ceiling and were then placed on the assembly line so that each cutter could perform their specific tasks. The car design was standardized to one model painted in one colour, black. Using far fewer employees Ford was able to manufacture considerably cheaper cars in his factories than the competition, 90 per cent of which were sold before they left 'the marriage point' where the bodies were mounted on the chassis. One thousand identical Model T Fords were produced every day just in his flagship factory in Highland Park, Detroit. A few years later it is estimated that about 80 per cent of all the world's cars were in the United States and that about 60 per cent of these were Ford cars (Houltz 2005).

Great emphasis was placed on hygiene in Ford's factories. Corners and recesses were painted white to prevent dirt from hiding and a staff of about 700 people made sure to continuously clean and maintain the premises (Brunnström 1990). There was every reason to prioritize hygiene, not least in Sweden. Many widespread diseases had affected the country; diseases that not only caused great suffering but also affected the economy and became part of many people's everyday lives. It has been estimated that tuberculosis alone killed about 1 million people a year in Europe at the beginning of the twentieth century (Puranen 1984). Hygienics became a leading theme in design and production. Telephone manufacturers took steps to reduce the spread of infection, not for the body of the machine itself, which through the intro-duction of new sheet metal pressing techniques had been given a protective cover, but to protect the mouthpiece, which was of course held near the mouth. Removable hailers were offered in materials that could withstand disinfection by boiling. Another solution came from the Stockholm-based company AB Monofon that had from the outset in 1907 built its entire business on the 'non disease carrying' telephone mouthpiece. This crookedly cut mouthpiece allowed one to speak freely into space instead of directing the mouth towards a funnel or membrane (Brunnström 2006).

A product that radically eased sanitation and the proliferation of bacteria was the vacuum cleaner. For the few that could afford it vacuum cleaning of the home was already available in the late nineteenth century, but with the help of large and heavy pumps operated by hand or by steam. The horse-drawn vacuum-cleaning wagon was parked on the street and long hoses were pulled up along the facade and in through the windows. With the introduction of electric drive and new fan technology the machine size was quickly reduced and the first devices for indoor use made by German and American companies started appearing on the market around 1906–8. In 1910 the Danish company Nilfisk introduced a vacuum cleaner in the form of a hose-fitted, vertical, shiny steel cylinder and in the same year the first Swedish vacuum cleaner patent was taken out for a similar device called Salus, which was really a variation on the American vacuum cleaner Santo. Considerably more famous is the vacuum cleaner production launched by the far-sighted but somewhat reckless industrialist Axel Wenner-Gren in 1912. The device, which was also built following the concept of a standing cylinder, was called Lux 1, weighed 14 kilograms and laid the foundation for the large company Electrolux. But it was still too expensive to supply anything other than industries and hospitals.

The breakthrough in the war on dust in Swedish homes did not come until the 1921 model, the torpedo-like Lux V. The torpedo shape with its tapered front was a variant of the largely American-developed streamlined shape. Lux V was fitted with an innovation in the form of gently curved runners, which facilitated moving over carpets and thresholds. A pistol grip at the rear and a carrying strap also made it easy to lift and carry. This horizontal, torpedo-shaped floor unit with the fan behind the dust container became the archetype for numerous subsequent vacuum cleaner models, and it also featured in an unusual marketing context. In the 1920s, a large number of 'vacuum cleaner cars' shaped like the Lux V were manufactured, which were used on the streets of Stockholm, London and Berlin as rolling billboards. But it would still be a long time before Electrolux fitted its vacuum cleaners with wheels. In the 1950s they were still made of plastic film-covered laminated steel tubes, which were fitted with plastic caps on the ends and stainless steel runners underneath (du Reitz 2002).

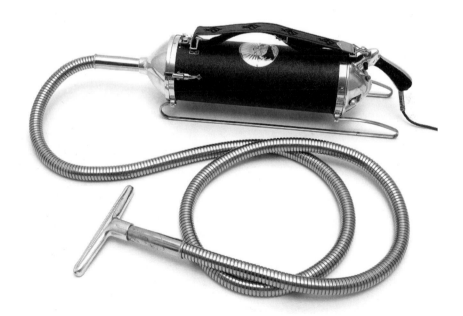

Fig. 2.1 The vacuum cleaner underwent major changes once it was fitted with an electric fan, and Electrolux was one of the leading companies in this development. Their first portable model Lux V from 1921 became, with its practical steel runners, very popular and inspired the future development of horizontal torpedo-shaped vacuum cleaners.

Symptomatically enough, the vacuum cleaner cars were made in Germany. Sweden had remarkable difficulty establishing a functioning car production despite its many talented innovators and industrialists. But there were many who tried, including Sweden's first aircraft manufacturer Thulinverken in Landskrona, which by the mid-1920s had built about 500 cars based on a Belgian design. In the end a genuine attempt was made with the financial support of SKF in Gothenburg and inspiration from American car production, which developed into a lasting business. From the parent company they took the name Volvo, actually a dormant ball-bearing patent that means, 'I'm rolling'. In 1927 the first model was launched, which was designed by the car enthusiast, artist Helmer MasOlle. 'Suddenly Swedish industry was at the forefront' writes Björn Linn (1997: 346). MasOlle had designed the open sports car Volvo ÖV4 at the same time as General Motors (GM) hired the first styling expert in the American automobile industry: Harley Earl. The similarities ended there. For Earl, it was the beginning of a legendary career as the design director of GM, while MasOlle received 500 Swedish kronor for his troubles. Although he designed the two follow-up models PV 651 and 652, subsequent models were designed by the company's engineers, who were responsible for design over the next twenty years (Schönbäck 1997).

After the radio and airwaves had been reserved for the armed forces until 1922, regular broadcasts were begun in 1924 by AB Radiotjänst (Radio service). There

Fig. 2.2 It was Volvo in Gothenburg who first started large-scale car production in Sweden following American models. The picture shows a prototype of the first model, ÖV4, parked at Götaplatsen in Gothenburg with the art museum from 1923 in the background. It, as well as a couple of the subsequent models, was designed by the artist Helmer MasOlle.

was a large pent-up demand to acquire the new culture-spreading device, which is why amateur radio construction developed early and ran parallel to factory production. AGA was one of the more prominent players, knowledgeable as they were in the audio technical area. At the time radios were manufactured with loose batteries and separate speakers, but in 1927 AGA presented an AC-powered radio with built-in speakers. It was mounted in a dovetailed and mahogany-stained wooden chassis with a high finish, which had been achieved by the female polishers at the modern AGA factory in Lidingö. Polishing was done in several stages with grinding in between. Scratches and imperfections were evened out with shellac, which was melted into the recesses. Then razor blades, grinding machines and polishing fluids

"*You know, dear, I think my Aga has been alight ever since the last Coronation.*"

Fig. 2.3 The AGA cooker was designed by Gustaf Dalén and released onto the market in the late 1920s. The combination of cooking plates, water heater, high efficiency, coke burning and adaptation for continuous operation made it particularly desirable for wealthy Britons with big, draughty stone houses. This comment is taken from the satirical magazine *Punch*.

were used to produce the desired smooth surface that matched the otherwise very simple and clean device. Under the loudspeaker, which had no protective grill, there was only an on/off switch and a channel selector, which simultaneously controlled the volume. Their advertisement also states that AGA, with these devices, 'has managed to simplify broadcast radio reception to a staggering minimum of inconvenience and expense, they can be operated by any member of the family and require virtually no supervision' (AGA-journalen 1928).

The first electric stoves had begun being manufactured in 1921 by Husqvarna in cooperation with Svenska Elektricitetsverkens ekonomiska förening (The Swedish Electrical plant's economic association). But the era of the solid fuel-fired iron stoves was far from over. Based on a patent from 1922 a new, completely revolutionary type was released a few years later, which was constructed and designed by AGA's founder, the physicist and Nobel laureate Gustaf Dalén. It was an efficient combination stove and water heater that could heat an entire home. Unlike the conventional iron stoves the AGA cooker was better suited for continuous operation, it never became scorching hot on the outside and it did not cover the pots and pans with soot from its fumes. The principle was to accumulate the heat in a large metal mass, which was then effectively isolated. It was originally designed for burning coke but was later modified for other types of fuel (AGA 1954). The AGA cooker with its solid engineering and simplicity quickly became a design classic. Above all the cream-white enamel cast iron stove with the thick chromium-plated lids, which were closed to keep the cooking plates warm, appealed to all the proponents of functionalism. The British art historian Herbert Read described it in his book *Art and Industry* and wrote about its admirable proportions, while the head of the Museum of Modern Art, Edgar Kaufmann, installed one in his Villa Falling Water designed by Frank Lloyd Wright.

The AGA cooker has for many years now been manufactured in England where, according to advertising guru David Ogilvy, it is regarded as 'the Rolls Royce of the kitchen. It is appreciated not least for its excellent cooking qualities' (James 2002: 55).

The consumer goods industry had its breakthrough in the first decades of the twentieth century. They went from building individual pieces to serial production, from the tailored to the mass-produced. And there was a demand for cheap manufactured goods, both in urban and rural areas. It was at this stage that many mail order companies began operations and began to compete in earnest with peddling. One of these was Clas Ohlson in Insjön that from 1918 helped to increase the national interest in technology by selling, for example, technical manuals, fretwork machinery, cameras with accessories and, a few years later, designs and components for radios. An early best seller was a set of drawings of furniture decoration, which was printed in 1:10 scale. They had been developed with a carpenter from Insjön and in just a few years hundreds of thousands of drawings were sold (www.clasohlson.se).

The ready-to-wear clothes industry expanded during the 1920s and 1930s. The weaving mills' range of cotton sheets and dyed or printed curtains increased and Swedish people began to buy more ready-made clothes. One of the Swedish clothing industry's prominent men, Algot Johansson had started out as a hawker in Sjuhäradsbygden but later moved to Borås and started Algot Johansson AB in 1913, better known as Algot's. It began with his wife and mother sewing workwear (Blåkläder) out of denim, fabrics that he bought from local textile mills. Around 1920 he had about thirty seamstresses employed in his Borås factory and additionally as many as 1,500 home seamstresses. The traditional distribution system with home seamstresses who picked up fabrics and delivered ready-made garments was strongly rooted in the countryside, but in the 1930s Johansson phased out this system. Instead, assembly lines and a high degree of standardization of the garments were introduced. Turnover soon multiplied (Segerblom 1983).

With the introduction of standardization and assembly lines, there was no longer any doubt that the factory was the site where future prosperity would be created. It was to the factory's machinery that both the product and people must adapt. Arguably international functionalism's foremost proponent, the architect Le Corbusier, campaigned for the home to be designed like a machine and designed houses that were adapted to the emerging car society. For radical Swedish architects the streamlined factory with its flexible, functionally adapted floor plan became the model for virtually all building assignments (Brunnström 1990). The factory and the serially produced factory product represented the future, the modern. In 1922 the standardization work was given a formal organization with the founding of SIS, Svenska Industrins Standardiseringskommission (Swedish Standards Institute). The machine age had made its definitive entrance.

Fig. 2.4 During the 1930s, production increased in many Swedish workplaces through the introduction of assembly lines. At the assembly line of the clothing factory Algots in Borås up to 100 women could sit in a row and sew parts of shirts and workwear. The assembly lines led to increased noise and the placement of the machines, one after another, made conversation between the women difficult.

Swedish Luxury Production Excels

In 1920, with the aid of government grants, Gregor Paulsson was hired as the Swedish Society of Crafts and Design's first full-time director. The municipal leadership of Gothenburg was at this time planning for a major national, and partly international, exhibition on account of the city's upcoming 300th anniversary. The Swedish Society of Crafts and Design had undertaken to organize a section for contemporary crafts and applied arts and Paulsson now took the opportunity, following in the footsteps of Hemutställningen (the 'Home Exhibition'), to try to formulate a social programme for the design of a series of room interiors. But the management of the exhibition gave it the cold shoulder: 'We don't want to have any social rubbish in this show' was his account of the answer he got (Ivanov 2004: 202). Political divisions were acute at this time and the Gothenburg Exhibition, which, after being delayed finally took place in 1923, served as a celebration of and for the bourgeoisie. The labour parties were sceptical from the start and the exhibition could only be realized thanks to the often talked about so-called Göteborgsandan (Gothenburg spirit).

What was shown, celebrated and had an international impact was exclusive and refined work by the elite of Swedish applied arts. Orrefors's magnificent glass pieces were a hit and Nordiska Kompaniet (The Nordic Company) showed sophisticated interiors that exemplified space and luxury. Although the result did not completely conform to the Swedish Society of Crafts and Design's propaganda for more beautiful everyday goods, it still showed what Swedish industry was capable of with the benefit of artistically trained competence. There is strong evidence that the exhibition was more significant than the relatively modest position it has assumed in history. The British architect Edward Maufe summarized the general picture quite well in the *Architectural Review* some years later:

> One came away from the Gothenburg Exhibition with the firm conviction that there was no bad modern work in Sweden, that the whole country was inhabited only by good artists, and by cultured and wealthy clients who appreciated and employed them. What a result to have obtained; what an advertisement to have made for Sweden. (Maufe 1931: 102)

P. A. Norstedt & Söner, who were celebrating their centenary, were also represented at the Gothenburg Exhibition. Norstedts had hired Akke Kumlien as an artistic adviser for the renewal of the publisher's book covers and title pages through Förmedlingsbyrån (The Mediation agency). Mass-producing books was considerably easier than a lot of other things and Kumlien's written and illustrated covers received enthusiastic reviews. Norstedts was described as the democratic aristocrat of book printers. The talented book designer Anders Billow stressed the importance of real typographic innovation, and drew parallels with architecture:

> Framework, initials and vignettes ... no more constitute a noble typography, than ornamental, niche decorations and capstones make good architecture. Furthermore, it is not an individual place that makes a city beautiful and pleasant

to live in, and nor are we very well served by only a few books being good enough, instead it is a mass effect, which in both cases it depends on. There is thus the task; whole neighbourhoods, whole districts and in the other case, whole printers, whole publishers. (Gram 1994: 96)

More exclusive Swedish design had its definitive breakthrough in connection with the first major exhibition for architecture and applied arts, *Exposition Internationale des Arts Décoratifs et Industriels Modernes à Paris 1925*. According to reports from the exhibition curator Gregor Paulsson in the Swedish Society of Crafts and Design's 1925 yearbook, Sweden won the most first prizes (after the host nation France). A lot had undoubtedly happened during the roughly seventy-five years that had passed since the first World's Fair and here the dogged educational work of the Swedish Society of Crafts and Design had certainly played a central role. 'The Swedish became essentially an ideal and role model in the foreign architectural and design environments' writes the Norwegian art historian Ingeborg Glambek in her review of the Paris exhibition's legacy and further argues that Swedish 1920s architecture and design 'was perceived as something completely special, as an original and creative mix of old Swedish tradition and modern innovation' by foreign observers (Glambek 1997: 64, 76).

So, what was it that aroused so much admiration in Paris? According to its title, the exhibition was supposed to demonstrate the range from decorative craftsmanship to the industrially machine-made. The Swedish exhibit, however, focused on more exclusive industrial art production, where they now had a relatively long experience of using well-known designers as selling points. Among the most acclaimed were the Swedish Pavilion, which was designed by Carl Bergsten in a severe classicist style with a domineering loggia supported by rather manneristic elongated Ionic columns, and Simon Gate's engraved glass for Orrefors, in particular his magnificent, almost 75-centimetre-high trophy in crystal, which had been given to the host city by Stockholm. Many other things also received praise, such as textiles from Handarbetets Vänner (The Association of Friends of Textile Art), Wilhelm Kåge's ceramic works for Gustavsberg, living room furniture by Carl Malmsten for Nordiska Kompaniet (The Nordic Company) and a study fastidiously decorated with bookcase, desk and high-backed chair by Gunnar Asplund. Particularly noteworthy was the generous, leather-clad chair where the seatback transitioned into the seat in an unbroken, sweeping line, inspired as it was by finds in the recently opened tomb of Tutankhamun in Egypt (Plate 4). The cast iron products from Näfveqvarns bruk in the shape of park benches and stools by the architect Folke Bensow were also significant (Plate 5), as well as urns by the artist Anna Petrus and the sculptor Ivar Johnsson.

The Swedish illustrator and writer Akke Kumlien was also praised. His works were inspired by eighteenth-century classicism and set with the noble French typeface Cochin that Norstedts had purchased a few years earlier. Typical of Kumlien's approach was a predilection for italicized upper case letters, which he readily spaced out and supplemented with small vignettes. This gave it a touch of ephemeral elegance, which matched the finest glass and porcelain (Bowallius 1999: 18).

Overall, the pieces on display were high quality. The emphasis on the decorative, the predilection for the slender and graceful, the simple, thin, smooth, almost two-dimensional surfaces and the black and white colour scheme, preferably enhanced with a touch of silver were characteristic. These examples were usually taken from classical antiquity, forms which were then reinterpreted. The Arts and Crafts pavilion at the Gothenburg Exhibition, designed by the architect Hakon Ahlberg, with its decorated but simultaneously large, unbroken surfaces had already epitomized many of the ambitions of Nordic Classicism. According to John Sjöström (Paulsson and Rudberg 1994: 26) it came to play a crucial role in the design of Sweden's best urban environments.

There was no doubt that the Swedish contributions were considered to be, at least considering their circumstances, luxury production with strong craft elements. However, the exhibition's French secretary-general, with a different perspective, considered them to possess an aristocratic simplicity and appeared to be good examples of Swedish folk art (Ivanov 2004: 229). But the real everyday objects that had been the guiding principle for the Swedish contribution were still scarce. Moreover, it was too gracile, refined and a touch too decadent or mundane, a fitting expression of the ideals of the time, which was about conveying a taste of the good life. But one has to remember that behind all these achievements stood a staff of collaborators who were not given the same chance to bask in the limelight. Particularly glass manufacturing, where the blown glass was refined by grinding on so-called grinding chairs and then engraved or etched, was dependent on a variety of artisans. It is an accepted fact that, for example, Simon Gate and Edward Hald would never have been able to create their masterpieces without the help they received from, above all, the two glassblowing brothers Knut and Gustav Bergqvist (Widman 1998).

One commentator who was not impressed by what he saw at the Paris Exhibition was the architect Uno Åhrén, who in a famous observation in the Swedish Society of Craft and Design's 1925 yearbook called *Breaks* thought time had stopped. Åhrén complained:

Forms, forms, forms … I felt the same drowsy weariness that I think one must experience in a tropical forest, where the air hangs heavy with suffocating scents from vegetation that spills out in flaccid extravagance.

A few lines later he highlights what he considers to have been the problem; a lack of a practical functional thinking:

That the chair and table and bed should have such difficulty finding modern designs is because people have not realised that they are also apparatuses. Does it not seem distantly absentminded to make chairs to this day that are ornaments impossible to sit in comfortably? What shall we do with practical things, unless we master them? How can we forgive a chair that hurts our backs at the same time as we resent a water pipe that leaks or an elevator that is stuck between floors! Because it is beautiful … If only it had never dithered between the desire to become a chair and the desire to become an imaginative work of art. (Åhrén 1925: 15)

The only thing he really deemed worthy to highlight was Le Corbusier and Pierre Jeanneret's advanced exhibit Pavillon de L'Esprit Nouveau, which displayed a completely new residential ideal with space, large expanses of glass and simple and sparse furnishings.

Fig. 2.5 Alongside all the magnificent engraved collectors glass at the Paris Exhibition Orrefors also displayed a simpler but somewhat luxurious everyday production. Practical glasses of this type, made at Sandvik's glassworks, which was rented at the time by Orrefors, were highly appreciated by visitors and critics according to Helena Dahlbäck Lutteman (1991). The goblet, whose foot is entwined by a leaf with a stem, was designed by Simon Gate in 1922.

Uno Åhrén's ideas were radical for the time and foreshadowed the radical aesthetic cleansing that would come a few years later. But the sophisticatedly gracile would hold out for some time yet and ran through almost everything, in architecture and in typography, in the slender figures of fashion and the shingled hairstyles. Even a company like Ericsson latched on to the trend and had their sheet metal desk telephone, originally from 1909, remade into a real beauty according to the spirit of the time. The high-gloss, black-lacquered casing was moulded in a single piece with smooth corners while the handset was chromed and had been given a typically languid and elongated Mannerist shape. This exclusive design, which was named after the new director Wincrantz (long-time close associate of the dominant owner and financier Ivar Kreuger), recurred frequently in Ericsson's marketing (Plate 6). It fitted perfectly as an eye-catching device on posters along with images of skyscrapers, smoking cigarettes, swan-necked young women with short hair styles and other markers of modernity (Brunnström 2006).

In praise of all this modernized classicism the British architectural historian Morton Shand, in an article in 1930, coined the often-used term Swedish Grace. At the same time he highlighted the Gothenburg Exhibition, which he said had laid the groundwork for a remarkable international interest in Swedish design and crafts (Shand 1930). Within architecture the period has come to be known as Nordic Classicism. Even more internationally viable, but closely related to Swedish Grace, the term Art Deco can be traced back to the Paris exhibition (an abbreviation of the exhibition's name *Arts Décoratifs*). Art Deco was a colourful, slightly jaggedly aggressive and decorative style in architecture and design that, above all, was linked to the luxurious urban culture of the 1930s. There was nothing like that in Sweden yet, except perhaps on the luxury cruise ships that sailed the Gothenburg-New York voyage. Sweden's successful efforts at the major exhibitions had made Americans curious about Swedish design and Swedish crafts. It was therefore no coincidence that the interior of the Svenska Amerika Linien's (Swedish American Line's) Atlantic cruiser M/S Kungsholmen has been identified as perhaps the best example of Swedish Art Deco. This floating travelling exhibition, that contained much of the best that Sweden had to offer in interior design, was completed in 1927–1928 under the direction of the architect Carl Bergsten. The unimaginable luxury on board permeated everything, from the Roman style swimming pool to first-class music and lounge rooms decorated in gold and precious materials, pigskin wallpaper and walnut panels (Plate 7). There was furniture, carpets, tablecloths, porcelain and glass by many well-known designers. A dozen artists completed the mostly fixed interiors with tapestries, stained glass, reliefs, intarsia and sculptures (Ericsson 2005).

The Stockholm Exhibition Paves the Way for the Factory Product

Five years had passed since Swedish design and architecture saw their great success at the Paris exhibition. Another important housing exhibition had taken place in 1927, organized by the Deutscher Werkbund in Weissenhof, outside Stuttgart. The elite modernist architects of the time took part with the graduates of the radical Bauhaus school in the lead. It was a breakthrough for the new function-driven factory style, a crescendo of steel, glass and concrete in stark, geometric, elementary forms; an almost Cubist idiom. In the same year the telephone manufacturer H. Fuld & Co in Frankfurt had launched a competition to design a people's device, Der Deutsche Fernsprechapparat. When the device was released the following year, they congratulated themselves on having been able to peel away all decoration and every single curved surface that was not absolutely justified for technical reasons. The detailed and sometimes overloaded design that characterized the older styles was not particularly well-suited to industrial production processes. Achieving streamlined and economically viable mass-production required simpler forms, and indeed the construction itself was elevated to an aesthetic norm. This development in Germany inspired similar efforts in Sweden (Brunnström 2006).

It was May 1930. Large parts of Norra Djurgården, Stockholm along Djurgårdsbrunnsviken, from Strandvägen all the way to the present day Tekniska museet (the National Museum of Science and Technology), were filled with exhibition halls, pavilions, cafés, kiosks, and brightly coloured billboards. The most conspicuous was a magnificent and airy, almost floating, restaurant made from steel and glass. There was also a residential area with a dozen small white buildings. The buildings, villas and terraced houses looked more like 'cardboard boxes or simple wooden huts' to borrow the critic Gotthard Johansson's description. The board-like roofs were practically flat, the walls were thin and the room dimensions usually minimal. The wind blew, a myriad flags rippled and well-dressed visitors strolled along the promenade. The Stockholm Exhibition had opened: functionalism (or *funkis* as it was often referred to in Swedish) was modernity materialized. The exhibition had been organized by the Swedish Society of Crafts and Design with Gregor Paulsson as the general director and Gunnar Asplund as the principal architect. The functionalist exhibit took place over four months in the hot summer of 1930 and it was a resounding success – at least in terms of visitors, with four million attending (Rudberg 1999).

'Where Gothenburg whispered, Stockholm shouted', observed the previously cited Edward Maufe (1931: 102). The striking contrast between the selective, aristocratic Gothenburg Exhibition and the Stockholm Exhibition, where everything was included and '"everyone" was represented', was a political one, he said, referring to the rise of social democracy. All sorts of serially produced staples in the new factory style were also shown at the exhibition. There were, for example, stackable pots from AGA, portable electric hot plates from Elektro Helios, a portable gramophone from the firm Symfonic, furniture series from Gemla and Bodafors designed by architects, glassware from the Målerås glasbruk cooperative, curtain fabrics designed by Greta Gahn, simple tableware by Hald and Kåge, a rich supply of lighting fixtures from ASEA and Böhlmarks and buses from GM designed by Sigurd Lewerentz. At the Bauhaus school in Dessau, Germany, which was the leader in design education at the time, they had been experimenting for some years with spring steel furniture. Now a Swedish take on this was also on display, from a blacksmith's workshop from Grythyttan in NK's booth. There the owner, the blacksmith Artur Lindqvist, had built a simple but extremely comfortable and popular garden armchair made from solid, red-lacquered horseshoe steel with seat, back and armrests of varnished beech or ash. In the spirit of the times it was simply called Modell A2. It is still in production today albeit with minor changes (Plate 8). Steel tube furniture for indoor use, represented above all by the KF architect Erik Lund, was met with some scepticism. The general feeling was that the chrome-plated metal tubes gave, both visually and tactilely, a sensation of hardness and coldness.

The radical architects and their related international role models in the housing section particularly excelled. The architectural historian Per G. Råberg (1970), who has described early opinions about the Stockholm Exhibition, explains that a great deal was epitomized by a formalistic modernism, which bordered on 'posturing machine romanticism'. The production apparatus could not yet accomplish any aesthetic miracles, machines and processes were inadequate, in terms of today's perspective. The factory style was simple and only somewhat effective.

The exhibition demonstrated great breadth, at the same time as it was, thematically, quite coherent. The ascetic puritanical permeated everything from architecture and design to arts and crafts. The silversmith Wiwen Nilsson, who had received much criticism at previous exhibitions for his eccentric style with geometric undecorated pieces and poor material expression, was vindicated here in a prime setting. After the Stockholm Exhibition talk instead focused on his consistency and daring and mathematically precise, flat polished surfaces (Wiwen Nilsson 1975).

In spite of its everyday goods and exclusive arts and crafts the Stockholm Exhibition was largely a building architect's exhibition. A case in point was the rapidly growing cooperative movement's architectural office, which showed some variations on fastidiously modernist co-op shops. The radical faction that Gregor Paulsson had gathered around him led by Asplund was responsible for the spectacular elements. Even the posters for the exhibition had been designed by an architect: Sigurd Lewerentz. His posters were as bold as the exhibition buildings, with print-to-edge text in self-drawn sans serif and with the diagonal as the main theme. The symbolism was clear: one poster was revolutionary red, another was interpreted by many as a razor that effectively cut away all the old.

Paulsson's motto, that the purposeful represented beauty, held true for the radicals. Mass production needed simple shapes and smooth surfaces that were easy to clean. Small houses needed cheap, space-saving and comfortable standard furniture. The home's interior design had to become a utility design; it should be practical and rational like in the workplace. The manifesto *acceptera* (Accept), which was published the year after the exhibition, stated that the factory/everyday article should serve humans, be primarily effective and inexpensive, and secondarily characterized by good form. In actuality, it could do without the professional artists. The critic Gotthard Johansson wanted to draw a dividing line between art and industry. Art had

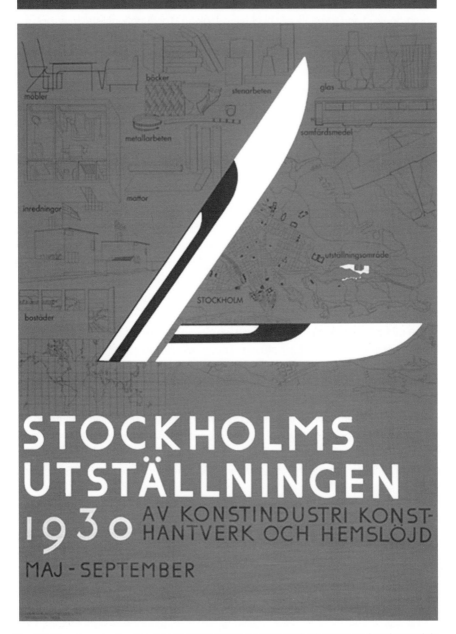

Fig. 2.6 The razor on the Stockholm Exhibition's posters and other promotional materials was meant to symbolically cut away all the old and outdated to make way for modernity. The poster was printed in a red colour which emphasized the radical message. This poster was designed by one of the exhibition's leading architects, Sigurd Lewerentz.

nothing to do with the fabrication of knives, plates and glasses. The coupling of art and industry had led to an exaggerated showmanship instead of simple effectiveness.

Even though the arts and crafts were represented their invitation to be involved had been rather half-hearted. In *acceptera* the arts and crafts were accused of being person-centred and romantically backward-looking. The functionalists' message was that the crafts had to step aside to make way for industrial production. Of course, not everybody liked this one-sided focus on the functionalist factory product: especially not after Gregor Paulsson – in a somewhat biased way – tried to influence the art industry's representatives to create some new objects for the exhibition in the functionalist spirit. The most powerful criticism came from Carl Malmsten, who was the era's leading interior designer and who had furnished two of the 1920s most prestigious buildings in a traditional style: Kreuger's Tändstickspalats and Stockholms Konserthus (Stockholm Concert Hall). He considered the new style to be far too 'unSwedish', untraditional and doctrinal, claiming that you could not use an industrial idiom to design housing and intimate conditions. The home was a place for relaxation and refreshment; it should not look like a workplace – especially in the Nordic countries where people spent so much of their time indoors. Many agreed with this criticism, which created the lively so-called *funkis–tradis* (functional–traditional) debate, particularly concerning the doctrinal elements of the exhibition programme (Råberg 1972). It was in this context that the term *funkis* was established, although it is not used today as a synonym for functionalism in the same way as it was in those days.

The radical management of the Swedish Society of Crafts and Design finally got the avant-garde exhibition they craved. They now had an exhibition that to a large extent took note of the social dimension, which was intended for the less affluent as opposed to the craft-centred luxury aesthetic that dominated in Paris. But at the same time they deprived themselves of the avant-garde role in accepting the present reality, as they themselves wrote in *acceptera*. Generalizing slightly, one could say that the contemporary reality was about accepting that Sweden had entered the machine age, accepting art's adaptation to industry, the only true, and above all fast, road to future prosperity for everyone, at least related to taste, aesthetics and a classless society.

Functionalist Ideas Pervade Society

Many saw the Stockholm Exhibition as a modernist bombshell, but it was really just a confirmation of the radicalization that had already occurred in many areas of art, but which had not yet affected the general public. Already in the 1910s and 1920s there had been a steady flow of international modernist art to the large galleries and Liljevalchs konsthall after its opening in 1916. Several artists had also travelled to Berlin and Paris where they were inspired by metropolitan city life and the great masters. Back in Sweden they depicted the pulse of Stockholm life. Even at the big exhibitions it was possible to become acquainted with modern art. Otto G. Carlsund exhibited a selection of avant-garde non-figurative paintings under the heading *Art Concret* at the Stockholm Exhibition by artists such as van Doesburg, Léger, Arp, Mondrian and Ozenfant; however, it was panned to such an extent that the artworks were confiscated after the exhibition closed (Widenheim 2000).

In the field of architecture the shock was in a way bigger in that it affected the shared public living space. The flat roofs were seen as an extraneous element, the plywood, Masonite, concrete and other innovations as common and cheap and the tight kitchen spaces as 'unSwedish'. Much of the functionalist message was deeply rooted, however, in Swedish building traditions. The architectural historian Eva Rudberg (2000) highlights the need to catch the light by, for example, adding windows to the facade and using lightly coloured walls in cities, which in both cases was prescribed for Stockholm's old building ordinances. Rudberg also emphasizes the importance of Swedish poverty for the simple, efficient solutions, as well as the drawn-out battle against bed bugs, tuberculosis and other endemic diseases as the background to functionalism's light rooms and shiny, smooth, easily cleaned surfaces in kitchens and bathrooms.

That functionalism had a relatively rapid, broad and long-term impact in Sweden can largely be attributed to its message of enlightenment, which quickly took root in the country's growing fascination with social democracy. An efficient manufacturing industry that produced good, cheap housing and everyday goods for the disadvantaged fitted the Social Democrats like a glove. When the party came to power in 1932 solving the problem of overcrowding became a priority. A measure of how the housing question was viewed in most circles in the 1930s, even the aesthetic stronghold of the Röhsska Museum, is given in the catalogue for the first of a series of housing exhibitions that the museum produced from 1937 to 1945: 'The home is first and foremost a social problem, only then an aesthetic problem' (Vår bostad 1937).

Traditional building techniques had offered a relatively stable framework for design and use. Loadbearing masonry and unstandardized timber dimensions made things more expensive and limited. Similar rooms, regardless of purpose, organized in rows one after the other with passages in the middle of the walls dominated. The almost always-symmetrical facade design governed the outcome of the room. It is true that it gave elegant and representative room cohesion, but the passageways reduced comfort and made the building harder to furnish. The materials and building techniques of the twentieth century, in the form of, for example, sheet glass, steel, reinforced concrete and pillar and beam constructions, meant that the room layout was no longer dependent on the walls as in the old masonry structures. For the first time technical prerequisites now existed enabling a distinction to be made between loadbearing and protective elements of the building. With loadbearing pillars houses could be built taller and slimmer, reducing the function of walls to just weather protection, which allowed for liberal piercing and glazing.

The emergence of a consumption-driven middle class, in connection with the great migration to the cities, made new demands on more informal housing. Inspiration from the ideal kind of housing in England had reached Sweden around the turn of the twentieth century. Here was a greater emphasis on comfort and a freer room placement, often around a centrally placed room. Lavish villas and simpler crofts were built on the outskirts of the cities and in central areas the rooms were differentiated by function in the growing number of apartments.

In many ways the Stockholm Exhibition set the standard for new housing, although it was not until the late 1930s and into the 1940s that these ideals were more readily taken on board across the country. The plain and simple – free from ornamentation – gradually made its way into Swedish homes. Texture and material effectively replaced patterns and superficial decoration. Wallpaper, for example, was increasingly manufactured without patterns and suitable for wiping clean. Many new housing estates were built with tall, narrow freestanding high-rise buildings, so-called *lamellhus*, which in true democratic fashion gave plenty of light and air to all the small, rational apartments. The ultimate functionalist ideal in the 1930s was one room for one function. Large old farmhouse kitchens were being replaced by small, almost laboratory-like kitchens. At the same time several hygienic appliances became standard, such as the broom closet, the balcony for beating carpets and garbage chutes. The former drawing room or salon, which was usually only used for special occasions and when guests came, was replaced with a cosy living room as a gathering place for the family. This was the place to rest after the day's troubles, read, write and have a nice time.

The manifesto *acceptera* emphasized the importance of furnishing according to the individual's needs rather than following old standard patterns. In particular, it

Fig. 2.7 Ericsson's Bakelite telephone was called 'The Swedish type of telephone' when, in the 1930s, it spread across the world and set the standard for how a modern plastic telephone should look. When the Bakelite telephone replaced the old sheet metal telephones with the fitted dial the turnaround for manufacturing went from one week to about seven minutes.

turned against the usual furniture groups, that is to say the complete suite of dining room furniture, bedchamber furniture or furniture for a study. Lighter, pliable and more flexible furniture was needed, especially for smaller apartments. And they would be made cheaply through mass production. As in architecture, the advocates of functionalism were striving for a standardization of furniture's different functions. Furniture should not only be beautiful and comfortable or perform some ceremonial function. It was equally important for it to be practical, hygienic and that it could be easily moved.

In contrast, the furniture industry took a generally cautious view of these innovations. Furniture decoration remained popular well into the 1940s, which offset a rationalization of the furniture industry. Only a few manufacturers, such as NK and AB Svenska Möbelfabriken in Bodafors, had employed their own architects (Eklund Nyström 1992). The new small apartments required practical tableware that could be stowed in the kitchen's limited storage space. In 1933, Wilhelm Kåge designed the Praktika tableware for Gustavsberg with white enamel, small brim and exceedingly simple and plain decoration. It was a service that was stackable for the first time and whose different parts could be combined in a practical way.

Telephones were now being installed in more and more homes since Televerket (Royal Electric Telegraph Agency) in 1933 signed an extensive agreement with Ericsson for permission to build the new Bakelite telephone and make it the new standard of the Swedish telecom network. When Ericsson's Bakelite telephone went into production the year after the Stockholm Exhibition it more than fulfilled the functionalists' ideals. It had a unique design that was objectively simple with smooth planes and sharp edges; the skewed front looked like the wind spoilers on a contemporary streamlined diesel locomotive. It was made in the new completely synthetic plastic material, Bakelite, which was smooth, shiny, hard and easy to keep clean. It was made using a technique that was itself as streamlined as possible. The new telephone had a fixed cradle, cradle switch and an integrated dial, which meant that they did not have to manufacture the casing and the cradle separately or recess the dial. In addition, no post processing was needed; the sheet metal telephones had previously required about ten different stages of surface treatment in the form of priming, plastering, grinding, dust removal, lacquering with black paint, decoration and finally varnishing. All this was replaced by a single manufacturing operation: the die-casting itself. The total time savings were huge, roughly from seven workdays to seven minutes. In addition, the Bakelite telephone was designed by an artist who had been brought into the industry. The development work had taken place at Ericsson's subsidiary Elektrisk Bureau in Oslo where the constructer Johan Christian Bjerknes had engaged the artist Jean Heiberg to do the design; this was after they had rejected proposals from a number of prominent Norwegian architects who had been competing for the assignment. Heiberg's integrated design language was radically different from the traditional additive approach, where component was added to component, that the engineers normally applied (Brunnström 2006: 179).

The functionalist winds of change could also be observed by the general public in Sweden in terms of what was happening in the field of graphic design, particularly in magazine typography and book art. The influence of the modernist Bauhaus school had left clear marks on the Lagerström brothers' publishing house in Stockholm, who published the journal *Nordisk boktryckarekonst* (Nordic art of printing). In a couple

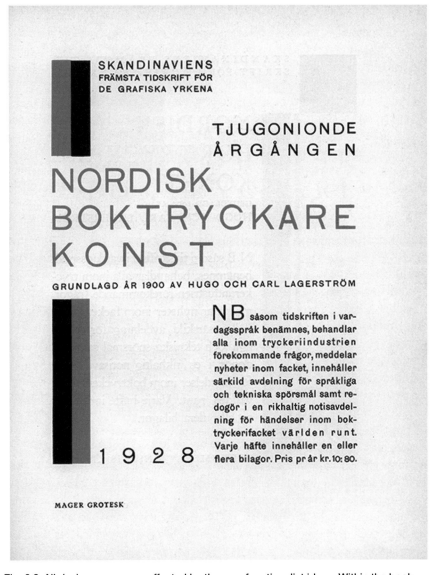

Fig. 2.8 All design areas were affected by the new functionalist ideas. Within the book arts typography was supposed to be simple, lucid and readable. The new so-called elementary typography was tested already in 1927 by the printer Hugo Lagerström in a couple of issues of the journal *Nordisk boktryckarekonst* (Nordic art of printing) (Lagerström 1928: 433). A few years later, Anders Billow radically transformed the Svenska Turistföreningens årsskrift (the Swedish Tourist Association's annual). See also Fig. 2.9.

Fig. 2.9 Cover of the Svenska Turistföreningens årskrift (the Swedish Tourist Association's annual) illustrated by the painter Otte Sköld. See also Fig. 2.8.

of booklets from 1927 Jan Tschichold's elementary typography and the geometric Bauhaus style with only lowercase letters in sans serif font were presented. The following year Hugo Lagerström presented a Bauhaus-inspired proposal for a new cover for the magazine. He also spoke about the importance of a simple and rational graphic design and of replacing ornaments with a decorative effect, which would be produced by 'the use of font, white space, sharp colours and possibly some abstract ornamentation' (Gram 2006: 56).

The breakthrough for the new typography came with Anders Billow's work for Nordisk Rotogravyr (Nordic Rotogravure) and in particular the transformation of the widespread Svenska Turistföreningens årskrift (the Swedish Tourist Association's annual) in 1932. In addition to an innovative typography that broke with tradition using centring and wide margins, Billow focused on photographic illustrations. Here he had unique access to Nordisk Rotogravyr's advanced rotogravure techniques, which allowed him to give plenty of space for C. G. Rosenberg's exquisite pictures (Gram 2006). That same year, 1932, the Swedish Society of Crafts and Design's organ changed its name to *Form* and got a new modern font and brand new layout.

Furniture Design Is Renewed and Professionalized

Urbanization and the development of technology created a market for new types of furniture. This applied to, for example, telephone tables and radio tables as well as smart folding chairs, which after a large event could be gathered and removed in their thousands in just minutes. Other more outdated types of furniture such as washstands with a frame for loose basins, smoke boxes and column pedestals were gradually phased out. In the decades after the Stockholm Exhibition the broad traditional and the narrow, more experimental furniture production developed in slightly different directions. A review of the catalogue of large furniture factory, Gemla's, reveals that the increase in wealth had brought a clear shift towards more upholstered and also more numerous types of furniture. The un-upholstered and thin so-called flat-upholstered furniture of the early 1900s was replaced gradually by sofas and armchairs with thicker coil spring upholstery (Designarkivet). Many manufacturers also continued to advertise furniture garniture and even their suites of period furniture that maintained their grip on ordinary people, not least during the war years. Against these – which were seen as not functional, but heavy and dark – turned both the traditional Malmsten supporters and the more radical proponents of functionalism with an intense propaganda campaign. Aside from the assiduous work of the Swedish Society of Crafts and Design, the Röhsska Museum took on an active role in propagating good taste by organizing well-attended exhibitions on the theme 'Vår bostad (Our house)' during 1937–1945. The slogan was modern furniture for modern people.

Permanent features at these Gothenburg exhibitions were bright, light works by Carl Malmsten, Bruno Mathsson, G. A. Berg (1891–1971) and Axel Larsson (1898–1975), the latter from 1925 employed at AB Svenska Möbelfabrikerna in

Bodafors. The furniture was displayed against a background of textiles and wall-papers created by, for example, Edna Martin, Josef Frank, Estrid Ericson and Elsa Gullberg. The delicate furniture in light cellulose-lacquered birch or acid-stained pine was upholstered in light, pale fabrics or braided webbing. The three produc-ers who in 1937 showed their steel tube furniture, however, did not appear to have much success and were missing in subsequent exhibitions. When museum director Gustaf Munthe looked back at previous exhibitions in the 1945 catalogue, he lamented that the manufacturers had had too much control over the supply. He noted that the exhibitions' non-profit objectives had worked in one direction and the profit interests of the exhibitors in another, and argued for the need to move forward with clear signals and tougher measures. What he felt was missing above all were ideas and suggestions on how less affluent families, with a large number of children, should arrange and furnish affordable apartments (Munthe 1945).

Here Munthe touched on the classic problem of why so many people with low incomes fell into the clutches of unscrupulous furniture dealers and salesmen. The new and the forward-looking on display at the exhibitions belonged almost completely to the exclusive range. In addition, many regarded the new furniture as far too simple, meagre and difficult to fit in with older existing decoration. The relatively small-scale furniture industry also lacked qualified designers for broad production; in this respect, it was significantly worse off than in the likes of the glass and porcelain industries. Instead, they borrowed and copied or relied on proven models. At the same time, it became increasingly clear that a cadre of theoretically and practically trained furni-ture designers were needed to provide the industry with blueprints for the standard furniture that was needed in all of the new smaller apartments being built in the cities (Frick 1986).

It is difficult to define the exact moment when it was possible to train as an inte-rior architect or furniture designer. For a long time furniture designer was a title that you just assumed. Students at Konstfack were specifically trained in a specialized department for furniture designers in 1907 and HDK in 1909, and in the 1920s the first, but unsuccessful, attempts were made to form a professional association. It was not until the 1930s that Sweden had a guild of self-employed interior archi-tects and furniture designers. An important driving force was the debate and interest that the Stockholm Exhibition had generated. The Swedish Society of Crafts and Design, however, was accused of obstructing the issue by its close collaboration with the building architects on furniture and interior matters. In the early 1930s large batches of graduating students initiated a steady growth of the profession. This led to a group of furniture designers, above all graduates from Konstfack and HDK, forming SIMS, Sveriges inrednings- och möbelarkitekters sammanslutning (Swedish association of interior and furniture architects), in 1933 (renamed in 1953 as SIR, Svenska inredningsarkitekters riksförbund [Swedish national association of interior architects]). The main issue was about improving economic conditions and raising the status of the profession. The latter was not completely straightforward and led to heated discussions with the building architects' association (Swedish Association of Architects), especially after they switched from the common name of furniture designer to calling themselves furniture architects. But membership granted legitimacy and the association grew rapidly. In 1939 SIMS had eighty-two members (Eklund Nyström 1992).

Many of the architects' names we encounter in the new association's registers are relatively unknown today. It was a tough labour market, forcing some to work in the furniture trade while others had to continue designing the heavier, old style furniture. But in the emerging welfare state, public construction and office development increased and consequently interior and furnishing assignments did as well. It was also with these types of assignments that the era's dominant figure of furniture design, Carl Malmsten (1888–1972), started his career. The breakthrough came in 1916 when he, largely unknown at the time, won both first and second prize in a competition to supply furniture for the ongoing city hall construction in Stockholm, hosted by the Swedish Society of Crafts and Design. The commission enabled him to open his own workshop in the capital and in the years following he delivered many prized furniture suites to the Swedish Society of Crafts and Design exhibitions. He also wrote about beauty and comfort in the home in the spirit of Ellen Keys and cooperated extensively with textile artists, in particular Märta Måås-Fjetterström whose carpets and fabrics in saturated earthy tones harmonized with Malmsten's interiors. Carl Malmsten has in later writings been most noted for his extensive luxury furniture and educational efforts; among other things, he started Malmstens Verkstadsskola (Malmsten's Workshop School) in 1930 for the training of furniture architects and qualified cabinetmakers. His extensive production of standard furniture has been forgotten, however. Even though Malmsten fought on the barricades during the Stockholm Exhibition, he had the same goals as the functionalists in their social and rational aspirations, albeit with different methods and softer shapes. Much later one of functionalism's prominent theorists Gustaf Näsström expressed it thus:

> He fashions each item of furniture to maximise its effectiveness in people's daily life. As someone who was in the battles around the 1930 Stockholm Exhibition where Carl Malmsten was the brave patriotic soldier on the traditional-redoubt it feels ignominious to call him a functionalist, but he is certainly a master of combining function and beauty, and I suppose that was what we most wanted in 1930, while we uncertainly embraced the cold steel tubular chairs. (Näslund 1988: 42)

Malmsten initiated a lasting partnership with one of Sweden's largest furniture manufacturers, Svenska Möbelfabrikerna in Bodafors, as early as 1922, for the mechanized serial production of simple everyday furniture, and a few years later he would eventually change the standards of Swedish office furniture in an extended collaboration with Åtvidabergs Industrier.

A substantial part of furniture production was aimed at the ever-growing office workplaces that started to be established in the 1920s, with banks and later insurance companies in the lead; Handelsbanken in Stockholm, for example, had 700 employees in the mid-1930s. The examples were found in the United States both in terms of labour, mechanization and room separation, and of furniture and office equipment (Bedoire 1981). Already at the London Exhibition in 1851, American manufacturers exhibited, as mentioned earlier, pioneering designs for future office landscapes in the form of comfortable swivel chairs and in the 1870s Remington introduced the first typewriters. AB Åtvidabergs Snickerifabrik, a major Swedish manufacturer of office supplies, was established in 1894. The idea behind the company came from the young owner of Åtvidaberg's centuries-old copper works, Theodor Adelswärd, who needed a substitute industry for the mining operations, which were languishing. There were large oak forests on its vast estates and after a visit to the 1889 Paris World's Fair the decisive step was taken after he had been impressed by American woodworking machines for the serial production of office furniture. The business quickly developed into a major European industry with significant export and special assembly plants in St Petersburg and Moscow for the large Russian market (Adelswärd 1963).

Fig. 2.10 By the early 1900s AB Åtvidabergs Snickerifabrik had developed into a major European producer of office supplies. They manufactured, among other things, magnificent oak desks. The intricate model above from the 1900 catalogue with foldable side panels and lots of drawers and compartments was based on American models. It weighed an impressive 175 kg and required an additional 150 kg of packing. The brochure's picture in Fig. 2.11 shows a considerably simpler desk, which was part of the standardized office furniture that Carl Malmsten co-developed.

Fig. 2.11 Simpler desk co-developed by Carl Malmsten. See also Fig. 2.10.

Popular products during the first decades were large, heavy desks made of solid, highly polished oak. These were supported by drawer units with pull-out boards and drawers and had an upper part that was practically divided with compartments and small boxes for paper and stationery.

Several of the models came with roller shutters that were pulled down over the table top and locked with a security lock; this was done in order to make it possible to leave working materials out but still protected. With the desks were screw-lift stools or swivel chairs which could be tilted, with a ball-bearing construction. The Åtvidaberg factory also offered special typewriter tables where the typewriter could be pushed down under the table top in a clever way so that it turned into a regular desk that was modelled on the treadle sewing machine; also available was an office supply that used to be important but is alien today: letter copying presses designed as furniture. The waste wood from the carpentry was used to manufacture parquet, which through the Åtvidaberg factory was soon transformed from a luxury product into a beautiful and hygienic everyday item.

With Carl Malmsten as the furniture designer the company developed the heavily promoted so-called Malmsten types; simple, standardized but still solid oak furniture, which was also well suited to the growing municipal administrations. The company's focus on the office workplace naturally led to manufacturing of various pieces of office equipment such as typewriters and adding machines as well. Here the company secured a dominant position through the acquisition of the famous brands Facit, Halda and Original-Odhner. A completely redesigned Halda typewriter with protective cover in a frost green, anti-reflection colour, which was gentle on the eyes, was presented in 1941, designed by Malmsten in soft, rounded forms (Diverse affärstryck Kungl. Biblioteket [Miscellaneous business press Kungl. Biblioteket]).

Åtvidabergs Snickerier, which also hired, for example, the talented furniture architect Carl-Axel Acking (1910–2001), soon dominated the market for office equipment, but similar furniture was also being manufactured at, for example, the factories in Edsbyn and Gemla. Like the major company in Åtvidaberg the latter company had an extensive range of office furniture 'in American-style' after ideas that the management and foremen had gathered from catalogues, trips and exhibition visits (Engman 1999 and Artéus 2006).

In many ways Carl Malmsten represented the general public's tastes. In a sense, his opposite number was the self-taught furniture designer Bruno Mathsson (1907–1988) whose radical furniture ideas have really only recently been incorporated

Fig. 2.12 The typewriter soon became an indispensable tool in the large office workplaces. Sweden's most legendary machine is the completely enclosed Halda that Åtvidabergsbolaget had Carl Malmsten redesign in 1941. Malmsten himself said that he had sought to give the new machine a harmonious exterior that suited its function, but it is also an early example of how, following American examples, one consciously sought to improve working conditions through encapsulation and anti-reflection surface treatment.

into Swedish cultural heritage. Bruno Mathsson, like one of the functionalist role models Gerrit Rietveld, had the advantage of being born into the furniture business. The family ran a furniture company in Värnamo and when, in the 1920s, he started working in his father's workshop it was as a fifth generation cabinetmaker. In order to educate himself about historical furniture styles and modern trends, he borrowed difficult to find technical literature over several years from the Röhsska Museum. Ingrid Böhn-Jullander (1992) quotes a letter in which Bruno gratefully gives the museum

Fig. 2.13 The bentwood chair Gräshoppan (The Grasshopper) with a suspended webbing seat from 1931 was Bruno Mathsson's first in a long suite of chairs that broke with the prevailing eclectic style ideal in his father Karl Mathsson's joinery. The chair was made to order for Värnamo hospital but it was not an immediate success. A few years later, Mathsson sketched the seating curves for the three models: office chair, recliner and lounger, which were the foundation for his continued design work (see Fig. 2.14).

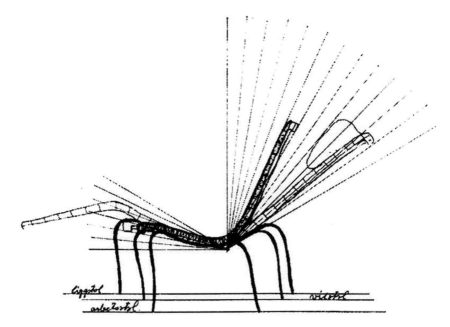

Fig. 2.14 Mathsson's sketch of the seating curves. See Fig. 2.13.

much of the credit for his newfound insights. In another letter he writes that it was a visit to the Stockholm Exhibition, as well as journals from Röhsska, which liberated him from taking a style-focused approach.

In the small community where he lived, Värnamo in Småland, characterized by non-conformist religion, Bruno Mathsson was considered an oddball. As a nature lover and naturist he broke from the usual pattern of life, especially as he also liked to sleep outdoors at his self-designed house. He was a man of vision who was not content just following in the family business's well-trodden footsteps, but always experimented with simplifying and reducing. It is said that he researched the basic shape of his chair suite by transferring his own body impression from a snowdrift. He divided the chair into an upper piece with back and seat and a base in the shape of a leg-stand. The principle, which emerged in the years 1933–1934, broke with conventional sitting furniture production and was instead related to deck chairs and rocking chairs. The result was an office chair, a recliner and a lounger, all with the base in laminate, that is to say a glued multilayer, bentwood covered with braided webbing. Bentwood made from laminated birch had been developed by Alvar Aalto a few years earlier in his work with Paimio Sanatorium, and webbing was cheap and readily available by the metre and also had the advantage of being breathable (Cornell 1967).

The breakthrough came in connection with an acclaimed exhibition at the Röhsska Museum in 1936, where he showed, in addition to his chairs, an ingenious folding table. The following year he was invited to furnish the Swedish Pavilion at the World's Fair in Paris. There the head of the Museum of Modern Art,

Edgar Kaufmann Jr – interested in functionalist approaches – was fascinated to the point that he ordered several Mathsson chairs for the extension of the newly established New York Museum. Thus Bruno Mathsson's name was forever put on the international design map and this was really only for a few products that he steadfastly adhered to and diversified over four decades. But they, along with Alvar Aalto's work, came to be seen as excellent representatives of the softer, more organic version of functionalist furniture that became a hallmark of the Nordic countries during the 1930s and 1940s; similar chairs were also designed, incidentally, by G. A. Berg and Axel Larsson for their respective companies, where, above all, Berg's work was notable for a more thorough ergonomic study (Perers 2003). This direction, sometimes called Swedish Modern, can be seen as an attempt during the war years to recreate a more Swedish national distinctive character, at the same time as it marks a rejection of the colder German tubular steel aesthetic.

During the 1940s, children's right to living space and development became an important issue in the housing debate and among residential circles, according to Monica Boman (1991). Several manufacturers began to provide children's furniture that was no longer just miniatures of adult furniture. Also at the Röhsska Museum's *Vår Bostad* (Our House) exhibitions children's room interior design was a permanent feature. Here they showed so-called Lekmöbler (Play-furniture), which was a combination of furniture that could be assembled and playground equipment; the first as early as 1938, designed by G. A. Berg and a few years later by the architect Erik Ahlsén, at the time employed at the Kooperativa Förbundets (The Swedish Co-operative Union's) architect office. The furniture was seen as an important pedagogical tool in the training of motor skills, orderliness, cooperation and construction capability.

Prominent Defenders of 'Good Taste'

Following influences from mainly the United States, NK (Nordic Company) opened its doors on Hamngatan in Stockholm in 1915. It was Sweden's first department store and the number of employees exceeded a thousand when it opened. NK, designed by the architect Ferdinand Boberg, quickly became an institution, as important for commerce, fashion and advertising as an arena for the enforcement of 'good taste'. In addition, it had the country's largest lighting system, a seven and a half kilometre long mailing tube, central vacuum cleaner and the country's first escalator.

Fashion shows with the latest models from the French fashion houses were held at the large department store. For the men, there was a barbershop, a cigar shop and an English tailor. Everything that was needed to decorate a first-class home was shown at NK. For many years, NK dressed the Swedish Olympic teams and it featured quality garments from Bohus Stickning, a distribution service for skilled craftswomen from the West Coast that was started by Emma Jacobsson during the crisis year 1939. At regularly recurring exhibitions on the premises the most modern art glass, ceramics and silver were also on display. After the war, NK received numerous prestigious assignments to decorate embassies, legations, executive offices, meeting rooms, business houses, banks, showrooms and major international hotels. To meet these demands for high quality furniture production NK built up its own workshops in Nyköping with several hundred employees. From here they supplied everything from iron beds in large quantities for Swedish hospitals to luxurious, architect-designed interiors. For a few years they also exported pompous furniture suites to the NK branches in St Petersburg and Buenos Aires. But, until the closure of the workshops in 1973, it was perhaps its furniture series that would make NK famous in a design context.

It all began in the 1930s when the architect Axel Einar Hjorth was engaged to draw cheap and modern birch furniture. NK had been criticized at the 1930 Stockholm Exhibition for their extravagant room interiors, with luxury furniture designed by top architects in exotic wood types inlaid with silver and ivory. The big break for NK's furniture series came in the 1940s, beginning with a contest for new furniture for family homes that had been organized by Svenska Möbelfabrikerna i Bodafors together with the Swedish Society of Crafts and Design in 1943. The contest was won by the versatile architect Elias Svedberg (1913–1987) together with his co-workers Lena Larsson and Erik Wørts with their proposal for a simple but sturdy furniture series, which the buyers themselves would assemble. The following year NK decided to take up production of the furniture under the name Triva-Bygg.

The Triva furniture should be seen as, for the time, a radical attempt to design a concept that was adapted to increased mobility in society. An accelerating urban immigration and changes of apartments, as households grew or shrank, demanded lighter, more flexible and less expensive furniture. Triva-Bygg was shipped in flat packages with attached instructions several years before IKEA started its similar winning formula. The designs were clever and the idea was to save the boxes so that you could disassemble the furniture and reuse them during a future move. This was something completely different from the many prestigious specialized interiors, and it is doubtful whether the NK manager Ragnar Sachs understood what he was getting into when he purportedly muttered to Svedberg, 'I did not know you wanted to sell me a lumberyard' (Larsson 1991: 70).

Triva-Bygg received a lot of attention at the Boutställningar (Living Exhibitions) that the Swedish Society of Crafts and Design organized in the mid-1940s. To begin with, the range included the absolutely necessary, such as chairs, tables and cupboards, but there was also a supplementary assortment of armchairs and small nesting tables.

The considerable interest in contemporary furniture led to NK, from 1947 and for a decade or so onwards, in addition to their regular expensive and exclusive range, also running a special interior department, called NK-bo (NK-live), on separate premises. It became a new, more experimental type of furniture store that mainly appealed to the younger market. Here the interior designer Lena Larsson

Fig. 2.15 Nordiska Kompaniet (The Nordic Company or NK) was known for its exclusive interiors. The contrast with the furniture series Triva-Bygg that was launched in 1944 in the form of flat boxes, long before IKEA, was sharp. The woman in the picture is holding the parts for a chest of drawers.

(1919–2000), who had been hired as the artistic director, with the help of screen walls created different sample arrangements of the new furniture series together with, among other things, textile prints by Stig Lindberg and upholstery fabrics by Astrid Sampe. The Triva series developed gradually with the help of many well-known Swedish and international architects, including Carl-Axel Acking, Eero Saarinen and Harry Bertoia.

The textile artist Astrid Sampe (1909–2002) had been employed by NK in 1936 and the following year became the head of the store's so-called Textilkammaren (Textile Chamber) where fabrics were woven using new techniques and patterns. Sampe was educated at Konstfack and the Royal College of Art in London and quickly acquired a large and useful international network of contacts. Filled with a desire to experiment, she introduced woodblock printing in the style of William Morris and a few years later the modern screen-printing, which opened possibilities for complicated multi-colour prints as well as larger patterns. In 1951, the first fibreglass fabrics were woven at Textilkammaren and in 1970, the year before Textilkammaren was shut down, she presented, in collaboration with programmers from IBM, the first computer-based textile patterns in Sweden; a contact she had made through her friend, Eliot Noyes, chief designer for IBM. The subsequently produced fabrics were used, among other things, for the Triva furniture and for rugs to put them on. The interior collaboration between Sampe and Elias Svedberg had already had a major impact at the 1937 World's Fair in Paris and their success was repeated at several later international exhibitions (Astrid Sampe 1984). Astrid Sampe was the great organizer, inspirer and perfectionist. An often-used quote is the journalist Marianne Höök's statement about her capacity: 'the blonde's head is systematised like an automatic card-index' (Herlitz-Gezelius 1992: 127).

On Strandvägen, not too far from NK, Firma Svensk Tenn (Swedish Pewter Firm) opened in 1924, which was yet another commercial arena in Stockholm with leanings towards exclusive design. The initiator was the drawing teacher Estrid Ericson (1894–1981). To begin with the company focused on objects made of pewter such as candlesticks, chandeliers, trays, mirrors and vases created by Ericson and her teacher, the artist Nils Fougstedt. After just five years she employed twenty-five workshop staff and ten female shop assistants, in addition to a number of artistic collaborators, the most prominent of whom were Björn Trägårdh (1908–1998) and Anna Petrus (1886–1949).

When the smoothly shaped grey pewter faded in popularity under the influence of functionalism it was polished and tightened into new expressions. At the same time Svenskt Tenn was expanded with a furniture and carpet department. On the furniture side Estrid Ericson cooperated with Svenska Möbelfabrikerna i Bodafors and the models were designed by, among others, the architect Uno Åhrén (Boman 2000). Gotthard Johansson (1952) argues that Ericson had an ingenuity that 'above all lay in the ability to select and compile, to create, often from simple materials and standard models, a unity of refined taste, to give a soft personal touch to functionalism's, in many eyes, far too naked and sober new objectivity'.

The cooperation with the Austrian architect Josef Frank proved to be crucial to the future of Svenskt Tenn, which began in 1932 and which led to him two years later arriving in Stockholm to escape from Nazi rule. Josef Frank (1885–1967) was a revered name among adherents of functionalism on the continent, especially after his efforts as a building architect at the Weissenhof Exhibition in 1927. In Sweden, as early as 1924 he designed through contacts, via his Swedish wife, the first of several functionalist villas with an emphasis on experimentation in Falsterbo, but it is as an interior designer in collaboration with Estrid Ericson that he has gone down in Swedish design history. Commissioned by Ericson for her store, Josef Frank created patterns, furniture, fixtures, glass, candlesticks and so on until his death. As a pattern designer, he was inspired by William Morris and the Art Nouveau artists' vegetative nature motifs (Plate 9). The patterns, which very much live on and inspire Swedish interior design, are usually very colourful with large-patterned motifs, fresh as a Nordic summer meadow, yet luxuriant as an exotic wildwood, to borrow Gotthard Johansson's words (Johansson 1952).

At the same time as Josef Frank made use of a richness of detail, he preached the importance of a room's cleanness. 'The modern dwelling has white walls', he stated and continued, 'it is the only possibility we have to preserve our freedom in it and to there introduce whatever we want. Against white, you can allow colours and patterns to bloom, white brings out the beautiful and drives away the boring' (Ericson 1968: 27). Frank was early in his quest for ergonomic values, to adapt objects to the human body.

In a manifesto-like article in the journal *Form* from 1934, he rejected functionalism's fashionable geometric shapes, tendencies towards primitivism and lack of functionality. 'The shape of a chair has to be tailored to the human body shape, whose negative it is' was the simple message. His own furniture often had a vigorous and delicate quality, as if he had chiselled the features out of the body's own framework. Of course, they were made from the natural material wood; steel was for him unthinkable. He also wanted to 'free housing from being condemned to always want to be art or reformatory'.

Svenskt Tenn evolved gradually into an interior design firm with a combination of rigorously selected imports and exquisite in-house production, which successfully participated in the many international exhibitions during the 1920s and 1930s. In 1975 the company became a foundation and six years later Estrid Ericson passed away. The memory of her lives on, particularly through the research foundation that bears her name and with whose help this book came about. The store has been expanded over the years and continues to operate. As does NK whose subsequent evolution has, however, been much more turbulent.

The Folkhem Vision Materializes

The Stockholm-based NK and Svenskt Tenn are all very well, but they primarily appealed to an affluent clientele or at least one that was interested in design and was quality conscious. If you were going to be able reach out to the masses, however, a distributor that covered the whole country and a producer that consciously put all its efforts into the good and cheap everyday product were needed. They got that in Kooperativa Förbundet (The Swedish Co-operative Union or KF). It is difficult to imagine today how important KF's role was in the realization of the Social Democrat and later Prime Minister Per Albin Hansson's Folkhem vision (welfare state vision) from 1928, of solidarity and consensus. Without exaggerating one can say that KF from the 1930s to the 1970s was involved in the average person's life, from cradle to grave.

What had started, inspired by British models, in 1899 as an association between forty-odd independent cooperative associations to lower the cost of food for the common people and reduce dependence on private retailers, grew into a colossus that built a whole host of industries and co-op shops across the country. In 1924 they were forced to establish an architect office to plan and keep abreast of the business; according to Gregor Paulsson this was initiated by Elsa Gullberg and himself. The primary reason was to achieve a rise in the standard of grocery store interiors, but soon the foundation of this modern project was being designed under the supervision of the architect Eskil Sundahl: spacious, modern homes, preferably terraced houses with their own little plot, functional and hygienic workplaces, standardized stores with cheap, mass-produced necessities and for edification and enjoyment Folkets hus (the People's House) and Folkets park (the People's Park), all in accordance with Sundahl's motto: 'A healthy sense of taste and a democratic building culture'. The office became a nursery for Sweden's architectural elite and also had a large international team of colleagues. Both the assignments and staff quickly grew and already in about 1930 KF's architectural offices were the largest in the Nordic countries (Brunnström 2004).

During the inter-war period, Sweden was one of the fastest growing economies in the world; around 1950 it even had the world's fastest economic growth. This had been achieved through taking advantage of natural resources, a rationalization of industry and a reform effort, which had made diligence and steadiness into virtues. But the most significant factor was certainly that this development could take place without the devastation of war that large parts of the rest of the world had suffered. KF was a key part of this welfare project and part of a broader collectivistic movement in Sweden, in which the trade unions, educational and interest organizations had also become increasingly important. Together they rapidly built a homogeneous, consumption-driven middle class that was both technology-oriented and progressive (Hansson 2002).

KF's breakthrough in the production of goods first came on the food side with the acquisition of two large mills, an oil factory and a cannery as well as the construction of a margarine factory, crispbread factory, oatmeal mill and a macaroni factory – all typical staples of the Swedish diet. An important driving force was the need to create a counterbalance to private trade, which was accused of forming cartels on a wholesale level and lending that created dependency in the retail trade. In 1938 it organized more than fifty-three meatpacking factories and thirty-two bakeries around the country (Brunnström 2004). They were also very early in streamlining grain and flour processing at the two mills Tre Kronor in Kvarnholmen in Stockholm and Tre Lejon in Hisingen in Gothenburg. For the storage of grain they built the country's most elegant and hygienic concrete silos, designed by Olof Thunström. The traditional method of filling, unhygienic and difficult to handle, 100-kilogram sacks with flour, which were then shipped to bakeries and grocery stores, was replaced in the 1930s with semi-automatic packaging machines that packaged the flour in 2-kilogram bags. The white, clean paper bags were decorated with the KF and flour brand's logos and thus became an excellent medium for advertising (Brunnström, Norling, Spade 2002).

Svea, KF's own major advertising agency, was responsible for the graphic design that gave the cooperative the possibility of entering the commercial advertising market, which was less common in other countries. But arguably Svea's main function was to sell the vision of the future welfare society and build the movement's brand.

This was done through large-scale marketing and with the help of skilled designers. An important task was producing hard-hitting posters and staging exhibitions where KF was represented. Gunnar Orrby, hired in 1937, was the agency's most prominent poster artist. He was educated at Konstfack and like his colleagues Erik Heffer at Svenska Telegrambyrån (Swedish News Agency) and Anders Beckman he was inspired by contemporary surrealist art, including artists like A. M. Cassandre and Salvador Dalí. The surrealist approach with its symbols and fantasies combined well with a sales message and often resulted in a thrilling, rebus-like message (Bowallius 1999). The posters were distributed free of charge to the stores and used for publicity purposes in both storefront windows and outside. By the mid-1960s Svea had developed a graphical profile for the whole movement and made the Möbius strip or lemniscate, already launched in 1959, the new company symbol for the limitless KF (Krantz, Ryberg et al. 1955).

The transition to self-service shops, or supermarkets as they are usually known, was of crucial importance for the design of food packaging. Here the idea was that customers would pass a turnstile at the entrance and then wander around the store, picking up their items and bring them to the checkout. The idea, of course, came from the United States where this scientific concept of buying had been developed in the 1920s in the supermarket chain Piggly Wiggly. Suddenly products had to be packaged and speak for themselves on the shelves, which gave a considerable boost to graphic design and the packaging industry. KF was the Swedish supermarket pioneer and tested the system in some stores in 1941. Seven years later, they had eleven supermarkets in operation and several more were planned. Most innovation came from the USA, everything from the layout of the 'self-service-stores' and refrigerated display cases for meat products to packaging machines for vegetables and bakery goods. Self-service reduced the staffing requirements as well as the waiting times. At the same time hygiene improved considerably.

The stores were in general the key to the whole cooperative system, as well as the fact that they did not allow for the commonly occurring credit trading but inexorably accepted cash transactions. As early as the 1920s, Konsum's (co-op) service stores existed all over the country and their numbers were steadily increasing. KF's stores represented a pioneering effort in retail culture. They were well constructed, well-furnished and tidy and thus for a long time differed radically from private stores. However, it was not always easy to rent central store locations, partly because of the socialist label that the movement received from its competitors. Through a successful cooperation with the housing cooperative movement they managed to get co-op shops on the street level of the larger newly developed housing. In the countryside they bought or built their own properties for their stores. During the years 1922–1935, for example, 2,000 new co-op stores were added of which 600 were newly developed and by the end of the 1930s the number of stores totalled over 4,000.

A joint standard for the stores was developed in 1922 and when the architect office began operations two years later the main function was producing blueprints and a common interior design standard for all new stores. An exterior detail that differed

Fig. 2.16 Product distribution made up Kooperativa Förbundet's (The Swedish Co-operative Union or KF) core activity and the thousands of co-op shops were an important part of their identity. The interior design in the exemplarily organized self-service stores was standardized and signalled hygiene, comfort and communicability. The scale, cash register, stools for visitors and counters were central in this context. This is how the store interior was presented at the 1930 Stockholm Exhibition.

between the urban and rural shops was that the former were fitted with as large a shop-window as the wall structure would permit. KF quickly became internationally recognized as an innovator in retail culture and had requests for its recipe for success from, for example, Germany, Britain and the Soviet Union (Brunnström 2004).

KF did not just get involved in the food sector, however, but was also keen to counteract cartel formations and keep prices down for other staple commodities. Rural shops had a wide range of goods and when the first department stores began to appear around 1930 distribution opportunities increased. A shoe factory in Örebro, the first new class of commodity, was purchased in 1925. The following year a controlling interest in Svenska Gummifabriks AB in Gislaved was purchased, which manufactured, among other things, galoshes and bicycle tyres. Car tyre production was expanded and an assembly line was introduced as one of the first in the country in the early 1930s. In 1930, a large and advanced light-bulb factory became operational, Lumafabriken (the Luma factory), which the architect office had designed. The factory was placed on a hill along Hammarbyleden (the Hammarby channel) in Stockholm, and was fitted with a giant Luma sign and a glazed tower-like test chamber in which random samples of the product were tested. The tower was bathed in light and served as a brilliant advertising space both day and night.

Fig. 2.17 The Luma light-bulb factory in Hammarbyhamnen, Stockholm was one of the KF-empire's flagship buildings in the functionalist style. The factory, which was completed in 1931 and became an important weapon against the existing cartel formations in the light-bulb industry, featured in several posters. This one was designed by Gunnar Orrby at KF's advertising agency Svea in 1946.

The technocratic motif became an important part of KF's conscious brand building and emerged not only as a symbol for electric light, as such, but also a symbol for the enlightened consumer.

The acquisitions and construction projects within key sectors of the building of the welfare state followed in quick succession during the 1930s and 1940s: a porcelain factory in Gustavsberg with immediate investment in a new sanitary-ware factory, a building board factory in Karlholm, crisis-time investments in paper mills, for example, in Fiskeby, a chemical pulp mill in Älvenäs for the production of synthetic fibres, a gas carbon facility for, among other things, a coal gas generator in Lycksele, coal and coking plants in Malmö and an artificial fertilizer plant in Köping, important tools for the stores in the form of Hugin cash registers in Stockholm and the scales factory Stathmos in Eskilstuna, the clothing factory Slitman in Sala for the manufacture of work clothes, several oil refineries to gain control of the petrol prices, and so on. Many of the factories were exemplary for their time, both from a productivity and a working environment point of view. On the whole, KF was keen to appear progressive; they saw it as being equally important to use high-profile campaigns to improve the Swedish people's personal hygiene as to sell as many washbasins, toilets and bidets as possible from the ultra-modern sanitary-ware factory in Gustavsberg.

The designer Stig Lindberg (1916–1982) was a considerable boon to KF and during his forty-three years of employment at Gustavsbergs Fabriker, of which about twenty years were as an artistic director, he designed many very popular products. These were tableware, sanitary-ware, many plastic products, ornamental and utility objects in faience and stoneware for Gustavsberg, but also, for example, transistor radios and televisions for Luma, book covers and patterns for textiles and wallpapers. He also did a lot to make KF's, Gustavsberg's and his own brand famous, both internationally and at home. Helena Kåberg writes, 'he participated in commercials, lectured, agreed to interviews and made personal appearances at exhibitions and the regional Domus department stores' (Kåberg 2006: 52). Many of Stig Lindberg's sketches and wash drawings are preserved at Designarkivet (Design Archives) in Pukeberg that clearly show the ease and fluency with which he could sketch in one variation after another on specific themes. The colours and playful style are impressive and the material is a wonderful inspiration for pattern design and design studies for budding future designers.

Gustavsberg was in every way a model facility, which when it reached its peak in the 1970s had well over 2,000 employees. Many foreign visitors were guided here and to Kvarnholmen, with all its modern food management. It was not only close to Stockholm, but these places also had the largest areas of company housing and, of course, they were also exemplary according to the new functionalist ideals or in the later somewhat moderated Folkhem's Modernism. They had also built narrow blocks of rental apartments with consistently bright apartments, terraced houses and small homes in the form of angle built single-storey houses. In every respect KF appeared to be a centre for the functional, standardized everyday product. It was there in the construction, in the interiors, in the industrial production and in the graphic production. Rational, technocratic and engineering design ideals were certainly dominant, but during the 1940s and 1950s humanistic and aesthetic values were given greater leeway. Gregor Paulsson was, for example, a frequently hired educator on taste and lecturer about good and bad taste at KF's training centre, and at KF's architect office they took collective responsibility for issues related to both the external and internal environment (Brunnström 2004).

The interior design commissions increased gradually, especially with respect to shop interior design and the working out of standardization guidelines for, for example, joineries, kitchen sinks, plumbing systems and sanitary facilities. But they also designed furniture and fixtures. The architect brothers Erik and Tore Ahlsén were, among others, responsible for this, and their neat, practical and relatively cheap basic furniture range would live on and evolve over many years. It included, for example, storage furniture, chairs, garden furniture (Plate 10) and children's furniture. Under the leadership of Erik Ahlsén a special furniture department was established in 1939 and later the department collaborated with furniture designers such as Sigrun Bülow-Hübe, Gunnar Eklöf, Carl Malmsten and Carl-Axel Acking (Eklund Nyström 1992).

3 Soft Values Get Upgraded, 1940s to 1950s

Women's Understanding of Home Economics Is Utilized

The home played a central role in the idea of the 'Folkhem' itself, as a metaphor for the joint project of building a welfare state but also in the form of instructions for the shaping of the private home. As the Second World War loomed, a number of surveys of housing habits were conducted. It was already known that Sweden, after Finland, was the country with the second most overcrowded living arrangements in the Western world, at least in terms of the number of rooms. But surveys also showed that the overcrowding in many cases was self-inflicted, which indicated that building larger apartments was not enough. It also had to be ensured that these were used in a sensible way, and that apartments were being utilized to their full extent. 'Instead of distributing the sleeping quarters more or less evenly in the different rooms families were squeezing 4–5 people into one single room' explained one of the leaders of the survey, Gotthard Johansson:

> As a particularly dramatic example, an apartment with 2 rooms, kitchen and dining alcove, where the whole family, five people, lay packed in a 10.5 m² room, while simultaneously in both the living room and dining alcove there stood unused double beds. (Johansson 1945: 9)

The housing habit surveys were thorough, especially those carried out by the interior designer Lena Larsson. On behalf of the Swedish Society of Crafts and Design and the Swedish Association of Architects, she studied around a hundred families living in newly built narrow blocks and tower blocks constructed in the functionalist spirit on the outskirts of Stockholm. During visits to these apartments the interiors were photographed and furnishing plans were drawn up but, above all, long, impartial conversations were held with the families. Apart from the distribution of sleeping places and their design, they discussed, for example, how and where meals were taken, what storage possibilities the apartment offered, how the housework was done, when furniture had been purchased, the laundry, how often they had guests, homework and other child-related issues. The results were published in the journal *Form* in 1945, where Lena Larsson complained about the small apartments, the shortage of closets, the 'baroque' sized small kitchens in the larger apartments, but also about the almost total ignorance that was prevalent regarding the relationship between the dwelling and its use. At its core, argued Larsson, Swedish overcrowding was a sleeping issue: families crowded together in a small space while a large living room stood uninhabited in anticipation of potential guests. Far too often furniture was purchased 'with an unconscious desire to impress friends and acquaintances' instead of fulfilling functional needs. The housing question was, in other words, as much an interior design question (Larsson 1945:15).

During the 1940s and well into the 1950s interior decoration was regarded as a public education issue and was included in virtually all the adult education associations' range of courses. The aesthetic propagation of good taste from Ellen Key's days had been reformulated with more easily defined and measurable benchmarks, such as rationality and functionality. The modernist ideal of beauty with simple, smooth and unadorned shapes could be justified on the grounds that it was practical and hygienic as opposed to the ornate, which was impractical and therefore ugly. The spirit of good general education was associated with democracy, modernity, morality and a high degree of civilization and it was also manifested in how you decorated your home. People with good taste made their choices based on reason and educated knowledge, a knowledge that above all was conveyed by the Swedish Society of Crafts and Design's advice and propaganda activities (Göransdotter 2005).

Not only interior decoration but also housework became a focus, largely through the extensive work of various women's organizations. This also strengthened consumer influence in many areas. Hemmens forskningsinstitut (The Institute of Home Research or HFI) was founded in 1944 by housewives and the domestic science teachers' associations together with the newly formed Aktiv hushållning (Active Housekeeping), which was a predecessor of the public institution Konsumentverket (the Swedish Consumer Agency). HFI was working for a systemic rationalization of working conditions in Swedish homes. Their activities would be conducted through research, time studies and tests. As a result the industrial streamlining principles of Taylorism had reached all the way into Swedish kitchens and children's bedrooms, even though this may not have been directly expressed (Åkerman et al. 1984).

At the time, women were responsible for virtually all of the housework and it was also where much of the knowledge about the home's arrangement, interior design and utensils could be found. Of the housewife's working hours it was estimated that about 30 per cent were spent on cooking while dishwashing and cleaning accounted for 15–20 per cent each. The vast majority of Swedish kitchens in the 1940s and 1950s were cumbersome and furnished with inadequate workspaces. While the functionalist architects may have shown small well-equipped and laboratory-like kitchens at the Stockholm Exhibition with linoleum flooring, stainless steel kitchen sinks, refrigerators, modern stoves and many handy storage spaces, they had hardly been an instant success. In addition, understanding of the real users' needs was far too vague; it was about more than just technology, hygiene and space to heat up the odd tin. Where were you supposed to sit and eat and where were you supposed to put the cherished kitchen bench? Preparing and eating food in the same room was considered contemptible by the architects and master builders. But the reality showed that many still preferred a large kitchen instead of a small dining alcove.

Gotthard Johansson, who was one of the few men on HFI's board, provided the analysis:

> The habit of eating in the kitchen is deeply rooted in the Swedish working class, where it is a legacy from the countryside, but as the housemaid issue has become increasingly difficult even within the middle class, where it used to be considered a mark of social class, many have discovered that eating in the kitchen is fine, provided it is big enough to accommodate a proper dining area. (Johansson 1945: 10)

The 1940s and 1950s were a period of transition with many innovations in the consumer market: for example, plastic materials for tools and surface treatments, machines for household use and the breakthrough of quick-freezing technology. Carin Boalt, who led HFI's research operations, has given an account of all the surveys and user studies that HFI launched to examine housing and market supply. They considered materials for countertops, working heights, working processes, design of stoves, refrigerators, vacuum cleaners, washing machines, cooking utensils, knives and other utensils for cutting up food, including Electrolux's newly developed Assistent (food processor) which was supposedly the only electric food processor available on the Swedish market. The working methods were largely taken from agriculture and industry, including Statens maskinprovningar (the State's Machine Testing Agency), in terms of the measurement of energy consumption, risk, timescale and efficiency. The housewife organizations also contributed with knowledge about working equipment and methods. The home was now the focal point of standardization measures and HFI became an important platform in terms of the radicalization of women's conditions. A number of suggestions for improvements and standardization measures were gradually developed and published in a series of pamphlets. The recommendations were also spread through numerous brochures and leaflets, exhibitions and lectures (Åkerman et al. 1984).

A study of dishwashing found that on average 1–1.5 hours a day were devoted to dishwashing, that the work was considered tiring and tedious and that the most appropriate working height was up to 95 centimetres as opposed to 85 centimetres for, for example, the kneading of dough. Studies of laundry habits and washing machines revealed that about 70 per cent of all washing was still done by hand in the early 1950s, which was very demanding work. An oxygen uptake study had shown that the first hand-operated machines that came into use did not facilitate handling but, if anything, required more energy. When small electric washing machines started to appear on the market in the 1940s, under the influence of the USA, they therefore quickly became popular. After only a few years, there were some eighty models on the Swedish market. Of the three different machine types, cylinder machine, pulsator machine and agitator machine, HFI recommended the first for Swedish households. The cylinder washing machine consumed less water and did more laundry per cycle, about four kilograms compared with one and a half

Fig. 3.1 Hemmens forskningsinstitut (The Institute of Home Research or HFI), which was established during the Second World War, focused on the domestic environment and through its systematic research and tests came to mean a lot for the Folkhem (welfare state) housing plan. The kitchen was the focus of the rationalization work.

kilograms, than the small pulsator-type washing machines that were popular in US households (Plate 11).

Around fifty different types of kitchen utensils were studied, for example, wooden tools, hand whisks, pans and knives. The knife study that HFI conducted had few if any international examples. A historical retrospective showed that the industrial production of kitchen knives started in the 1870s in Sweden. The following decade there were about ten main types on the market, a number that had increased tenfold by 1944. These one hundred types were in turn available in nearly 300 different sizes and designs of varying quality. The knives' design, handle material and construction were all tested on twenty volunteers with varying hand sizes and housework experience. When the subjects used the knives in various cutting situations it emerged that the handles were generally uncomfortable, far too thin, flat and angular. The results provided the foundation for the development of a trial series with new comfortable handles modelled in plastic. The prototypes that were later made and then quickly converted to serial production by several companies all had larger dimensions, softer rounded edges and rear finger guards. For the handles hard, dense, oily wood types were recommended, which should not be stained or painted so as to survive the test's 300 dishwashing cycles. The attachment was best made by allowing the extended knife blade to go through the handle and join them by means of, for example, metal rivets.

During the Second World War homes also needed to conform to household crisis management. To this end, the government created the organization Aktiv hushållning (Active Housekeeping) under female leadership in 1940, whose primary task was to collect and communicate knowledge about diet and clothing. In 1944, a children's clothes committee was established, which developed simplified models suitable for clothing manufacture in large batches. The standard models were supposed to be comfortable for children to wear at the same time as they had to be easy to wash and mend. Children's clothing was usually manufactured in the form of reduced copies of adult formal wear. Now designs from working life, which were suited to playing and sports, were chosen instead. These were loose and comfortable garments such as bib-and-brace overalls, collarless shirts and woollen sweaters (Åkerman 1984).

In 1954, Aktiv Hushållning was merged with HFI, which was nationalized a few years later and was the forerunner of today's Konsumentverk (the Swedish Consumer Agency). The manufacturers had alongside the Swedish Society of Crafts and Design received an additional counterpart, which used empirical arguments to examine and compare different products.

The Industrial Designer Demonstrates His Talents

In both Swedish and international design history, it is often the consultants who are highlighted; that is to say the prominent designers with their own companies that for various reasons have managed to make a name for themselves. The manufacturing industry's in-house designers are generally much less familiar, the traditional applied arts excepted. It is not until the last few years in Sweden that there has been any direct interest from management to strengthen a brand by capitalizing on the name of individual designers. Certainly, one reason is that companies have long been driven by technology and staff designers have generally been in a weak position; another is that the information about design experimentation is hidden in the company archives and that there has not been any real attempt by design researchers to unearth pioneering Swedish innovation. It should also be noted that the corresponding foreign names that figure in design history have, as a rule, been active in design-intensive companies; for example, Harley Earl at the American GM, Dieter Rams at the German Braun, Louis Kalff at the Dutch Philips and Ettore Sottsass Jr at the Italian Olivetti.

But in Sweden, oddly enough, not even its most design-intensive major companies such as Volvo, Saab, Ericsson and Electrolux have shown any great interest in their own design history.

A Swedish industrial design pioneer whose efforts went unseen for many years was Ralph Lysell (1907–1987), or Rolf Nystedt, as he was originally called. Lysell's career was highly remarkable. During most of the 1920s and 1930s he stayed in America where he graduated in engineering while, apparently, also becoming an American university boxing champion. Lysell was outgoing, creative and had a rare talent for drawing, something that certainly helped shape his career as an industrial designer. He was arguably in the right place at the right time, as it is precisely in connection with the Great Depression and its aftermath that the definitive break-through of industrial design is usually dated. During much of his career, Ralph Lysell, both in articles and lectures, promoted this emerging profession, often with the help of American references. In addition, he was clearly inspired by his eminent colleague Raymond Loewy's dextrous ability to quickly draft an idea and convince his clients, using a felt-tip pen and plasticine.

Lysell also learned how to fully master these important design tools. His portfolio included lipstick tubes and pin-less price tags and his American career's crowning achievement was designing a white, sophisticated, streamlined sports car. After a brief sojourn as a test driver with Mercedes-Benz in Germany, Ralph Lysell returned to Sweden in the summer of 1939 and was employed by the telecom company Ericsson. At Ericsson they had experience of bringing in outside aesthetic consultants in the context of telephone manufacture. In the age of wooden caskets they had been aided by skilled master carpenters and when the enclosed metal telephones were adopted the architect Torben Grut was consulted. In connection with the development of the Bakelite telephone an artist was responsible for the shape and when the device was redesigned later in the 1930s the engineer Alvar Lenning, who was well versed in design, was brought in. But in Lysell, Ericsson had, as the first Swedish manufacturer outside the art industry, an in-house expert who also had fresh design experience from the leading country to the West (Brunnström 2006).

Ralph Lysell quickly acquired a stellar reputation and over the following years it seems as if virtually all of the company's newly developed products had been fashioned into different streamlined shapes by him: speakerphones, home telephones, telephone boxes, radios for the subsidiary Svenska Radio AB (SRA) and more. Ideas were usually visualized in the form of quick pencil sketches, but were later modelled in clay or worked into stylish airbrush renderings on black cardboard. As a person, Lysell was persuasive in many ways. A close associate has described him as something of a renaissance man, a charming man who was concerned with his appearance, had a way with words, a ladies' man and who was basically the biggest and best in whatever he undertook (Lindström 1997).

In 1943, Lysell established his own little department at Ericsson called Estestisk formgivning (Aesthetic design), which was directly under the company-wide construction department. Now he had to educate draughtsmen on issues related to colour and shape. He was also very interested in material issues. He had a good command of aluminium and tubular steel structures but was, above all, a specialist in different plastics including both Bakelite, or resin as it was called at the time, and the new thermoplastics. Lysell's lecturing, article writing and extroverted personality led to contacts with the directors of Swedish industry. In the spring of 1945, this 'Mr. Design' left Ericsson and started his own company in grandiose style. With support from an advertising agency, extensive marketing and a studio in central Stockholm, AB Industriell Formgivning (Industrial Design) was founded with around ten employees.

The agency received relatively few but nevertheless varied commissions: some Loewy-inspired fronts for standalone refrigerators for Electrolux, a new car model for Philipssons which was preparing a production in Augustendal at the inlet to Stockholm; but above all miscellaneous small commissions from creative but,

Fig. 3.2 Ralph Lysell was one of the foremost pioneers of Swedish industrial design and as such was clearly inspired by the USA. He worked as an in-house designer at Ericsson during the Second World War and in 1945 started his own design company AB Industriell Formgivning (Industrial Design) where the picture was taken.

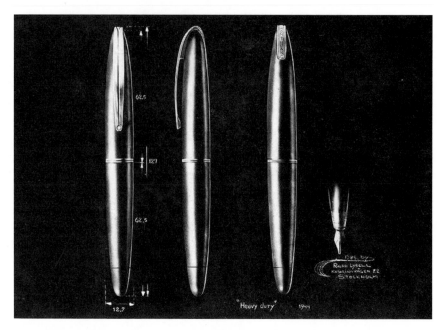

Fig. 3.3 One of Lysell's strengths as a designer was his ability to quickly present an accurate sketch or rendering to the client, as in the case of the pen Heavy Duty that he made in 1944 for Montblanc.

as a rule, not very solvent small business owners. When Swedish commissions were scarce Lysell turned his attentions abroad and signed a contract with the French company Japy, who manufactured clocks and typewriters. He also drew a torpedo-like fountain pen for the prestigious brand Montblanc, called Heavy Duty. But Lysell was at least ten years ahead of his time. Design was too new and unfamiliar a concept for Swedish industry to be able to support an operation of these proportions. In addition, Ralph Lysell's strength was the conceptual work itself, sketching, rendering, plaster and clay models. When it came to prototyping and the execution phase, taking into consideration the production requirements, finances, machine-handling and so on, his design agency lacked both enthusiasm and sufficient experience. After only two years this pioneering company went out of business and Lysell moved on to Paris and later Oslo in search of a fresh start (Lindström 1997).

Lysell's short but intense design career coincided with two other industrial design pioneers: Alvar Lenning and Sixten Sason. Of these, Lysell notably crossed paths with Alvar Lenning (1897–1980), a polymathic and inventive engineer who had also worked in the USA during the late 1920s, albeit on refrigerator construction for Electrolux. Lenning became more and more interested in design later in his time at Electrolux and was probably the one who first brought industrial design issues to the attention of the public. Based on a few articles in *Dagens Nyheter* from 1938 it appears that he saw 1930s functionalism as a thing of the past. He argued that hardly anyone bought tubular steel chairs anymore 'or cabinets that look like packing-boxes' (DN 31/1 38). He wanted to call the new style that was on its way *barockfunkis* (functionalist baroque), a synthesis between functionalism, streamlined shapes and baroque. He saw American movies as a major influence. What he was describing is what has sometimes come to be called Folkhemsfunkis (Folkhem's functionalism), a form of expression that materially described the majority of Swedish-made articles during the 1940s and 1950s. In a far-sighted lecture for Teknologföreningen (Technologist association) on the theme of 'Design development of industrial products', as referenced in *Dagens Nyheter* 17 November 1938, he said that he had high expectations for the new style: 'It will be easy to adapt to many materials' natures and to the articles' functions, at the same time it will provide new aesthetic values, a new plastic'. But this, he claimed, would make strenuous demands on the professionals, 'it will not be enough to have solely an engineering or solely an architectural education, what is needed is quite simply an architectural engineer, the man with two educations'.

Lenning himself provided an excellent early example of the new style when he was given primary responsibility for the design of Electrolux's stand mixer Assistent, which was launched in 1940. It came with a collection of recipes for times of crisis; the mechanization of household work became a central issue during the crisis years of the Second World War and the stand mixer facilitated heavy tasks like baking bread and grinding meat. The Assistent with its soft, simple design in beige and stainless steel has been one of the domestic appliance company's flagship products through the years and is still manufactured today, only slightly redesigned. In the following year, 1941, Alvar Lenning felt he was ready to set out and start his own consultancy. His commissions came from, in particular, the telephone and radio industry; in addition to the Ericsson commissions, he also designed a number of radios for Aga-Baltic AB and Center brand intercoms for AB Gylling & Co.

Lenning worked in a different way from Lysell and was in many ways his opposite, much more cautious and less grandiose. This was not about quickly assembled clay models but painstakingly developed wooden mock-ups made to scale. His idiom was stricter and less streamlined and Lenning was also not as anxious to use Bakelite as a manufacturing material. Both the intercoms and radios had casings made of wood and much time was devoted to the important task of studying the design of the edges. A few months after Lysell, with the help of an advertising agency, had opened his consulting firm, Alvar Lenning carried out a similar but slightly more modest design manifestation with his brother Einar. Einar Lenning, who early on was inspired by the functionalist movement's new typography and was responsible for the radical promotional material for the Stockholm Exhibition, was an advertising consultant at AB Svenska Telegrambyrån – one of the country's largest advertising agencies. In a promotional publication entitled *Industrial Design* (1945) it was recorded that 'the internationally famous engineer Alvar Lenning and employees' had been taken on by the advertising agency with the task of assisting the company's clients 'with suggestions for technical improvements and in connection with this the development of a more beautiful external shape of the products'. Ralph Lysell had competition and there would be more.

Fig. 3.4a and b One of the design pioneers of Swedish large-scale industry was Alvar Lenning who for many years was associated with Electrolux. One of his more important projects was the popular electrical domestic appliance Assistent. This stand mixer was developed during the 1930s, when it still looked like a workshop machine (above). In 1940 Alvar Lenning made an integrated redesign which turned the machine into a household product (top). It was produced in the same design for decades.

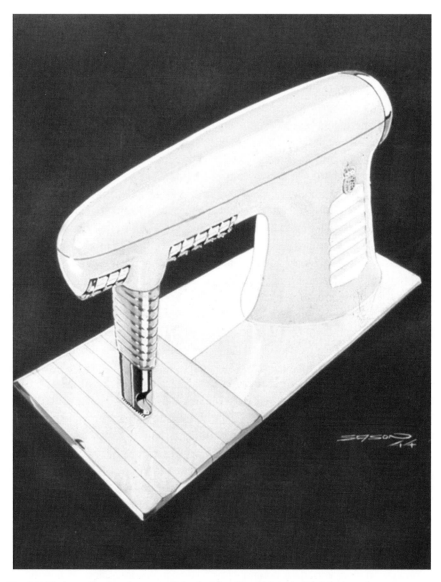

Fig. 3.5 Perhaps the most accomplished of the Swedish industrial design pioneers was Sixten Sason. He was a design consultant for several large companies and is best known for his work on aircraft and automotive design for Saab over many years. For Husqvarna he designed most things, including sewing machines. He sketched this elegant, white model in 1944, long before the Italian success story in sewing machine design.

At the end of the war a talented young Swedish artist and sculptor laid the foundations for a successful design career. His name was Sixten Sason (1912–1967) and he was in the process of creating Sweden's first real compact car, the Saab 92, one of the most important Swedish design projects of the twentieth century. Sason (born

Andersson) was an autodidact and something of a prodigy. Since his teens, he had supported himself by making engine drawings for different magazines while he was a sculptor's apprentice at his father's stonecutter's shop. With only a technical correspondence course and some painting studies with the artist Otte Sköld on his CV, he was hired in 1939 as the head of the drafting group at Saab. Sason's ability to, for example, make instructive X-ray drawings proved useful for the company's manuals and instructional materials, both in terms of early aircraft production and post-war car production (Sköld 1997).

But Sason was also technically gifted and had the rare ability to draw from the inside out so that technology and aesthetics worked in close cooperation. This made him a sought-after collaborator for various clients. Word spread that Sason was highly skilled and had the ability to design so that products could easily be put into production. He soon opened his own consulting firm with a couple of employees. In addition to the responsibility for designing all of Saab's car models up to and including the Saab 99, he had two regular customers in Electrolux and Husqvarna. This meant that a considerable amount of post-war consumer goods came to be designed by Sixten Sason and he soon emerged as the true designer behind most of the Swedish 'Folkhem'. For Electrolux's part this included vacuum cleaners, refrigerators, floor polishers, kitchen mixers and boat engines; and for Husqvarna it was sewing machines, irons, waffle makers, chainsaws, mopeds and more. Another customer was Victor Hasselblad, who he helped put into production the world's first single-lens reflex medium format camera with interchangeable lenses and magazines in 1948. The design was timeless and unusually durable, like many products designed by Sason. The design director at Electrolux, Hugo Lindström, has recounted how when he was commissioned to redesign a Sason-designed iron, he refused on the grounds that it was not possible to produce a better design. Sason was by all accounts easy to work with; he spoke the language of the technicians and was also an ideas man. He received offers for assignments from the automotive industry in Detroit but declined because, as he admitted himself, of his lack of linguistic skills (Sköld 1997).

Integrated Design Thinking Replaces Additive Engineering

Ralph Lysell's most important contributions to design history during his time as the head of design at Ericsson were the two one-piece telephones Ericofon (Cobra phone) and Unifon (Uniphone). When international design reviews give examples of what the new profession could achieve in terms of total aesthetic solutions, the American Raymond Loewy is almost always emphasized along with his redesign of Gestetner's duplicating machine from 1929. Lysell's slightly later but relatively unknown transformation of Ericsson's Unifon project from an engineering prototype to a design product is, however, just as illustrative in this context.

The pictures are a before-and-after illustration of this textbook example of what a designer can contribute when it comes to turning everything on its head and thinking outside the box. The Unifon project was developed by Ericsson in 1941 as an internally competing parallel project with the famous Ericofon. Like the Ericofon, it was about creating a one-piece telephone, that is to say a handset-like complete telephone in one piece. The man behind the idea was Hans Kraepelien who had long been thinking about this challenge during his time as technical manager at Ericsson's facilities in Warsaw. After he managed to escape through the German siege lines in the run up to the outbreak of war, work was able to continue at Ericsson's Stockholm office. Kraepelien was conceptually clearly influenced by the linesman's handset with a fitted rotary dial that the linesmen had started using as test handsets. But this project was more complicated because in a consumer telephone one has to be able to switch quickly and easily between transmitting and receiving modes. He intended to resolve this with a switch-hook that was affected by a steel wire with a hanging loop when the receiver was lifted off and hung up on a hook. The task of making this design attractive, user-friendly and marketable fell to the company's designer Ralph Lysell. What the designer had to work with was thus a cobbled together handset with a bent shaft that contained various components, a mounted dial and built-in hook-switch. Components were added and the device was meant to be hung on a hook on an office desk with the weight of the phone affecting the switch-hook function.

Lysell made use of the latter, but in a completely different way than the engineer Kraepelien could have imagined. Lysell's goal was to give the new telephone its own personality so that it no longer looked like a refurbished handset. The basic concept was thus changed from a hanging to a lying telephone meant to be placed on a table. The switch-hook could thereby be affected by the device's weight against the table top, constituting its own design element. It was designed in the shape of a springy microphone cover, whose movement from a retracted to an extended position was so great that the sound receiving part of the lid ended up in front of the lips during use.

Lysell devoted particular care to the grip in both his sketches and model studies. He used a strikingly modern ergonomic way of thinking based on the fact that fingers which hold a narrow shaft give rise to a cramped grip, something one avoids when the hand remains half open. These considerations eventually led to a curved clothes-brush-like grip, which was adapted to the hand's anatomy through the design of finger grooves. The design also made it possible to grip the device far down, at the microphone end, so that it could rest comfortably against the inside of the palm – a particularly restful grip if the elbow is supported against, for example, an armrest while calling. The earlier handle had suddenly turned into a casing that could now be divided into two easy-to-manufacture halves, and there was even room for a simple signalling device. In order to fit inside the outer contours of the casing and be protected against knocks and bumps, however, the finger dial's diameter had to be reduced. This was the telephone's largest individual detail and completely determined the casing's width and the comfort of the grip. Ericsson's engineers solved the problem by introducing a revolutionary so-called movable finger stop, which decreased the finger dial's diameter by 13 millimetres.

Fig. 3.6 The engineering prototype of the Unifon (Uniphone) from 1941.

Fig. 3.7 The designer's version of the Unifon (Uniphone) from 1944.

The whole telephone now had a streamlined design that had obvious similarities with the more advanced automotive designs of the time. The selected pilot model was lacquered a matte green colour and the Unifon was registered as a trademark based on descriptions and drafts in April 1944. Patents were obtained for the switching device in Sweden and the important competitor and export markets – the UK and USA. They planned to manufacture the casing in 3-millimetre thick Bakelite, which would have given it a weight of just over a pound, or roughly the same as the handset of a contemporary standard Bakelite device. The pilot model was made of wood and there were some concerns about whether the harder Bakelite would mark the table top, but solutions were found for this problem as well.

Everything was ready for production. The model was tested in the autumn of 1944 by both men and women in one of Ericsson's offices. It was disassembled and demonstrated a hundred times and everything worked flawlessly. Everyone seemed happy, but suddenly setbacks occurred. Due to mobilization because of the war, Ericsson lacked available personnel because the company was focusing their main effort on the production of weapons and signal equipment. The remaining manpower was only sufficient for one major project at a time and at that time the company was concentrating its energies on material replacement and the redesign of the standard Bakelite telephone. Then it was the turn of the standing Cobra phone, Ericofon, which the engineer Hugo Blomberg, along with Lysell's assistance, had developed in parallel with the Unifon. Largely thanks to its standing design it was considered more appropriate for the waiting US market; after all, the Americans were still used to the design of Bell System telephones which were upright like a candlestick. In addition, when the Unifon's constructer, Hans Kraepelien, was appointed head of Ericsson's New York office in 1945, and Hugo Blomberg became the chief engineer for the development department a year later, it was the final nail in the Unifon's coffin (Brunnström 2006).

Colourful Plastic Replaces the Black Era

That the Ericofon and Unifon would be manufactured out of plastic was quite obvious to Ericsson. However, it was unclear which kind of plastic they should use. When Lysell's Ericofon prototype was shown in 1941, the intention was to produce it in black Bakelite like their other telephones (see page 125). In 1956, however, when, after numerous delays, the serial production of the Ericofon went into full swing, it seemed better to choose bright and colourful plastics to products that were not too large. The material was both cheap and practical to use. Admittedly, a selection of colours was a major departure from the industry standard of black but came in response to the demands of customers who wanted a richer selection of colours. The new colour schemes were symbolic of a more positive and promising new era.

Plastic was originally dark in colour. The first completely synthetic plastic, Bakelite, or synthetic resin as the revolutionary material was also known when it was introduced in Sweden around 1920, was a major contribution to product design for the decades which could be christened 'the black era'. Black was a colour that was not only associated with industrial machinery; it also echoed the dark-suited world of the factory directors or all of Ford's cars. During the 1930s black was also a fashionable colour, for example, in ceramics. Hedvig Hedqvist (2002) highlights Edward Hald's black tea service for the Stockholm Exhibition and Arthur Percy's successful porcelain with black glaze for Gefle Porslinsfabrik. Indoors, walls were decorated with a rapidly increasing number of electrical plugs and sockets of black Bakelite. Wooden door handles and toilet seats were replaced with Bakelite handles and equally comfortable but much more hygienic black Bakelite toilet seats. Then, in the place of honour, there stood black Bakelite telephones and the occasional radio set made from the same material. Even the first laminate sheets, the Perstorpsplatta, were black. Black (or very similar drab colours) was the only realistic colour for Bakelite objects, as the colour of the Bakelite resin and the necessary filling agents (usually wood flour) made dyeing with bright pigments practically impossible.

It was only the restrictions imposed by the Second World War, which included a lack of Bakelite resin that caused people to seriously start experimenting with new plastics, primarily the two closely related thermoset plastics urea and melamine. They were admittedly more expensive – urea was also more brittle and less heat resistant – but they were colourless and could therefore be manufactured in any desired colour. At last it was possible for plastic objects to compete even in terms of colour with household porcelain, and the extensive range of cream-coloured enamelled metal objects, particularly from Kockums's enamel works, that were on the market. This development was particularly pushed forward by AB Alpha in Sundbyberg, which had to maintain its large deliveries of casings for Ericsson's telephones. In 1942, a third of Ericsson's new telephones were manufactured in the new pressing plants (Brunnström 2006).

The country's other major pioneer in plastics manufacturing, Skånska Ättikfabriken in Perstorp, also felt compelled to find a substitute for its Bakelite substance that was called Isolit. A statement from Hemmens forskningsinstitut (The Home Research Institute or HFI) concerning the Perstorpsplatta (a laminate with an outer layer of melamine and formaldehyde) revealed that although it had excellent qualities, it had to be made in bright colours. After years of testing melamine with different grades of paper they managed to make the pattern resistant to wear and in 1950 the new tiles were approved by HFI, resulting in HSB (the Savings and Construction Association of the Tenants) ordering 120,000 square metres to be included as standard in their comprehensive housing programme. It was a hygienic and practical material that was equally suited to the kitchen counter, the bathroom wall or laundry room. A series of new patterns could now be developed, the most famous being Virrvarr, designed by Sigvard Bernadotte's design offices (Lindblad 2004).

The Swedish plastics industry had its breakthrough after the Second World War. The development was explosive and remarkable. In 1948 there were 150 thermosetting resin presses. In addition, there was also a rapidly increasing number of companies specializing in the injection moulding of thermoplastics, the real materials of the future. In 1961, the number of plastic manufacturers in the country had risen to 1,100 and according to the trade association Svenska Plastföreningen (The Swedish Plastics Industry Association), in 1956 Swedish people were the world's second largest consumer of plastics after the Americans. At the time there were about twenty different types of thermoplastics for manufacturers to choose from, including the strong and increasingly popular ABS plastic that the Ericofon was injection-moulded from.

The plastic industry's rapid development provided further opportunities for the new profession of industrial designer, who soon became something of a specialist in the field. When it came to the design of metal objects, there existed a long engineering tradition that was more difficult to break. For its part, plastic required the highlighting of its sculptural qualities. A thermosetting resin like Bakelite set specific design requirements for soft sweeping lines in order to be as strong as possible and not crack during the die-casting. It was a requirement that was constantly trotted out by the Bakelite manufacturers' information offices and thus came to control its design ideals. It was therefore no coincidence that the heyday of the streamlined product occurred at the same time as Bakelite was at its most popular in the 1930s and 1940s.

Plastic was also the material of major production. The dyes, which were supposed to remain precisely constant for possibly hundreds of thousands of pressings, were very expensive to produce. It was essential for the colours to be exact because it ensured that the products would sell, that they would be sufficiently attractive to customers. It was in this way that the industrial designer in collaboration with the marketers could enrich engineer-driven Swedish industry (Brunnström 2006).

One of the first to venture into the plastics industry was the artist and designer Folke Arström (1907–1997) who in 1943 received a consultant contract with Perstorp, a collaboration that lasted almost a decade. He was at this time well-established, working as the artistic director of Gense AB in Eskilstuna and had exhibited in both the World's Fairs in Paris in 1937 and New York in 1939. His experience was, however, restricted to metals like pewter, silver, nickel silver, bronze and stainless steel, which led one of the owners to give him a lesson in the importance of studying plastic's special properties. This centred on bending and impact durability, water and heat resistance, the impact of crack formations in the object and so on. He was also given a copy of *Gestaltung von Kunstharz Pressteilen*. His first commissions were salad servers and a paper knife. The latter he believed he would be able to design in half an hour, but it subsequently took three days. Arström's production at Perstorp was extensive and varied. Everything was manufactured in the thermosetting resins of Bakelite, urea and melamine, including a spice scoop in a stylish colour palette, a steering wheel for the Volvo 444, a toilet seat in Isolit that Gustavsberg ordered 100,000 copies of in 1948 and a popular melamine mug in white, pale blue and yellow for the military, schools and hospitals, which replaced a heavy porcelain mug from Gustavsberg (Lindblad 2004).

In 1957 Perstorp employed its first full-time industrial designer, Hugo Lindström, who had started his career with Ralph Lysell at AB Industriell Formgivning. He was responsible for the design of the factory's moulded goods until 1960 and was stationed at the company's Stockholm office. Perhaps the most important product that he was responsible for designing during this period was a new letter box for Postverket (the Postal Service) in dark green moulded polyethylene; it was at this time that Postverket, in the same way as Televerket, provided the Swedish people with standardized products. The soft, rounded plastic box replaced a heavy, angular and rust-prone metal box. There were three types of plastic that were judged to meet all the requirements for outdoor durability and mechanical strength; polyethylene was chosen because it was the cheapest. Postverket's expectations were realized when it was the world's first postal service to have a plastic letter box (Lindström and Ljungh 1958).

At the porcelain company Gustavsberg, owned since 1937 by KF, they realized, even before the war was over, that many of the articles manufactured in their household porcelain factory would soon be replaced by plastic. To meet the new market demands, they had already in 1939 built a modern sanitary-ware factory and in 1945 they launched their own plastic production, which soon became very significant. The then CEO Hjalmar Olsson has subsequently explained the essential difference when the more than a century-old ceramic tradition was making way for the completely different plastics technology:

> The technical process, the expensive tools and the, eventually, ever more expensive raw materials demanded a more rigorous type of planning and discipline for the organisation of the product range, purchasing machines and machine load than what had characterised household porcelain. On the other hand, the inherited professional skills of the porcelain manufacturers was not required of those who worked with the machines … Learning to manage an injection-moulding machine does not require especially long training … The product development and the production of porcelain is very much a trial and error process that allows for the production of unique products as well as small series and mass productions. But the cost of the moulding tool for a simple household article in thermoplastic may be in the millions and requires a mass production. It places great demands not only on the tool designers, other technicians and designers in the product development and production, but also requires an integrated marketing. (Hald 1991: 146)

The United States was the leading country in the plastics field and the first CEO of Gustavsberg's new plastics factory had to go there for a year to learn how to manufacture plastic objects first-hand. In the beginning they focused on the domestic sector and sanitary ware, for which they already had working sales channels through KF's vast network of stores. One of the first products was a set of measuring spoons made from thin white polystyrene, which was developed

Fig. 3.8 When buckets were made of galvanized or enamelled steel they were always round, but with the help of plastic it was possible to give buckets other more practical forms. At Gustavsberg's new plastics factory Carl-Arne Breger got the opportunity to design a square bucket with domed cover, which he poses with here. It was made of polyethylene, was easy to pour from and was perfect for household rubbish.

together with KF's test kitchen and would later become a classic. While most new plastics manufacturers had to look for collaborations with an at that time limited group of design consultants, Gustavsberg had the advantage of already having their own team of designers. They also had modellers and experience of producing prototypes in plaster and clay or making porcelain models for full-scale tests; the drawback was that the porcelain artists did not always have the technical knowledge needed for plastic. Gustavsberg's superstar, the always-creative Stig Lindberg, was one of the first to get to grips with this new field of work, but the equally productive Carl-Arne Breger (1923–2009) was responsible for the most lasting efforts of the 1950s. His square bucket from 1957, sculptural watering can from 1959 and, later, a beautifully shaped citrus press have all become plastic classics, both for their cleverness and their beauty.

During the 1950s and 1960s Gustavsberg entered a productive period. The plastics section was soon afforded as much attention as the porcelain tableware. The editor of the Swedish Society of Crafts and Design's magazine *Form*, Arthur Hald, was hired as the artistic director in 1956 and the marketing profile became progressively more aesthetically coherent. The Italian office supply manufacturer Olivetti was the model. When Breger moved to Bernadotte Design he was replaced by the ceramic-trained Peter Pien. A few years later, in the late 1960s, three industrial design graduates from Konstfack were hired. Sven-Eric Juhlin and Per-Olov Landgren were attached to the plastics factory, while Jan-Olof Landqvist began at the sanitary porcelain factory. A new era began with a string of celebrated products that could be used in everyday life: double-walled mugs and pitchers in various colours (1969), a shopping basket for supermarkets in bright red polyethylene (1970), a measuring jug with clear decilitre markings in translucent SAN-plastic (1977) as well as numerous practical, stackable letter trays, magazine racks, drawer units and other paper storage in polystyrene plastic. It was also here that Juhlin together with Henrik Wahlforss developed a gripping device for the disabled (1973), which laid the foundation for a later successful business at the design consultancy Ergonomidesign (Ergonomic Design). One of the final product types were the floppy disk boxes (1985), designed by Landgren, with the lower part in polystyrene, a lid in colourless SAN-plastic and a locking bolt in bendable polycarbonate plastic; but then the plastic manufacturing was moved to Borås and changed its name to Idealplast only to be sold in 1987 to Gislaved AB and later moved to Estonia. This development was symptomatic of KF's dwindling industrial empire and one which was completely phased out in 2001 (Hald 1991 and interview with P. O. Landgren).

Mobility Increases and the Leisure Sector Expands

After the struggles of the Second World War there was not only an overall desire for colour in life, but also for freedom, lightheartedness and gadgets. Since 1938 Swedish people had the statutory right to two weeks paid vacation, and this was increased to three weeks in 1951. Many people wanted to spend their time in nature. The more widespread use of internal combustion engines facilitated simple and rapid transportation. On the race track Husqvarna Vapenfabrik had gained a world-wide reputation as a manufacturer of elegant and powerful motorcycles as early as the 1930s but the motorcycle never became a popular vehicle, not even when the company introduced its lightweight model in 1955, the legendary Silverpilen (Silver Arrow) designed by Sixten Sason. A vehicle with a less powerful engine would however have its breakthrough in connection with a new law concerning the licence-exempt so-called mopeds which came into force in 1952. The Swedish bicycle industry then began to supply bicycles with small two-stroke engines, and just five years later it is estimated that about 400,000 mopeds were being ridden on Swedish roads. As a result the Swedish worker had a cheap and reliable vehicle to get to work on and rural isolation was broken. Manufacturers experimented and competed with advanced streamlined moped designs by above all Björn Karlström and Sixten Sason. Karlström designed for Nymanbolagen in Uppsala, whose Crescent 2000 from 1955 had a sheet metal encapsulated frame and a headlight built into the fuel tank, while Sason designed the two-tone lacquered and speedy models Roulette, Cornette and Corona in quick succession for Husqvarna Weapons Factory (Johansson 1997).

The active outdoor life very much included the maritime traffic that was now starting to become motorized. Rowing boats, dinghies, canoes and yachts were now equipped with simple, small outboard engines. Soon the rattle was as loud in the archipelago as on the country's streets. In Sweden, there was a strong, established boat engine industry with brands such as Penta and Archimedes, but it was only when outboard motors began to be fitted with a protective cover and recoil start (automatically reciprocating starter rope) that they became manageable and significant as leisure items. The first widely popular Swedish maritime engine went on sale in 1953 and was based on a moped engine with the cylinder in one end of a tube while the other end was fitted with a bevel gear drive and a propeller. It was designed by the illustrator Björn Karlström (1921-2006), who designed all of Crescent's outboard engines and mopeds up to the mid-1960s. Nymanverken in Uppsala were responsible for the manufacturing and would later become Europe's largest outboard industry. Being able to design stylish and exciting marine engine cowlings attracted a number of 1950s designers. Sixten Sason, Peter Maddock and Sigvard Bernadotte's office designed for Electrolux and Rustan Lange for Husqvarna (Biström and Sundin 1997).

At this time small cheap cars were being built all over Europe; in Italy a great number of even cheaper Vespas were also rolling out of the factory in Piaggio. It had been a difficult time for Volvo with weak sales and no really successful model. However, they got one in the popular Folkhelm car PV444. The numbers represented a four-seater with a 40-horsepower four-cylinder engine. It came into production in 1947 but interest was so great that some customers had to wait for three years for their car. The design was soft and curved with a streamlined pulled-down rear, which was common in many contemporary European and American cars. The influence of Ford's latest models was clear, but the Volvo was considerably smaller and had a more refined design.

The demand persisted until 1965 when the last relatively modernized PV544 came off the assembly line: 440,000 cars had been sold, some for export to the United States.

The streamlined shape was well established at this time, particularly in the American automobile industry but also in American and European industrial production in general. It is easy to agree with Alvar Lenning, who in 1938 saw it 'as the USA's functionalism, although it happened to become round instead of square like in old Europe' (DN 17/11). It unquestionably emerged as the ultimate design symbol of modernity, representing speed, freedom and success. In fact, Ralph Lysell even claimed in an article in *Form* in 1943 that it was 'the aeroplane and its streamlined shape' that formed the basis of all industrial design. The shape itself, however, was older than that. Its roots as a design principle are closely connected with the history of aerodynamics and hydrodynamics in which eighteenth- and nineteenth-century innovators had been fascinated through nature's effective designs for the flight of birds and the movement of fish in water. The minimized air resistance and low turbulence of the streamlined shape, softly rounded front and tapered tail section was confirmed by wind tunnel experiments carried out in the late nineteenth century. The military industry embraced the idea for their zeppelins and submarines, and in 1914 the Italian coach-builder Castagna hand-built a famous teardrop-shaped car on an Alfa Romeo chassis that had a top speed of over 130 kilometres per hour (Bush 1975).

The design of the PV had been produced by engineers from the drawing office but in 1950, Volvo took the decisive step of establishing its own design department. It consisted initially of only two people, Rustan Lange (1921–1980) and Jan Wilsgaard (1930–2016); the latter was recruited from HDK before he had even had time to graduate. The work of developing a completely new model at Volvo happened in roughly the same way as at the big American car factories. The working process in the 1950s has been described by Rustan Lange as follows:

> The factory management gave directives for the car's size based on experience gained from previous models. After the engineers had prepared a dimension sketch with certain specified minimum and maximum internal dimensions the designer took over, first with rough sketches of the vehicles silhouette. At the same time, based on the measurements an 'insidesattrapp' (mock-up) was built with seats, moving steering wheel, pedals and gearshift lever in the correct positions, dashboard, openable doors and floor at the right height off the ground. The car could thus literally be designed around the human body so that you could test getting in, the driver's position and the instruments' readability. After the silhouette sketches, coloured renderings were made that showed the finished car in perspective. Then it was time to build a model in scale 1:4. It was supposed to be made as accurate and lifelike as possible with, for example, chrome bumpers, glazed headlights and number plates. When it was evaluated in terms of its interior and exterior, a realistic full-scale model was made in plasticine, with a 5 cm layer of clay, on a wooden frame. It was now that one had the greatest potential

for assessment and modification. It turned out that the enlargement of the quarter scale model resulted in some shift displacement, which necessitated changes from both an aesthetic and production point of view. At the end of the design work, a full-scale wooden or plaster model was made with the same precise finish as a sheet metal body. Then it was time to call in the management to see if they wanted to give the green light for production. (Lange 1953)

In the same year that the PV began to be delivered to its first customers a pre-production model of another Swedish compact car was presented. It was an even more streamlined car from the firm Saab. In this case, the design was fairly obvious as Svenska Aeroplan Aktiebolag (Swedish Aeroplane Limited), which was the company's full name, had built aircraft for the Swedish Armed Forces and now, after the war, had to convert to civilian production. After many discussions about direction it was agreed that they would produce an uncomplicated front-wheel-drive car built around a small two-stroke engine with few moving parts. The driving force behind the Saab 92 project was the engineer Gunnar Ljungström with the help of Sweden's most talented designer at this time; at least he had a high opinion of Sixten

Fig. 3.9 That the small country of Sweden managed to create two relatively strong automobile brands must, from an international perspective, be seen as remarkable. The breakthrough for both Volvo and Saab came after the Second World War with the models Volvo PV 444 and Saab 92. This photo shows the more American influenced PV 444 model 1:4. See also Fig. 3.10.

Fig. 3.10 This photo shows the drivable prototype of the Saab 92, which was designed in a European tradition and came more to resemble an aeroplane wing in profile. See also Fig. 3.9.

Sason, who he described as 'a genius, an engineer with the artist's talent or an artist with the mind of a technician'. The little car took the form of an aircraft wing in profile and was built with a whole-welded monocoque body, in the style of an aircraft and almost excessively strong. The shape together with the flat bottom resulted in a sensationally low aerodynamic drag (cW 0.32) for its time. The car's interior was as functional as the exterior, even though space was limited. For instance, the seats and backseat could be easily converted into a two-person bed (Tunberg 1997).

Suddenly, Sweden had two independent car manufactures, which of course was remarkable for such a small country. As the car industry expanded, caravan production also increased after the war. The first mass-produced Swedish caravan, or mobile home as it was called, was finished in 1948. It was an egg-shaped little creation with four beds weighing 370 kilograms. The body was made of oil-treated Masonite and the caravan was manufactured by SMV in Örebro in the late 1950s.

Civilian air traffic was in full swing in the mid-1920s. Swedes had by then already been able to travel by air, first in the German-built pontoon equipped seaplanes, and from 1937 also in the larger and more comfortable American Douglas DC-3s. A pioneer of Swedish civil aviation was Aktiebolaget Aerotransport (Aerotransport Limited or ABA). That same year the first Swedish-built commercial aircraft was flight-tested, a twin-engine short-range plane named Saab 90 Scandia, which would replace the DC-3s. It had been developed by Svenska Aeroplan AB (Saab), which had been formed in 1937, in close cooperation with ABA's technicians. Sixten Sason, at the time established as a designer at Saab, was responsible for the interior design. One of his young colleagues was Rune Monö (1920–2007) who in 1943 was recruited by ABA to lead their drafting department. There he designed streamlined aircraft stairways and aircraft decals. Also at ABA was the graphic designer Anders Beckman (1907–1967) who was responsible for marketing the airline with striking posters with dramatically cropped images (Plate 12). When the Scandinavian airlines merged in 1946 and the first scheduled transatlantic flights began, it was Monö who had made the graphic profile in the form of a Viking ship emblem along the airframe and a dragon's head on the nose. But aviation was at that time reserved for the business world or something that was recorded in the exclusive travel and entertainment reports. Its real importance to the consumption-driven holiday Swede came with the cheaper charter flights in the mid-1950s.

The Foundation Is Laid for the Swedish Safety Philosophy

The safety philosophy of the Safety Movement and the concept Safety First may have been rooted in American industry's profit optimization in accordance with the scientific teachings of Taylorism, but it was in the Swedish welfare state that post-war safety philosophy found its clearest expression. Given that safety has been an important focus of Swedish design ever since, it is perhaps no coincidence that the country has been described as obsessed with safety (Sund 1993).

Snow, cold and long distances are often seen as obstacles to the development of society but can also be turned into something positive. Just think of what all the foreign car manufacturers' winter testing facilities mean for the development of Arjeplog in rural Lapland today. As early as the 1940s the extreme weather conditions in Sweden proved to be a competitive advantage for the emerging automotive industry. Here, if anywhere, warm, protective cabs and equipment for safe transport were needed. It was for the commercial vehicle that the first crucial efforts were made and it is not an exaggeration to say that the truck cab laid the foundation for the celebrated Swedish safety design. The cabs, which after the Second World War were produced by specialized body plants, were among the worst workplaces imaginable; the drivers having to sit in small, damp, cold, draughty, noisy and vibrating, almost shed-like, structures. The cabs were normally made of sheet metal-covered plywood, which in the event of a crash turned into a death trap. The thin birch framework held together by screws and nails would quickly give way, rupture and the space would be filled with razor-sharp pieces of plywood. But the danger came not only from the front; the driver also had to contend with a displaced load pushing in from behind.

The leading Swedish manufacturer of this type of truck cab was Be-Ge Karosserifabrik (Be-Ge Body Plant) in Oskarshamn, which began mass production in 1947. The same year, Gösta Nyströms Karosserifabrik (Gösta Nyström's Body Plant) in Umeå presented the so-called safety cab, a completely new design approach in which the cab was designed as a steel cantilever structure with an extra-reinforced rear end; inspired by, among others, the Swedish National Railway (SJ) which had switched from wood to steel for their fleet. Thus the foundations of a bitter feud were laid, followed by an intensive development effort over the next few decades in which the two partially different cab philosophies were pitted against each other. Nyströms waged an aggressive scare campaign that showed the devastating damage caused by a displaced load. The science was based on specious statistics of the number of truck drivers killed. For its part, Be-Ge focused on developing ever more comfortable cabs and accused the Nyström cabs of being draughty and poorly insulated, with resonant sound and condensation. Since Be-Ge was the main supplier to Scania-Vabis (today Scania) and Nyströms to Volvo and these were later incorporated into their respective companies, both unions and authorities were quickly dragged into the feud. In 1961 the argument culminated in new regulations on inspection of truck cabs, including crash tests. There are many indications that it was here in this power struggle over how the optimal truck cab should be designed that the foundations were laid for both Swedish trucks' success in later years and Volvo's image as makers of inherently safe vehicles.

The self-taught farmer's son Gösta Nyström (1906–1988) was an innovator and product developer who worked with a user focus that today is mainly associated with a designer's method of working. At the same time as the safety cab, he developed the first roll bar for tractors and a little later also a tractor cab that was entirely built out of steel sections. This type of rollover protection was intended to effectively protect the driver if the tractor tipped sideways or reared and flipped. In the mid-1950s tractor-related deaths were widespread across the country. During the harvest season an average of one death per week was attributed to this. In this safety-related work Nyström, in cooperation with Arbetarskyddsstyrelsen (Workers Protection Authority), managed to pass a law on mandatory cabs or roll bars for tractors in 1959. The production of tractor cabs was sited at the Volvo subsidiary Bolinder-Munktell (BM), which dominated the Swedish tractor market. The next generation of tractor cabs were manufactured in the style of cars and trucks in a double-shell of moulded steel sheet to meet new demands for heating, seating comfort and noise reduction.

The tractor is a low-speed vehicle where the advent of the cab was driven by demands for increased safety, but Swedish work on safety was also at the forefront for high-speed vehicles. In particular, during the 1950s new types of restraining seat belts were developed, which would replace the substandard lap belts that had existed for both cars and aeroplanes for a long time. Vattenfall, which was in the middle of a large hydropower expansion programme in Norrland with an extensive transmission grid to maintain, had noticed an unacceptable increase in serious car accidents among its linesmen. The actual cause was long road haulage on lonely roads of poor quality with an abundance of reindeer, but focus was put on trying to increase the passive safety of the company's fleet of cars. Of particular interest was the seat belt issue, but there were no seat belt studies or crash tests to rely on. Instead they had to arrange their own crash tests using a car chassis with a restrained dummy that was dropped from a high position by a crane. Different belt designs were tested and photographed with a high-speed camera. After employees from Vattenfall had also taken note of the American space programme's tests on how acceleration

Säkerhetsringen
*I nya Volvo-hytten är
föraren säkert placerad
inom ett kraftigt ramverk
av väl utprovad säkerhets-
konstruktion.*

**Volvo-
hytten
i stål**

Fig. 3.11 The success of the Swedish truck production by the Scania and Volvo brands is largely due to the development work that has been devoted to the cab's safety and ergonomics. With the safety cab's steel cantilever structure with an extra-reinforced rear designed by Gösta Nyström, Volvo had a design that could withstand the dangerous situation where the load is displaced in the event of an accident.

and deceleration forces affect the human body, it was decided that they should equip all their vehicles with diagonal belts in what came to be called System Vattenfall.

With the diagonal belt, as opposed to the lap belt, a jackknife movement is prevented, but there is a risk the body will slide under the belt in the event of an accident. If one could combine the two seat belt principles with three anchor points, one could restrain both the torso and the lap. The originator of the ingeniously simple idea of a three-point belt was Volvo's first and newly appointed safety engineer Nils Bohlin (1920–2002). He had a background in product development at Saab, where he had participated in the pioneering work on the development of ejector seats for a series of fighter aircraft, including the J21 Tvestjärten (J21 Earwig), the world's first mass-produced planes with such seats. In 1959, just one year after Bohlin had joined Volvo, the three-point belt was standard equipment in the front seats of passenger cars. It quickly became a global article that was patented in most countries and drastically reduced the frequency of driving injuries. When the German Patent Office was deciding on the eight patents in the world that they considered had most benefited humanity in connection with its centenary in 1985, Bohlin's three-point seat belt was chosen, alongside greats like Diesel and Edison.

The superiority of the three-point seat belt was confirmed in a doctoral thesis by the anaesthetist Bertil Aldman (1925–1998). As a research physician at Statens trafiksäkerhetsråd (National Traffic Safety Council) he was later able to build on this knowledge

Fig. 3.12 The three-point belt system, which has saved many lives, has been designated by the German Patent Office as one of the world's eight most distinguished patents in all categories. The picture shows the belt's creator, the safety engineer Nils Bohlin with Volvo, who in 1959 is demonstrating the belt in a PV 544. The Swedish product developers got the science concerning the body's placement and restraint when exposed to strong deceleration forces from American space experiments.

to develop his own product: the rear-facing child seat. It came into existence after he, in collaboration with consumer organizations in England and the United States, had tested all the known types of protective systems for children in vehicles without finding anything which did not risk damaging the stomach's soft tissues or could withstand the stress. The decisive impetus came after he, like his seat belt colleagues, turned his attention to the USA and studied the position they imagined the astronauts of the first manned space capsules would take during take-off and landing.

They were supposed to lie on their backs to cope with the stress on the body, which closely resembles that of a traffic accident. Aldman then realized that he had to design a cocoon-like device that caught the whole child's body at once. After some trial and error with cardboard models and then having a prototype produced and evaluated, he managed to convince a company from Småland to manufacture a test series. The year was 1965. Seven years later there was a rear-facing child seat in injection-moulded plastic as a standard accessory for Volvo's fleet and once again this was a first among all the world's car brands (Brunnström 1997).

The Human Dimensions and Requirements Govern the Design

Safety and the concept of ergonomics go hand in hand and to achieve them products must be designed from a user's perspective. This was understood by the American engineer and organization theorist Frederick Winslow Taylor who in the early 1900s studied the working human's performance ability. By examining where the problem areas were in specific tasks he was able, for instance, to determine how long it was possible for a worker in an industrial production process to inspect and sort before their attention started to dwindle, or how a shovel should be designed so that an averagely strong person could manage to dig for a whole workday without getting repetitive strain injuries. Since the 1920s there was sufficient documentation to show that it was financially profitable to try to prevent accidents in the workplace (Waste in Industry 1921). The key was to see the worker as a resource to be nurtured. But of course the message was anachronistic: if the working environment and tools were improved, not only would occupational injuries decrease but the worker's capacity was utilized better and the production rate could be increased, which ultimately gave the owner a better economic return.

The science of human interaction with objects, tools and machines, or in the computer age interfaces, has since the 1950s been included in the term ergonomics. The first to apply a systematic ergonomic design approach was the American Henry Dreyfuss, although he preferred the synonymous term 'human engineering'. In the 1930s Dreyfuss began collecting unarticulated user-knowledge as it proved to be the best way to get the honest truth about a product. When he was designing a new telephone for Bell he dressed in overalls and assisted the telephone company's repairmen, all in order to better acquaint himself with how the telephone worked and was handled in the field. In connection with the design of the driving environment of a new tractor for John Deere, he built a mock-up that was thoroughly tested in various stages and even assessed by a medical consultant. Through such simulated tests in real work situations, important knowledge was obtained about the continued design direction, such as the forward-leaning driver's seat and the angled foot pedals.

Since the early 1930s Dreyfuss and his colleagues in the design office had gathered quantitative data on men, women and even children's abilities in the context of handling various machines and objects. It could for example relate to seating comfort, grip, pull and push forces when driving a tractor or viewing angles in the context of typewriting; the user studies came to a head during the Second World War when Dreyfuss was recruited to not only examine every possible efficacy and safety requirement but also the probable effects that could hypothetically arise when the situation changed. The documentation eventually grew into an impressive systematic organization of data that was first used internally within the office but was also published in the years 1959–1960 in the widely distributed illustrated work, *The Measure of Man*.

In Sweden people also submitted themselves to seating comfort studies as early as the 1930s and 1940s. Both Bruno Mathsson and G. A. Berg tried with seemingly quite similar bentwood chairs to achieve the ideal seating curve by identifying the anatomically correct support points. For Mathsson it was more about achieving a statically optimal seating ergonomic while the graduate engineer Berg assumed a more dynamic ergonomic philosophy. Maria Perers (2003) especially emphasizes G. A. Berg's systematic work during the 1930s when designing chairs where you could change position and lean in different directions while resting the head. This was achieved through a broad and generous shape, integrated headrests that made it possible to turn one's head and high backward tilting armrests, which gave plenty of room for the elbows. Berg's collaboration with the physician Bengt Åkerblom also ensured that the chairs supported the lower back and had a low seat height to avoid pressure under the thighs that would have impeded blood circulation. Åkerblom also launched his own chair model that he designed, in collaboration with the interior designer Gunnar Eklöf, based on his extensive studies of the anatomy of sitting. The so-called Åkerblom Chair with its characteristic anatomical twist (a backward angle of approximately four degrees) of the back was, during the period 1949–1958, the height of fashion and 120,000 were sold (Gordan 2005).

Seating ergonomics were an even more important issue for office workplaces where people spent many more hours in more or less fixed positions. Åtvidabergs Snickerifabrik had, according to its brochures, several doctors and architects involved when they developed their Stöd-stol (support chair) in 1941. It was a desk chair with adjustable lumbar support, which reduced the risk of hunched so-called *kontorsryggar* (office backs) that were common among the machine typists. 'The correct sitting position increases the working capacity', they write in their advertising, clearly inspired by the teachings of Taylorism. The architects' task was to design the support chair so that 'despite all the technical considerations it was as aesthetically pleasing as possible and did not break with the style of the usual office furniture standard' (Miscellaneous Business Press, Kungl. Biblioteket). The latter definitely did not worry G. A. Berg, who some years later took a radical approach to overhaul the managers' workplaces. Berg claimed that his unconventional and comfortable working armchairs meant that desks could be scrapped; a low conference table was enough (Perers 2003).

Under the leadership of Brita Åkerman (1906–2006) the Swedish Society of Crafts and Design began specific furniture function studies following roughly the same approach that The Home Research Institute used. With the help of the furniture designer Erik Berglund (1921–2008) the operation started with a much-needed measurement standardization of bed furniture as well as table and seat heights. The work was carried on with greater weight by Varudeklarationsnämnden's (Commodity Declaration Committee or VDN) furniture committee and focused in the early 1950s on quality tests similar to those begun in the UK and USA. Berglund also played a leading role here and with the help of the testing laboratory that he had built for testing furniture sustainability and technical quality, it became possible to VDN-declare the furniture. Although only a few pieces of furniture from a limited number of manufacturers were in fact provided with VDN-facts the work attracted a great deal of attention. The operation was strengthened in 1967 with the establishment of the independent Möbelinstitutet (Furniture Institute), which until 1995 was operated with funding from the government and industry and had an office and laboratory linked to Konstfack's premises. When VDN was discontinued in 1972, Möbelinstitutet introduced the new tougher labelling system Möbelfakta (Furniture Fact) (Berglund 1997).

There is no doubt that the ambition of the quality measurement was to look after the interests of users and consumers but there was also a joint state and industry interest in being able to assure the quality of Swedish furniture exports and protect the brand 'Made in Sweden'. Particularly large corporations like KF and IKEA were keen to use Möbelinstitutet's standards and also set up their own testing laboratories in the early 1970s.

In heavy industry Atlas Copco, which manufactured air-powered tools and machinery, together with the electrical engineering company ASEA were the fore-runners in terms of user customization. As in so many other areas, Atlas Copco had after the war been strongly influenced by developments in the USA. The company was represented in a Swedish industrial delegation that in 1955 was invited to get acquainted with the activities of American industrial design offices. What above all impressed the Swedes was their work in human engineering; for example, adapting machines to the human body, designing handles that were easy to reach and grasp and instrument scales that were easy to read. Few areas were more appropriate than compressed air management when it came to applying an ergonomic approach and designing with the focus on the user. It was certainly an extremely efficient, but also noisy and vibrating activity that at this time was used for everything from starting jet engines to powering rock drills, dental drills and hand tools. The following year the talented artist and engineer Rune Zernell (1921–2009) was hired from Volvo to build a design department at Atlas Copco and take on all of these design challenges.

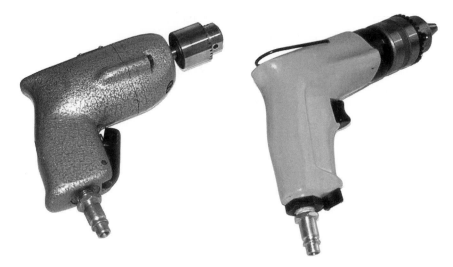

Fig. 3.13 Rune Zernell's most notable design work was the development of Atlas Copco's pneumatic drill LBB33 with the so-called eight-hour grip. The work was carried out in close cooperation with medical expertise to achieve a drilling machine that was adapted for use during an entire shift. The picture shows the clumsy RAB 300 from 1940 to the left and the new, ergonomically elaborate LBB 33 to the right.

Rune Zernell was heavily influenced by Henry Dreyfuss's work and photographs from the 1960s show that he also had Dreyfuss's posters from *The Measure of Man* on the wall by his drawing table for support and inspiration. He is one of very few Swedish industrial designers who are represented in the international design reviews and particularly highlighted is the pneumatic drill LBB 33 which was fully developed in 1960.

Pneumatic drills had undergone a dramatic evolution from heavy and weak-engined two-handed machines to a nearly three times lighter, yet stronger single-handed machine with a pistol grip. It was this machine from 1940 that Zernell was commissioned to further develop as it was still front heavy and awkwardly shaped, as well as having a cramp-inducing grip. He contacted Dr Fritjof Sjöstrand at the Karolinska Institute for help with the science concerning the hand's anatomy, muscles and nerve centres in connection with his experiments with different grip models in plaster and plasticine. The result was a radically new approach, known as the eight-hour grip, which made it possible to handle the LB 33 for an entire shift without being affected by static or dynamic injuries to the hands and forearms, entirely in the spirit of Taylorism. What Zernell found was that the grip should be distributed across the whole hand and the pressure force from the machine's centre should have a linear continuation through the inside of the hand by the base of the thumb and all the way up to the forearm for the finger grip to be relaxed. This also allowed the stronger middle finger to work the throttle control instead of the forefinger (Brunnström 1997).

At about the same time as Zernell at Atlas Copco, John Meilink (b. 1923) was charged with building a design department at ASEA in Västerås. He had an optimal educational background with both a Master of Science in Engineering and a diploma from an art academy in the Netherlands. Meilink's mindset was just like Zernell's in that the design should proceed from human needs and physical capabilities and that ergonomic studies had to be done on a scale of 1:1. His industry background, combined with an educational interest, also made him an important figure in the first educational efforts that were made to meet the industry's growing need for industrial designers; these were courses that were carried out at Konstfack during 1957–1959 in cooperation with the Swedish Society of Crafts and Design and Mekanförbundet (The Metal Trades Association). ASEA's design office soon comprised of a number of specialists in various fields and the operation received ample premises in a separate building with space to handle full-scale models. Here they designed motors, generators and transformers, electric trucks, grinders, power stations, etc., tasks where safety as well as human dimensions and needs were vitally important.

The Swedish Society of Crafts and Design Attains Their Goal of More Beautiful Everyday Goods

The international critical reception was already in relative agreement, in relation to the Stockholm Exhibition in 1930, that the Swedish version of Modernism differed from that of Central Europe. It was not as doctrinaire but instead had a stronger connection to crafts and natural materials. Its humanistic features were also linked to the democratic and social aspirations of the emerging Swedish welfare state. Sweden was somewhat romanticized as an ideal country in the 1930s; it was regarded as a kind of utopia in a world hit by the depression, having forged a middle ground between capitalism and socialism. The journalist Marquis W. Childs contributed to Sweden's reputation in 1936 with the best-seller *Sweden the Middle Way*, which had a big impact, was published in several editions and was even translated into Chinese. The book particularly emphasizes Swedish social democracy, KF, HSB and the Swedish Society of Crafts and Design as key players in the creation of the good and beautiful society. This reinforced the Swedish Society of Crafts and Design's ambition to enhance the image of the Swedes as a people brought up to appreciate quality. Long stretches of Childs's book could have been taken from their propaganda brochures, argues Jeff Werner in *Medelvägens estetik (The Aesthetics of the Middle way)* (2008).

The self-image of Swedish designers and architects was further strengthened following the successful exhibitions in Paris in 1937 and in New York in 1939. As the range of products was broadened and the classicized features were smoothed out, the terminology also shifted: Swedish Grace became Swedish Modern. The new concept was promoted in massive marketing campaigns after the Paris Exhibition and was associated to an even greater extent with the Swedish contributions in New York.

Works by, among others, Bruno Mathsson, Carl Malmsten, G. A. Berg, Axel Larsson, Astrid Sampe, Elias Svedberg and remarkably even the internationalist

Josef Frank's textiles and furniture, helped to characterize a lasting and very success-ful image of what was typically Swedish. The style, which was very well received by the Americans, was a softer version of functionalism with lightwood in organic shapes set against colour accents in textiles and ceramics as well as slighter furniture, all distinguished by a general cosiness. To further emphasize national characteristics in the Swedish Pavilion the exhibition architect Sven Markelius and graphic director Anders Beckman placed an almost three feet high orange Dala horse – a wooden, painted horse from the Dalarna region of Sweden – in front of the entrance, while inside snacks were served on a rotating smorgasbord designed by Alvar Lenning (Stavenow 1939).

A large number of books and pamphlets were published in connection with the New York Exhibition. KF and HSB took the opportunity to communicate their activities and in their design department's lavish catalogue stated that Swedish design was a manifestation of the ideology behind the welfare state. Swedish Modern was defined as healthy, sober and beautiful everyday objects that were manufactured with modern technologies in close collaborations between artist and industry. The message was a confirmation that the Swedish Society of Crafts and Design's propaganda operation of many years had borne fruit, even if the propaganda to some extent still preceded the reality; it only concerned products in the household goods sector and furniture in particular. Significantly, Jeff Werner points out that smart American businessmen stole the successful Swedish Modern concept as early as the 1930s and made it their own. What we mean by Swedish Modern is not what Americans associate with the concept. The reason was, he says, that Swedish marketing and production were aimed at the upper middle class, in part because of lack of faith in ordinary people's tastes. Given that the distinctive Swedish furniture with its simple shapes and uniform materials was easy to mass-produce, it created space for a domestic, slightly Americanized, cheaper production but rendered in Swedish style (Werner 2008).

According to Ingeborg Glambek (1997), in New York the spotlight focused on Swedish design while the other Nordic countries were completely overlooked. After the Second World War the situation was different. Even though Sweden's usually excellent political reputation was tarnished, the war had brought the Nordic countries closer together. Scandinavism grew in strength and the Nordic Council, formed in 1952, established itself as an official coordinating body for Nordic parliaments and govern-ments. Interest from America had grown and it was seen as an important future export market. There were advanced plans for a joint manifestation of Scandinavian design at the Museum of Modern Art in New York (MoMA) during 1947–1948. The initiative came from the museum's director Edgar Kaufmann, Jr, who was greatly interested in the region. When MoMA suddenly changed its programme, according to Harri Kalha (2003), partly due to the fear of communist overtones, taking a travelling exhibition to a number of North American rural towns was suggested instead. This idea is supposed to have come from Elizabeth Gordon, editor-in-chief of the magazine *House Beautiful* in connection with a visit to the Milan Triennial in 1951, where Denmark, Finland and Sweden participated with great success. The triennials were to the 1950s what the

Aktiebolaget
Ekmans Mekaniska Snickerifabrik
Stockholm.

Central-Tryckeriet, Stockholm.

Plate. 1 The rapid urbanization associated with the rise of industrialization gave the large joineries the opportunity to supply all kinds of prefabricated buildings. Ekmans Snickerifabrik's 1890 catalogue presented, among other things, a simple church in the then-popular Gothic Revival style. The church was sold to several locations in the upper part of Norrland.

Plate. 2 The early twentieth century was the golden era for the building of the large bank palaces. The picture shows a detail of the lavish entrance to the Skåne enskilda bank (Skåne individual bank) on the corner of Fredsgatan and Drottningatan in Stockholm. The bank was erected in the year 1900 and was designed by the architect Gustaf Wickman and the ornaments that were intended to take visitors' breath away depicted the rich farming communities in Skåne.

Plate. 3 The textile artist Märta Måås-Fjetterström was the head of the Malmöhus läns hemslöjdsförening (Malmö county handicrafts association) and had there learned of the treasure-trove of patterns in the traditional peasant textiles from Skåne. Her breakthrough came in 1909 with the tapestry 'Staffan Stalledräng', which was an independent interpretation of an old Swedish religious motif. Ten years later she started her own textile workshop in Båstad, which is still in operation, specializing in rug weaving.

Plate. 4 The architect Gunnar Asplund was given the opportunity to decorate an office in his refined style at the 1925 Paris Exhibition. The room's most elegant piece of furniture was the leather-clad Senna chair with a relaxed curvature and armrests adorned with antique ivory medallions. The copy in the picture was made by the Italian Cassina S.p.a in the 1980s.

Plate. 5 One of the Swedish items that was highlighted at the Paris Exhibition was a park bench, or garden bench, which had been designed by the architect Folke Bensow. It was cast at Näfveqvarns bruk and had already been shown at the Gothenburg Exhibition in 1923.

Plate. 6 Inspired by the Swedish success at the Paris Exhibition and influenced by French Art Deco the phone manufacturer Ericsson in 1929 redesigned its twenty-year-old sheet metal telephone. This occurred during a period of expansion when Ivar Kreuger had a majority share and the desk phone was launched with the help of a couple of posters that refer to modern urban life. The skyscraper in the background (Södra Kungstornet in Stockholm) was Sweden's first and housed, among other things, Ericsson's headquarters.

Plate. 7 The Atlantic cruiser M/S Kungsholmen was from 1928 until the Second World War used as a floating travelling exhibition of the finest Swedish interior design in Art Deco style. The interior design work was led by Carl Bergsten, who was assisted by a number of the architects, artisans and artists who had participated in the exhibitions in Gothenburg and Paris. The image shows the luxurious, bordering on vulgar entrance to first class, 'Grand Entrance', which was designed by the architect Rolf Engströmer.

Plate. 8 The springy steel tube chairs, so popular in Central Europe, did not, due to their streamlined coldness, prove popular in the Swedish interior design of the 1930s. However, a customized outdoor chair made of solid spring steel was shown at the Stockholm Exhibition, which would become a big seller. Designed by the smith Artur Lindqvist at Grythyttans verkstad, the chair originally had a dark red frame and later became known as the A2.

Plate. 9 The Austrian architect Josef Frank had an extensive production behind him when he came to Sweden in 1934. He added vegetative motifs and fresh colours in the spirit of William Morris to the Swedish pattern flora. Aralia from the 1920s is a good example of this.

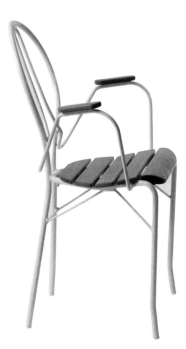

Plate. 10 The Pia-chair is a pretty, white-lacquered tubular steel chair for outdoor use from 1942. It was designed by Tore Ahlsén for KF and has a practical foldable seat that makes it easy to stow away. The chair is still in production as are other products in the Pia-series, for example, the airy, delicate Pia-lamp.

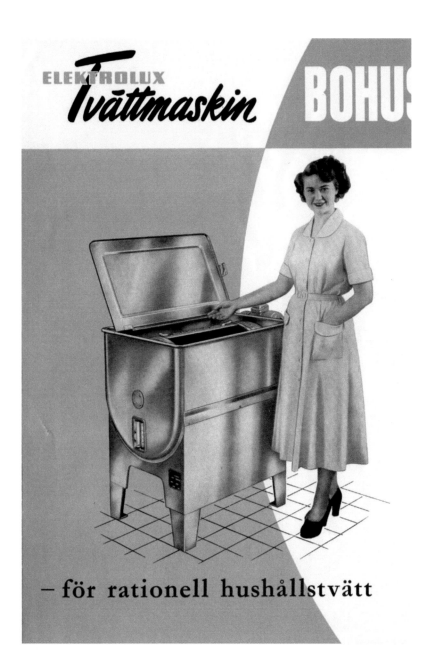

Plate. 11 Washing by hand was one of the hardest aspects of housework. The first washing machines arrived at the end of the 1940s, after inspiration from the USA and some common brands were Calor, Alfa-Laval and Bohus. The latter machine was of the recommended cylinder type. Brochure photo from 1955.

Plate. 12 Passenger flights developed in parallel with the professionalization of the designer corps, which is one of the reasons that so many designers have been given commissions from airlines. ABA, which from 1946 was included in SAS, employed Anders Beckman to market the company with the help of striking posters.

Plate. 13 The large Helsingborg Exhibition in 1955 was the definitive breakthrough of the beautiful Swedish everyday product and a manifestation of the Swedish Society of Crafts and Design's half-century-long effort to bring together artists with industry. Anders Beckman was in charge of the graphic design and in the theme of H55 he had in chemical formula managed to merge the city and exhibition year into a powerful slogan.

Plate. 14 Few had the ability to market their projects with the help of striking visionary sketches as Ralph Erskine could. Here he excels in an advertising brochure from 1954 showing a future 'Europe's first Shopping Centre ... a complete miniature city with a controlled climate, which would give comfort and enjoyment ... with streets, alleys and squares, where the trees flourish and diverse flowers shine all year round ... even if the thermometer "outside" shows severe freezing temperatures'. Even though the supply of electricity appeared to be assured by all the hydropower in northern Sweden that was under development, the reality never lived up to the expectations. Luleå in the north of Sweden did get its shopping centre, but a considerably more modest one.

Plate. 15 The co-operative idea was concerned with minimizing costs for households. It was therefore logical that KF was at the forefront in terms of a standardized generic low-price range where you only paid for what you got. KF's so-called Blåvitt (Blue-white) range of staple commodities that spoke for themselves in simple packaging and uniform decoration was introduced in 1979. Blåvitt was an immediate success and the range was extended several times.

Plate. 16 Geometric patterns, preferably in grey scale, dominate Ingrid Dessau's textile work. At her debut exhibition at Galerie Moderne in 1953, she showed among other things the drapery Manhattan, where she skilfully interprets the big city's regular city plan with the cars hurrying down the straight streets or, if you like, the light shining from the windows in the equally straight rectilinear skyscrapers.

Plate. 17 The artist Sture Johannesson's provocative poster, popularly known as 'Haschflickan' (The Hash-girl), was made for the exhibition Underground at Lunds Konsthall in 1969. It was a paraphrase of Eugène Delacroix's painting Liberty Leading the People in the spirit of drugs and liberalism. The poster was seized by police, the exhibition was closed before it opened and the art gallery manager was forced to resign.

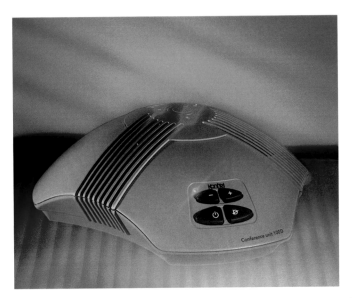

Plate. 18 The establishment of the Umeå Institute of Design in 1989 came to be very significant for the establishment of design awareness in northern Sweden. Some of the first graduated design students started the consultancy Struktur Design, which got off to a flying start with the innovative design of a conference phone, Konftel 100 from 1994.

Plate. 19 The concept car Saab EV1, which was developed in 1985 under the leadership of the chief designer Björn Envall, was one of the decade's most interesting car projects. It was made fully drivable and was in many respects ahead of its time. Based on the popular Saab 900 Turbo platform, a red four-seater sports coupe was created with deformation resistant front and rear sections of plastic, black panel-type dashboard, extremely light and ergonomic seats, and last but not least a spectacular solar cell-fitted glass roof where the solar cells powered a fan that ventilated the coupe when the car was parked.

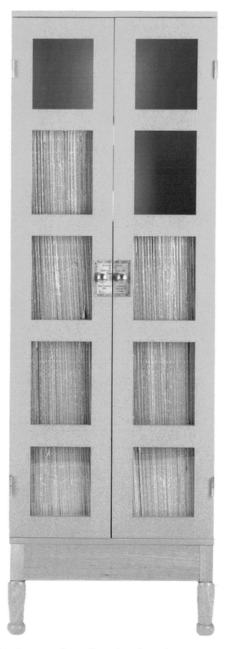

Plate. 20 Källemo's furniture producer Sven Lundh took on a whole team of designers with strong personal styles. One of these was the innovative Mats Theselius who made this cabinet congenially suited to twenty-five years of the magazine *National Geographic*.

Plate. 21 BD1 for David Design from 1996 appears almost to be a graphic character. Björn Dahlström's background as a graphic designer is evident in much of his wider production.

Plate. 22 Lei by Officeline might be the world's first ergonomic office chair for women. The chair is a result of a lengthy study on female sitting posture. Designed by Monica Förster Design Studio 2009.

Plate. 23 Ecolean is a super-light packaging material: a one-litre beverage package weighs just less than half what a gable top or pet bottle weighs. The material consists of 40% degradable calcium carbonate (chalk). The image shows Ecolean in practical use.

Plate. 24 The design process and exploration are at the heart of the internationally acclaimed design group Front, founded by Sofia Lagerkvist (b. 1976), Anna Lindgren (b. 1977), Charlotte von der Lancken (b. 1978) and Katja Sävström (b. 1976). Furia Rocking Horse for Gebrüder Thonet Vienna was launched in 2016, when Front only consisted of the first two designers. The project stemmed from a thorough study of the company's long tradition of working with bent wood.

World's Fairs had meant up to the Second World War: an international forum where countries could compare themselves, be assessed and ranked (Wickman 2003).

Design in Scandinavia, a travelling exhibition, toured twenty-four American and three Canadian cities between 1954 and 1957. This was the first time that the modern Nordic democracies had shown on a large scale what they could achieve when art and technology met in the arena of industrial production. Some 700 items were presented in five different themes, ranging from interiors and everyday goods to contemporary craft and exclusive art handicraft. Here serially produced bentwood chairs by Bruno Mathsson and Stig Lindberg's Gustavsberg products sat side by side with glass sculptures by the Finn Timo Sarpaneva. The social-political rhetoric had been toned down, as had the countries' internal differences. The objects were more central compared to the exhibitions in the 1930s and were related to the home and family. Links to natural materials and the local traditions remained, while at the same time the idiom became more elegant and refined. The sculpted, almost, constrained elongated shapes tended at times towards the abstract, indicating an influence from the inter-war radical European sculptural tradition, with names like Constantin Brancusi, Henry Moore and Jean Arp.

The exhibition met with an extremely warm reception among critics and the public and helped to create interest and goodwill towards the Nordic countries, according to the American design historian Claire Selkurt (2003). Over 650,000 people visited the exhibitions and through massive media coverage, lectures, and films on the Scandinavian theme it is estimated that around 13 million people were exposed to the exhibition's message. These events created a strong purchasing interest among American consumers and as early as 1954 there are supposed to have been more than 3,000 retailers for these products in the USA.

The success also continued in Europe, where Swedish and Nordic designs were presented to an international audience at the Swedish Society of Crafts and Design's large H55 exhibition in Helsingborg and later received numerous awards at the Milan Triennials. H55 was not like the Stockholm Exhibition a utopian or experimental exhibition, but rather an account of how functionalist heritage had been nurtured and refined to what in an architectural context is called Swedish Empiricism and what in a design context can be described as Scandinavian Design. At the same time it was a manifestation of the Swedish Society of Crafts and Design, a kind of crescendo for a half century's efforts to encourage artists into industry to create more beautiful everyday products. The location of the exhibition was spectacular: large parts of it had been put on Parapeten, a 33-metre wide and 800-metre long breakwater that stretched out like a spit in the ocean.

The man responsible for the graphic identity was Anders Beckman, who at the time was an experienced and acclaimed exhibition designer, not least after New York in 1939. In a clever move Helsingborg and 1955 were merged in the style of a chemical formula into the successful conflation H55 (Plate 13). The graphical leitmotif served as the main theme throughout the whole exhibition in everything from posters to Stig Lindberg's souvenir ashtrays. And not just in the exhibition, but also throughout the city, on streets, buildings and in flowerbeds; in fact the catchy logo was even seen in the form of cakes. According to the British specialist on company profiles, F. H. K. Henrion, Beckman's efforts at H55 were 'the first and most complete corporate design for an exhibition and a town ever seen' (Bowallius 1999: 44).

Most things were represented at the exhibition, in particular the household goods sector with all things related to the home. A special hall was dedicated to electricity with the latest in refrigerators and freezers, stoves, fans and domestic appliances. Hemmens forskningsinstitut (The Home Research Institute) had its own department for practical children's clothes and in a hall for school meals, children were served food that had been flash frozen; they also got to eat Raketost (soft cheese) and drink milk from Tetra Pak's new tetrahedron-shaped milk cartons. For book lovers there was Kajsa and Nisse Strinning's smart and popular string shelf consisting of shelves that were hooked onto supports made from plastic-coated steel wire. Graphic design was also represented, by among others Svenska Telegrambyrån (Swedish News Agency). Many of the objects were brand new; for example, Gense's innovative Focus cutlery, Björn Hultén's practical recliner H55, which was even named after the exhibition, and Stig Lindberg's flame retardant stoneware Terma. The latter consisted of frying pans, pots, teakettles and coffee pots that were so elegant and heat resistant that they could be taken directly from the hot plate to the table and vice versa without cracking. The Terma series was not manufactured out of regular ovenproof material, but rather a new high-tech material, Norvarlit, which had originally been developed in the factory's laboratory to be able to withstand the rigours of a rocket launch. The media was in relative agreement that everyday goods did not get more beautiful than this, although there were some critics who wondered where the more pronounced industrial design was (Wickman 1995). But it would take another few years before Swedish industrial design had conquered the exhibition scene.

Everyday Items with Classic Status

Many of the everyday items within the category of Scandinavian Design are undeniably easy on the eye, as Källemo's founder Sven Lundh often put it. But the fact that products from the 1950s are so often cherished, as well as durable, is because they represent much more than visual aesthetics alone. For example, Eskiltuna-based Gense's stainless steel cutlery Focus and Ericsson's Ericofon – known internationally as 'the Cobra telephone' – deserve to be regarded as design classics.

Focus is an understated set of cutlery, its style reminiscent of the shape of a tulip and with clear sculptural qualities. The life-affirming tulip and hourglass shapes provided precisely the kind of desirable contrasts to the strict and restrained fashion that had prevailed during wartime. The new cutlery was designed by Gense's artistic director, the silversmith Folke Arström (1907–1997). Personally, I've been using this cutlery daily since it was launched and therefore dare to make a closer analysis of its qualities.

Fig. 3.14 Just in time for the H55 exhibition, Folke Arström and Gense were able to present a new comprehensive cutlery set in stainless steel that would attract admiration worldwide. The cutlery was called Focus and it also came in the luxury version Focus de Luxe with black, burgundy or grey nylon handles. The cutlery, which has been put back into production, is as beautiful as it is practical.

Focus was manufactured out of stainless steel and comprised 18 per cent chromium and 8 per cent nickel with the exception of the knife which was made of hardened chrome steel (14 per cent chromium). Stainless steel became popular as a cutlery material in the 1940s. It was strong and easy to wash and maintain, unlike older traditional cutlery made from carbon steel, silver or nickel silver. The handles came in two versions: a standard design made solely in stainless steel and Focus de Luxe which had handles made from black polyamide plastic (nylon), a modern version of the nineteenth-century's bone and porcelain handles. The product is well-dimensioned and tumbled, a process whereby all sharp edges are worn down and softened. This is a prerequisite to ensure that the cutlery is safe to use and, if put in the mouth, will not prick or cut the user. Accordingly, the Focus cutlery set represents a different, more modern post-war eating pattern, where food no longer has, by necessity, to be dropped into the mouth at the lips but instead can be placed deeper into the mouth. Eating is thus made easier as food can be consumed more quickly and more safely. Furthermore, food thus becomes a new sensory experience as its flavour is not altered because stainless steel has no taste. The effect of cutlery on the sensory experience of food is underestimated, given how often we use cutlery. Writing in one of Gense's brochures, design critic Ulf Hård af Segerstad estimates that we insert a fork and spoon into our mouths approximately 20,000 times per year through eating.

The design of the different cutlery components was innovative and requires closer description. The knife has a short blade, only a third of the knife's length and no more than is required for a table knife. The difference is striking when compared to the impractical blades that were commonly used for older cutlery and which could sometimes be twice as long as the handles, ensuring their full length could therefore not be utilized. The blade is also not straight but has been given a rounded shape on the ventral side, which creates a cutting angle that gives a longer actual cutting edge and increases its penetrative power. The cavetto itself, the transition from blade to handle, is made with almost surgical precision, while the handle has been given a sleek and simple form.

The fork also differs radically from contemporary traditional cutlery. With its three broad and short prongs it offers exactly the grip necessary to bring the piece of meat or fish to the mouth. The claw's shape also affords plenty of space left over so that some sauce or other condiment can be scooped up with the fork. Even the spoon has unequivocally functional qualities. The rounding, the heavy material and the soft edges contribute to it being comfortably put into even a small mouth. In addition, the bowl of the spoon is cupped in a way that is well adapted to the palatal curvature, which minimizes the risk of discomfort as a result of suction.

Folke Arström's Focus was one of many series of stainless steel cutlery sets produced during the 1940s and 1950s. He designed a further three more conventional sets of cutlery for Gense: Thebe (1944), the simpler Facette (1946) and Ellips (1953). Thebe was an extensive project that was initiated when he was hired in 1940. It ended up including 125 different pieces of tableware in total, according to the company the most complete series in stainless steel ever made. Gense's production was largely focused on the American market and the design of Thebe followed a trend that Arström was already familiar with from when he worked with more noble materials for G.A.B. (Guldsmedsaktiebolaget in Stockholm) during the latter half of the 1930s. Thebe was fitted with fluted handles on the cutlery and matching ridged decoration on the edges and handles of the platters, dishes and trays that are also included in the series. For the salt and pepper shakers American-inspired torpedo shapes were used.

Even master craftsman Sigurd Person (1914–2003), who like Arström was also a designer, designed a stainless steel cutlery series with lasting qualities. It was named Servus and was developed as an innovative everyday set of cutlery for KF for the H55 exhibition based on a two-year-old version in silver. Characterized by the spacious fork with four prongs, as a whole this angular cutlery does not possess the same elegance that distinguishes both Focus and other examples of Folke Arström's production.

The quality of the Focus cutlery series has been confirmed by the high prices they regularly fetch second-hand. Over the years this has inspired – and still inspires – other manufacturers to make similar models. Furthermore, Gense brought it back into production in 2006, although with slightly distorted and coarsened forms and with the handles of the luxury version made of dishwasher-resistant POM plastic.

The Ericofon (the 'Cobra phone') also has lasting qualities that deserve to be highlighted and which make it a well-deserved classic. Ericsson developed the Cobra between 1941 and1954, primarily for the American market. Hence its special appearance: a standing handset coiled like a listening cobra, ready to attack. The shape is also reminiscent of the look of the two hand-operated candlestick telephones, which were part of American culture until the 1940s–1950s (circa 1890–1950). But the Cobra was a much smarter so-called one-piece telephone. Making a telephone in one single piece and collecting all the components in the handset had long been a dream for the world's telephone manufacturers. The German company Siemens & Halske made an attempt as early as 1930 but the project never got further than a series of prototypes. However, Ericsson learned, more or less by chance, of the German experiments. This prompted feverish activity among the company's engineers, which led to the development in 1941 of a fully functioning prototype designed by Ralph Lysell.

For a variety of reasons, including the wait pending the development of a sufficiently strong coloured thermoplastic for injection moulding, the project was put on ice until 1949. When the work resumed a good deal of care was put into the ergonomic details, such as a supportive thumb grip at the bottom of the shaft as well as a handle shape that fitted the shape of the hand as well as the ear. In 1954, a trial series was released and when production started in earnest two years later, sales went through the roof. After about six months the number of orders exceeded the production capacity by 500 per cent despite minimal marketing.

The Ericofon became the world's first mass-produced one-piece telephone and was produced until 1982 in the new ABS plastic in about thirty different colours. Only five colours and 20 per cent of the production reached the Swedish market. One requirement was that the whole telephone would weigh less than the old

Fig. 3.15 Ericsson's Ericofon, or 'Cobra phone' as it is commonly known, was the world's first serially produced one-piece telephone. It was originally designed in 1941 by Ralph Lysell but was not put into production until the mid-1950s after ergonomic adaptations by a technical apparatus group led by the engineer Gösta Thames. The Cobra was originally intended to be manufactured out of Bakelite, but the demand for scratch resistance and the strong desire in the 1950s to be able to provide colourful telephones caused the switch to ABS plastic. The gorgeous colours and the material's high surface finish was a major break from the traditional heavy, black Bakelite phones. This picture shows the prototype of the 'Cobra phone'. See also Fig. 3.16.

Fig. 3.16 One of the 2.5 million copies of the 'Cobra phone' produced at the factory in Karlskrona, Sweden from 1956 to 1982. See also Fig. 3.15.

Bakelite handsets, which was achieved by a wide margin. In addition, it only took up a third as much desk space as a conventional desk telephone and could be put down anywhere without the need to search for a cradle or any other part of the appliance.

The spectacular phallic shape, combined with delicate colours and excellent finish completely broke with the black Bakelite era and as the design historian Arthur J. Pulos (1988: 309) notes: 'helped open the way for a new generation of telephones'. It is the first telephone where as much emphasis is placed on the aesthetics of its resting position as when it is in use. That it beautifies its environment – with its elegantly sculpted design even when not in use – was noted in the 1950s and 1960s. It became one of the favourite props of advertisers and photographers and was regarded as an important marker of modernity, even for film directors such as Fellini. Since I grew up with a mint green Cobra, I even remember the feeling of total control that it gave as you used it; there was no longer the risk of pulling a base unit down on the floor. Although by today's standards it was a little heavy at the base of the unit, it gave a sense of freedom of almost the same character as the one felt when the first cordless phones were introduced in the 1980s. This was also something that Ericsson took advantage of in its marketing, which among other things established how comfortably you could make a call even when curled up in bed with your Cobra.

It is no coincidence that the Cobra, preferably in flaming red, adorns the covers of both foreign and Swedish books about telephones. Scarcely any other Swedish consumer product – Mathsson chairs, the Volvo Amazon and the Tetra Pak milk cartons included – has had such an international impact. The reason is that the Ericofon represents an epoch, a paradigm shift in terms of international telephone design. A measure of the expectations that the company itself had placed on the new model is that it was the first Swedish telephone to be given a proper name and not just a number and letter designation; a first sign that it was regarded more as a consumer product than as a simple extension of telephony as a system.

The Cobra has not ceased to provoke reaction. In time for Ericsson's centenary in 1976 a sequel was released, redesigned by Carl-Arne Breger. The new model was slightly smaller and lighter than its predecessor and was fitted with a keypad instead of a dial. You might think, therefore, that the Cobra is a closed chapter, but such is not the case: it is very much alive. On the second-hand market this model is more sought after than ever, particularly among young people, and for telephone collectors worldwide, it is mandatory. The device has been given iconic status and is sold through all conceivable channels. It is plagiarized in low-income countries and the old covers house modern electronics. You even encounter the Ericofon in a cemetery in Förslöv, Skåne, carved on the polished gravestone of one of Ericsson's directors, which if anything demonstrates what emotions this innovation provokes. The Cobra has also gained many followers among the more serious producers, even Bang & Olufsen made a wireless version in 2001, Beocom2, which takes on a cobra-like shape when the slightly curved telephone in the form of an aluminium tube is placed in the bulbous charging unit (Brunnström 2006).

4 Broadened Design Commissions, 1950s to 1980s

The Industrial Design Profession Finds its Form

In December 1955 the newly graduated British industrial designer Peter Maddock arrived in Gothenburg by boat, carrying only a backpack, for the journey on to Stockholm. He had earlier the same year visited the H55 exhibition and was now firmly resolved to find a job as an assistant at a design office in 'design-conscious Sweden'. Interest in Swedish design was now sky-high throughout the Western world and especially in Britain. In 1953, for example, Gense's design director Folke Arström wrote that he had read a press release from London some time before in which Sweden was considered to have 'the highest artistic and qualitative standards in the world in terms of mass-produced objects' (Arström 1953: 130). No wonder Maddock came to Stockholm. However, it was considerably harder than he had imagined, even though he had learned a little Swedish from his wife. He was amazed that in Sweden, which had an international reputation for being a 'design mecca' there existed barely any, what he with his British terminology called, designers, except those that were doing work with more emphasis on craft in the domestic household goods sector. There were of course a few lone wolves and some industrial designers with direct links to the provincial industries, but no assistant jobs.

Peter Maddock had to bide his time. He managed to get some freelance work and tried taking an evening course in furniture design at Konstfack. He says himself that it was due to a lack of other things to do, as there were no opportunities in Stockholm to improve his knowledge in the industrial design sector. When their first baby came he stayed home for a year, but when their second child was born the family had to improve its income. It was 1958 when he visited Rune Monö's office, AB Industridesign, but there was no work there at that point either (Maddock 1996).

Rune Monö was a trained engineer and also a talented draughtsman, who had learned all about X-ray and cutaway drawings at Sixten Sason's drafting department at Saab in Linköping. Like his mentor, he soon mastered the technique of rendering light and shadow so well that the objects emerged as if they existed in reality. Like many of his generation, he was fascinated by streamlined shapes during the 1940s, which were not only used in his work with aircraft stairways for ABA, but also for objects that were far from being associated with speed. The fascination with the great pioneer country in the West was palpable. In the summer of 1952 he, together with colleagues from Sweden and the other Nordic countries, participated in a design course in Oslo led by five professors from the Institute of Design in Chicago. There they learned the latest in American design education, which used different materials to train the sense of proportion and observational ability. The rhythm of movement was stressed and simple structures were playfully developed into organic, abstract and random shapes. There was no longer any talk of a 'spreadable streamlined decor', instead it was now Henry Moore's sculptures that were the positive ideal (Arström 1953).

Monö had been working alone at the time when Maddock was refused employment, and had won, among other things, a prestigious assignment for the industrial magnate Axel Wenner-Gren: he was to design an ALWEG-system monorail train, one of the more grandiose public transport ideas of the post-war period. Monö designed not only the actual trains, but also the rail track on poles, stations and bridges. A test track was built on the outskirts of Cologne, and the system was then introduced in a few places in the Americas and in Osaka, Japan. The work with ALWEG had been taking place in parallel with various assignments for SAS until 1957 and bolstered by this he felt ready, after he had allied himself with a businessman with an interest in design, to transform his office into AB Industridesign in the same year. A German model builder was hired and soon also some young designers, marketers and secretaries.

1957 was an eventful year not only for Monö but also for Swedish industrial design in general. Monö's colleagues Hugo Lindström and Per Heribertson had taken the initiative to form a professional non-profit organization to preserve the quality level in this new professional field. When the organization Svenska Industridesigner (Swedish Industrial Designers or SID, now Sveriges Designer [The Swedish Association of Designers]) formed on 1 March 1957, Sixten Sason joined, as did Folke Arström, Atlas Copco's design director Rune Zernell, Sigvard Bernadotte and Rune Monö, who was elected president. Astrid Sampe, the first female member, also joined a little later.

There were many new issues to consider. Meticulous agreements were signed with the employees and as a designer at AB Industridesign one was not allowed to undertake personal commissions in the field of industrial design. Commissions within arts and crafts, however, were encouraged so long as it did not adversely affect their daily work. Staff were also allowed to participate under their own name in design and architectural competitions and retain any prizes. If the prize led to a commission, however, then it would fall to AB Industridesign, which would then take over the official responsibility for the work. They also had to commit to reveal absolutely nothing about the work of the company or any of the assignments they undertook, either during employment or after they had left. The working hours lasted from 08.00 to 16.45 with a 45-minute lunch and a 15-minute break for coffee. In addition to the monthly salary, a simple form of profit-sharing was included based on the agency's total fees charged (contract from 1963 in Monösamlingen, Designarkivet).

Being an industrial designer in the 1950s was no easy task. Contacts with clients usually occurred at low levels. Engineers often had a slightly indulgent attitude towards things that could not be calculated or expressed in numbers. Any idea, every line in fact had to be justified. Here Monö could draw on his technical background. Among

Fig. 4.1 An important milestone for the professionalization of Swedish industrial design was the creation of Svenska Industridesigner (Swedish Industrial Designers), SID, in 1957. The picture shows from the left some of the founders: Folke Arström, Rune Monö, the economic association's theorist Ulf Hård af Segerstad, Hugo Lindström and Rune Zernell.

the more high profile of Monö's hundreds of commissions were the intercom Centrum Futura (1958–1959) that matched the best in contemporary Italian office design and the delivery van Tjorven, with a body of fibreglass-reinforced epoxy (1965–1968).

Monö received his largest and most comprehensive commission from the supermarket chain ICA (Inköpscentralernas AB), which in 1962 wanted to tie its four regional purchasing groups closer together. It started with a logo, but as is so often the case, it ended with the assignment being extended to include a full corporate identity, with signs, prints, journal headers, car decals, staff uniforms, carrier bags, packages and more. But first and foremost ICA's twenty-year-old logo needed to be revamped.

What they had was the three capital letters compiled in a roman italic on a circular base: dull, anachronistic and also utilized by their dealers in a far too varied and inconsistent way. At the time the stringent sans serif had emerged on the international scene as the epitome of the modern and progressive. The functionalist typefaces Universal and Futura from 1925/6 and 1927 respectively and above all the most neutral, rational and clearest of them all, the Swiss Helvetica created thirty years later, had begun to be used by the major international companies. This was Monö's starting point when he designed a brand new sharp-cut emblem where the C coalesced boldly with a cropped A. The proposal was much disputed, Monö has recounted, before ICA's management committee finally approved it. The new ICA logo was introduced in 1964, around the same time that the ICA movement seriously began to compete with KF in the food trade. It proved through its simplicity and forcefulness to be commercially successful and has also survived the test of time (Monö 1997).

Returning to Peter Maddock; he finally got lucky and was hired towards the end of 1958. The big (in more ways than one) bohemian Sixten Sason needed an assistant. His office, or studio rather, was on the second-floor of his two-storey apartment in Solna. He was constantly travelling by car between his main employers Electrolux, Husqvarna Vapenfabrik and Saab. Although Maddock stayed in the studio for the most part, he got important insights into the work process. At Electrolux in Lilla Essingen Sason had a room that he shared with a development engineer, and most of the work was done there. It mostly concerned facelifts for outboard engines and development work on the vacuum cleaner, where a typical taskforce included developmental engineers, drafters and production engineers, sometimes with a representative from the sales department and an outside designer. When there were big differences in opinion, it was the designer who could bring the group together again. In the case of vacuum cleaners, the main focus was on saving weight by replacing metal parts with plastic. A prototype was also developed for a completely new vacuum cleaner, designed to operate like a soft suitcase on wheels that did not scrape against door edges and the like. By making use of polyurethane foam it could be made very light. The only problem was that it differed too much from ordinary vacuum cleaners and was therefore rejected. 'Developing the right design for the right time is an essential element in the art of developing new products' was something Maddock learned (Maddock 1996: 5).

Maddock was given a fairly free rein by Sason and was sometimes allowed to present proposals at project meetings. He recalls his experiences of advertising executives who he thought interfered in design issues with short-sighted reasons related to the current competitive situation, without reflecting on what the situation would look like in a few years when the product was out on the market. The work for Husqvarna Vapenfabrik consisted at this time of designing electric frying pans, knobs and handles for stoves and refrigerators in addition to the difficult to control colouration during the enamelling of appliances and cookware. The most important project, however, was to design the new best seller, the electric iron. Maddock noted that the work climate in the old mill outside Jönköping was more traditional than at Electrolux, with directors and director's wives having personal views on design issues that were usually irrelevant to customers.

The fledgling Saab at Trollhättan was an exciting environment for a newly appointed designer, providing interesting discussions with development engineers. A major department before computerization was the template office where the exact curves of the car body where scribed on aluminium plate, which was a more stable foundation than paper. The curves were created using long strips of hardwood held in place by lead weights.

When the curve was judged to be accurate it was verified using mathematical calculations. Several interesting new projects concerning light vans and various sports car prototypes were in the pipeline, although few reached execution. Maddock was allowed to help Sason on the Saab 96 and the practical family car, the station wagon Saab 95, but also in the preparatory work for the Saab 99. Taking part in a trainee capacity was the young car enthusiast and future head of design at Saab, Björn Envall.

Fig. 4.2 Sigvard Bernadotte, who belonged to the Swedish royal family, opened a design office in Copenhagen with the Danish architect Acton Bjørn in 1950. The operation grew to be probably the largest design consultancy in the Nordic region and in 1958 Bernadotte moved back to Sweden to open a branch in Stockholm. The many employees were responsible for relatively independent design work even though the signature Design Sigvard Bernadotte was often used as an important selling point. In this brochure photo for AB Moderna Kök (later Modernum) from the end of the 1950s Sigvard Bernadotte demonstrates a real best-seller, the so-called Bernadottekannorna (Bernadotte Jugs).

In 1962 the big adventure ended for Peter Maddock. Sason had financial problems and could no longer take responsibility for his assistant. Instead, he was employed by another lone wolf in Stockholm's design field, Per Heribertson. Unlike Sason, Heribertson was a trained engineer in the electronics field, and had for many years worked as the construction manager for the lighting department at Elektroskandia.

But over the years his interest in art took over and he began to specialize in the appearance of the fixtures. His lighting fixtures for offices, industry and roads were highly acclaimed and award-winning, for example at the Milan Triennials. In 1960 he became a design consultant under his own name (Monö 1997). Heribertson was an aesthetic connoisseur and could work with a shape for a long time to achieve a minimalist perfection: 'a master of the art of fine-tuning a curve or a colour' according to Maddock. During the roughly two years that Maddock worked with Heribertson, they received many commissions for fittings from different manufacturers, for both indoor and outdoor lighting. The most important commission, however, was for X-ray equipment and other electro-medical equipment for hospitals. The products were supposed to be ergonomic and manoeuvrable for the staff, at the same time as being attractive and not intimidating for patients.

In 1965 Maddock joined Bernadotte Design AB, which was a completely different type of workplace. It was at this time probably the Nordic region's largest design consultancy office with at its peak about fifteen employees and numerous commissions in the consumer goods sector. The office originated in Copenhagen where Sigvard Bernadotte together with the Danish architect Acton Bjørn had founded the firm Bernadotte & Bjørn Industridesign, Merkantil Design A/S in 1950. Sigvard Bernadotte (1907–2002), after graduating from Konstakademien (Royal Academy of Fine Arts), had worked as a silversmith and artistic director for Georg Jensen in Copenhagen. He was inspired to get involved in the industrial design business during a several-year stay in the United States in the 1930s where he visited the great American pioneering offices led by Henry Dreyfuss, Raymond Loewy and others. The fact that Bernadotte was the son of the then King of Sweden opened many otherwise closed doors and was also boosted by Swedish Modern and Scandinavian Design being widely appreciated and written about. Both designers and clients sought out the office; among the more famous were Jacob Jensen and Jan Trädgårdh as well as Åtvidabergs Industrier (with the brands Facit and Original-Odhner) respectively. The Åtvidaberg group was a faithful client and in the redesign of their office machines a family resemblance was created that was emphasized in the shape of the casings as well as in the silver-grey colour and typography. The office's workflow was, according to Jacob Jensen, that Bernadotte and Bjørn brought in the clients; the commissions were then dictated to the secretary who wrote down the information and conditions for the employees to base their work on; ideas and sketches were then presented to the owners who gave criticism and then a final draft was formulated. One of the secrets of their rapid success was the office's consistent working method to quickly compose a realistic model that would inspire the client to come to a decision (Bernadotte 1997).

In 1958 the company opened a branch in Stockholm managed by Sigvard Bernadotte. His network of contacts was wide and good language skills were an asset in the acquisition work, which also gave the office a number of international clients. Many employees saw the office as a stepping stone to further careers and the staff turnover was therefore high. Carl-Arne Breger was the first chief designer but resigned in 1959 to start his own business. Torsten Dahlin, Sven Bergman and Henrik Wahlforss laid the foundation for Ergonomi Design Gruppen (now Veryday AB) after a few years. Rolf Häggbom, who had succeeded Breger as chief designer, quit in 1968 to become the head teacher of Konstfack's newly established industrial design course. Hans Sjöholm, who was the office manager for consumer goods design, remained the longest. But Sigvard Bernadotte always had comprehensive control. His name was used in the marketing of many products, even though he was rarely behind the design himself, a not entirely unusual phenomenon in the related architecture industry. This led to disputes and discussions among the staff but also helped to promote the office.

When Peter Maddock entered the picture Bernadotte had the previous year broken away from Bjørn and was now solely responsible for the Stockholm office. Maddock was immediately impressed by the professionalism he found and began by designing saucepan handles and cigarette lighters, but soon moved on to office machines and household products for Husqvarna Borstfabrik. He eventually became the design manager and was responsible for most of the customer contacts. In 1969 the company merged with the British AID, which specialized in packaging and corporate identities, but the entire operation had to be shut down only three years later. The incipient energy crisis and recession hit the industry hard. Peter Maddock had to move on in his design odyssey and he did what most of the others did at this time: he started his own small-scale business.

Advertising Becomes Ever More Important within Design

In today's computerized design world it is easy to forget that hand drawing both is and has been the cornerstone of design, the fundamental premise of visual communication. Drawing is also a superb analytical instrument. It was therefore no coincidence that the automotive design at Saab started in a drafting department managed by Sason. It was also no accident that the other two industrial design pioneers, Ralph Lysell and Alvar Lenning, both started their consulting businesses under the protection of an advertising agency. Drawing was also the common ground for the collection of book artists, typographers, commercial artists, decorators, packaging designers, poster artists, pattern constructors and others who were part of the professional non-profit organization Svenska Affischtecknares Förening (Swedish Association of Commercial Artists, or SAFFT). The association was formed in 1936 (since 1986 Sveriges Reklamförbund [Advertising Association of Sweden] and 2009 Sveriges Kommunikationsbyråer [Swedish Association of Communication Agencies]) with the goal of promoting 'a clearer language of visual communication'. During the 1950s, other associations within the drawing industry had been added. For those who associated themselves with the titles of cartoonist and book illustrator there was the organization Svenska Tecknare (The Association of Swedish Illustrators and Graphic Designers) from 1955.

The narrow demarcations of cartoonist, poster artist, book artist, typographer as well as the professional titles advertising artist or advertising adviser, which were very popular in the 1950s and 1960s, are no longer as relevant today. They are now usually replaced with the name graphic designer or the management title within advertising of art director/AD, which in turn fit within the larger term visual communication which includes all the professional practices of drawing, graphic design, journalism, photography, advertising, television, film and so on. The term graphic designer comes like other design terms from English, where according to Megger and Purvis (2006) it was first coined in 1922 by the American book artist William A. Dwiggins. He used it to describe his own activities; that is, a person who brought order and structure to the visual design in printed communication, or to put it more concretely: to create an atmosphere using the format, fonts, type area, line spacing, margin proportions and paper, which complements the book's message. The term design, however, did not become more widespread in a graphic context until after the Second World War. Sweden awarded its first professorship in graphic design as recently as 1987 and in Swedish *grafisk design* has become a generic concept and an alternative denomination only in the last few years.

At the time of SAFFT's formation, there was no adequate graphic design programme in Sweden to speak of. The two design schools at Konstfack and HDK had for several years offered teaching in book art and typography, but the focus was on more general artistic training. According to Bowallius (1999), it was only when the newly created Grafiska Institutet (Graphic Institute) and Konstfack were co-located in 1944 that Sweden had a powerful centre for graphic design education. A few years later, the teaching of US-inspired subjects like design and advertising theory began to replace traditional book-craft. At HDK in Gothenburg teaching was also adapted to changing conditions and in 1945 the name of the old graphical department was changed to Bok- och Reklamkonst (Book and Advertising Art) with two different focuses: one on advertising and typography, and the other on fashion drawing and book illustration. 'The extension of the advertising art education would be of particular importance, an area, which in recent years has undergone a revolutionary development', stated the departed rector Sigfrid Ericson (1948: 173) in his centennial history.

In 1939 several other schools were started in Stockholm in order to capitalize on the great interest in the advertising profession and to meet the demand for skilled personnel in the field. Anders Beckmans Skola ([Anders Beckman's School] now Beckmans Designhögskola [Beckmans College of Design]) was set up by Beckman with support from his brother Per and the textile designer Göta Trädgårdh (1904–1984) after the acclaimed World's Fair in New York, while Skolan för Bok- och Reklamkonst (the School of Book and Advertising Art) (which was however forced to close after only seven years) came into being through the initiative of the Swedish Society of Crafts and Design and Svenska Boktryckareföreningen (Association of Swedish Book Printers). At Beckmans teaching soon took place in four areas: advertising art, book art, window dressing and fashion drawing, the latter with Trädgårdh as the supervisor. But the need was still not considered to be met and two years later yet another school was opened, Reklamtekniska Skolan ([The Technical School of Advertising] today Berghs School of Communication) by Gösta Bergh and his wife, Irma, on the initiative of the major advertising agencies. The new schools concentrated on maintaining close contact with the now rapidly expanding advertising industry, which went from 138 unionized workers in 1940 to 422 in 1964 (Bowallius 1999).

The 1950s and 1960s became the golden age of the advertising industry. Cinema advertising evolved into its own genre with many successful commercial directors and movie clips, above all from the confectionery manufacturers such as Marabou, Mazetti and Cloetta. Neon advertising, which in Sweden had its breakthrough at the Stockholm Exhibition, reached its apex. The most spectacular roof and facade signs were placed on the new Hötorgsskraporna in Stockholm, including a sign for Dux Radio, which was the largest luminous advertisement in Europe when it was lit up in 1960. Shop windows were, however, considered the most important advertising spot for retailers, and a number of Swedish trade journals devoted themselves to giving hints and advice related to signage and window dressing. 'Retail culture' had for some time been the watchword, embraced by the cooperative movement as early as the 1920s and with the USA providing the model. Many ideas were taken from the world of theatre and now that working on signage had become an established profession the task was to make the store look like a showroom, not a stock room. At the same time one had to try to awaken the viewer's interest with something striking. When Sweden's first shopping centre was opened in Luleå in 1955 it was spectacular (Plate 14), and with its range of stores and daring architecture by Ralph Erskine quickly became one of Sweden's biggest attractions (Kåberg 2003).

The printing industry advanced in the 1950s to become Sweden's fourth largest industry and commercial advertising expanded, encouraged by a new law against restraint on trade that came into force in 1954.

Ad spending per capita was soon among the highest in the Western world, prompting critical reflections in the form of, for example, Sven Lindqvist's book *Reklamen är livsfarlig* (Advertising is lethal) (1957) and *Sveket mot konsumenterna* (The betrayal of the consumers) by Åke Ortmark (1963). Although the commercial sector dominated, Bowallius (1999) argues that the advertising concept of the time was broader than today and could also include non-commercial activities. As the graphic designer's skills grew, new fields of work began to appear and the boundaries to blur between what had previously been considered as either beautiful book art or more utilitarian graphics. Not only ads needed to be designed, but also brochures, catalogues, posters, billboards, packaging, shop windows, exhibitions and so on. KF with its cooperatives built much of its success on consistently giving all of this a common profile and the larger companies designed graphic identity programmes inspired by the current international models such as Olivetti, Braun, IBM and Westinghouse.

This variation in graphical tasks was exemplified by the prominent contemporaries Karl-Erik Forsberg (1914–1995) and Olle Eksell (1918–2007). They had both completed their studies at the short-lived but recognized Skolan för Bok- och Reklamkonst. Between 1946 and 1947 they obtained supplementary education abroad in completely different environments, which contributed to both of them working primarily in different traditions within the graphic design field: book art and advertising respectively.

Karl-Erik Forsberg, like his almost equally renowned brother Vidar Forsberg (1921–1992), made a name for himself in particular with his book designs. He designed the covers for more than a thousand books, long-standing logos (for, for example, Volvo, Scania, Vin & Spritcentralen, Sveriges Radio and Gustavsberg), over 500 bookplates, royal monograms, stamps, playing cards, wine labels and fonts all with graceful elegance. He travelled to Switzerland to study and became an ardent supporter of the functionalist-inspired new typography movement linked to the likes of Paul Renner and Jan Tschichold. In 1949 he succeeded Akke Kumlien as the artistic director of P. A. Norstedt & Söner (now Norstedts) and would over many years leave his mark on the company's book publishing. His style gradually moved towards a calligraphic and classic direction, especially after 1951 when his self-designed typeface Berling Roman was developed at Berlingska Stilgjuteriet (Berlingska Type-foundry) in Lund (Lindberg 1987). This typeface was used, among other things, for the issue of one of his most important works, the Bible with pictures by Rembrandt, from 1954.

The idea of a Swedish typeface had been much debated during the early twentieth century. The issue was spurred on primarily by the book printers Waldemar Zachrisson from Gothenburg and Hugo Lagerström from Stockholm. One reason apart from the nationalistic ones, but also a difficulty, was the Swedish language's divergent vocabulary with its double consonants, many long words and the abundant presence of up and downward strokes. Berling Roman is considered in most contexts to be the first completely Swedish typeface, adapted to the Swedish vocabulary as well as being both designed and manufactured in the country. It is based on the classic roman type and was designed as an easy to read, composed and harmonious typeface suitable for reams of copy. Forsberg worked with the new typeface throughout the entire 1940s, resulting in several thousand sketches and drawings. Berling Roman has had an international impact and has not only survived all the technological shifts, from lead printing over Letraset's dry transferrable lettering to phototypesetting, but has also been developed to fit today's digital technology (Lindberg 1994).

Olle Eksell furthered his education in the United States. Together with his wife he attended The Art Center College of Design in Los Angeles (now in Pasadena), the leading school in graphic design, photography and industrial design at the time. During their stay in the USA they came into contact with some of the world's finest graphic designers, such as Alvin Lustig, Ladislav Sutnar and Paul Rand. The latter worked for IBM for many years and became both a source of inspiration and a close friend. Once the Eksells had returned home, they organized the first exhibition of American graphic design, at Nationalmuseum in 1947. The then museum director Erik Wettergren saw the North American advertising art as innovative but at the same time shocking. The suggestive and abstract dominated, influenced by the prevailing art movements of the time, surrealism and abstract constructivism (Eksell 1999). Olle Eksell would also make several book covers for various publishers, but in a completely different style to Karl-Erik Forsberg. They are considerably lighter and more figurative with a script reminiscent of Stig Lindberg's. But what would make him celebrated both in Sweden and abroad was, above all, his work with a corporate identity for Mazetti.

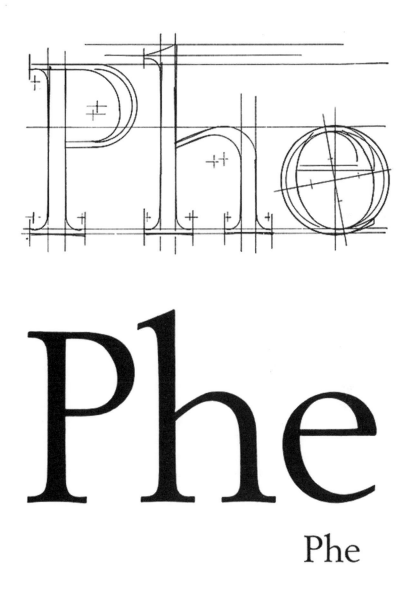

Fig. 4.3 A vast amount of sketch and design work preceded Karl-Erik Forsberg's Berling Roman from 1951. It is probably Sweden's main contribution to the international typeface flora and has for a long time been prescribed in the Government Office's graphical manual for all printed material. The typeface is based on the classical roman type and is particularly suited for longer texts with the Swedish language's uneasy vocabulary. The picture shows a scaled-down design drawing.

Mazetti was a chocolate and confectionery factory in Malmö (acquired by Fazer and shut down in 1992), which had been founded in 1888 by the Danish business-man Emil Mazetti-Nissen. Mazetti's slogan and logo was a pair of open, naturalistically drawn eyes, a symbol of honesty that they wished to be associated with. In addition to chocolate, nougat and other sweets, the company's main product from the outset was packaged cocoa under the brand Ögon-kakao (Eye-cocoa). In an attempt to recoup lost market share Mazetti launched an international design competition for a new corporate symbol in 1956. Olle Eksell won the competition with a compelling redesign of the old brand in the form of a pair of drawn, stylized eyes with an Egyptian touch. The new brand had the advantage that it could be enlarged or shrunk to any format with undiminished efficiency and could be printed in different colours on the packages; the text was also changed from uppercase to more legible lowercase letters. He also received a full-time assignment from the far-sighted CEO to create, over a couple of years, a new branding programme for Mazetti. The new eye symbol came to play a key role as a visual marker on letterheads, envelopes, invoices, business cards, packaging, wrapping, vehicles, flags, uniforms, curtains, signs and advertising. Everything was supposed to combine to create an effective unit. Eksell was even allowed to design the chocolate pieces in the boxes, which also resulted in adjustments to the production machines. The new cohesive graphical programme led, according to Eksell, to the company regaining its entire market share after only a year's change of management (Eksell 1999). Requests to use their materials in the classroom came from art and design schools around the world, and Mazetti's brand-ing programme was highlighted with an initial place of honour among 763 selected examples in the voluminous work *Trademarks and Symbols of the World* by the Japanese designer Yusaku Kamekura, from 1966.

Based on the results of Olle Eksell's work for Mazetti one could say *Design = ekonomi* (Design = economy). That also became the title of an acclaimed book by Eksell, published in 1964. Here he emerges as an early propagandist for the use of graphic design as a means to increase business profitability but also for getting Swedish advertising and graphic design labelled as art and culture. He argued that it is graphic design together with architecture that visually reflects a company's objectives and purpose. Based on his American and domestic experiences Eksell argued that companies cannot afford to make do with a blurred profile. More graphic designers were needed to 'create significantly more functionality in homes, in work-places, in the urban landscape, in communications and in education …'. In order to achieve results and be liberated from various so-called 'experts' in the organization, the designer must be placed next to the CEO in the company, and he gives a good deal of examples from different countries demonstrating the success of such collab-orations (Eksell 1964).

At the time of the publication of Eksell's book, Swedish advertising was domi-nated by three major advertising agencies that lived largely on commission income from daily press advertising. They were Gumælius (Sweden's oldest advertising agency that was founded in 1877 by Sofia Gumælius), Ervaco, and the largest

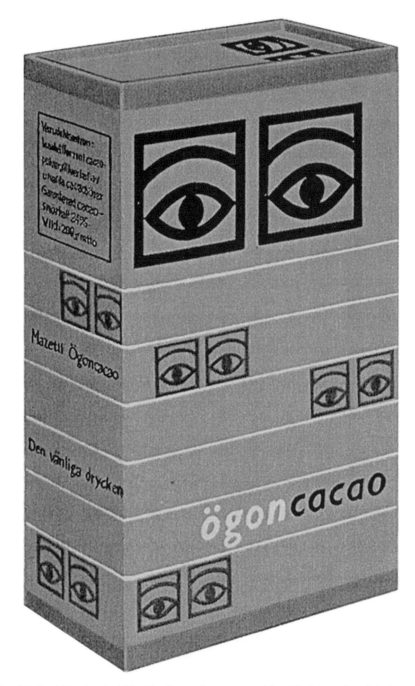

Fig. 4.4 The US-educated Olle Eksell won the company Mazetti's international design competition for a new corporate symbol in 1956. His pair of stylized eyes, which were a development of an already existing brand, was the starting point for a very acclaimed graphic identity programme that included giving all the packaging a uniform and powerful look.

of them all AB Svenska Telegrambyrån, with about 500 employees and its own design department in Malmö. The latter was managed relatively independently by John Melin (1921–1992), one of the greatest creators in the graphic field. Together with the artist and graphic designer Anders Österlin (b. 1926) he formed M&Ö, a signature that delivered innovative advertising with a trenchant graphic design. They made posters, packaging, brochures, catalogues, calendars, book covers and videos for clients such as Moderna Museet, Malmö and Lund's art galleries, large publishers and several manufacturing companies from the south of Sweden. Between them, they almost attained the industry's Guldägg (Golden Egg) Award and their honoured works include an innovative suite of posters for Trelleborgs Gummifabriks AB.

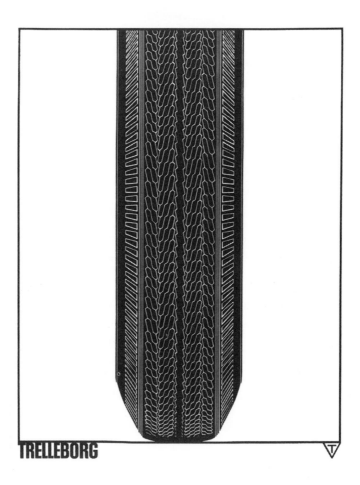

Fig. 4.5 Simple and rational, but graphically poignant and powerful. That was the characteristic of Melin and Österlin's many Guldägg (Golden Egg) winning posters for Trelleborgs Gummifabriks AB during the 1960s.

M&Ö's advertising constituted the culmination of a long period where the animated image was the main element of visual communication. During the second half of the 1960s the industry changed to a new linguistic way of communicating and with the photograph as the focus. Following developments in the USA the commission system was abolished and agencies were no longer dependent on how many times an ad was inserted. Instead, one was paid for one's creative work based on the time spent. The transition to an hourly rate gave rise to new, smaller agencies and the advertising industry turned into a consultancy business with professional titles like art director and copywriter. The recommendation to purchase, which had previously been the sole prevailing working method in advertising, was supplemented with new creative approaches. Across the Atlantic the American agency DDD was responsible for an epoch-making introduction to Volkswagen under the heading 'Think Small'. Leon Nordin at Arbmans together with Alf Mork created an ingenious ad campaign in the same spirit for the rather wobbly Renault 4L, depicting it as rather luxurious. Arbmans, which had been founded by Stig Arbman in 1953, became a nursery for young creators under the guidance of the successful but hard-nosed Leon Nordin. In the early 1970s, many broke away and started their own agencies, including the team Lars Hall and Jan Cederquist as well as Lars Falk and Ove Pihl. New challenges were waiting for them with the oil crises, the introduction of advertising tax and a social climate where the word advertising was exchanged for information (Sandberg 2000).

Breakthrough for Female Designers

The advertising agencies were for a long time a man's world, which is rather apparent from reviewing, for example, the pictures in the book *50 år med svensk reklam* (50 years of Swedish advertising) (Wigstrand 1999): men making advertising for other men, but also increasingly for a female clientele. Typical images are brainstorming sessions with men in suits around a table with small notepads and many ashtrays, a haggard advertising guru with the obligatory cigarette in his hand, or the agency's draughtsmen in white studio coats concentrating at their sloped drawing boards, illuminated by ASEA's practical, adjustable Triplex pendulum fixtures. Encounters with male faces in the pictures of workplaces were characteristic of virtually all design disciplines in the 1950s, more so than in areas such as the related arts and crafts. Class lists also show that men were numerically dominant in the design schools (Beckman and Widengren 1994). On the other hand, a number of women feature in the older, preserved class photographs and one wonders how their lives turned out. Many got married and changed their surnames, which may be an obstructing factor in the research.

The furniture and interior design area was popular among female design students. The art historian Sigrid Eklund Nyström has made an important contribution by bringing several women who were active in the profession in the 1930s and 1940s out of obscurity. Two of them, Greta Magnusson Grossman (1906–1999) and Margareta

Fig. 4.6 In 1950 Greta Magnusson Grossman designed an elegant and smart desk lamp called Cobra. The picture shows a re-launch in vintage red by Gubi.

Köhler (1901–1974), were both prominent designers and entrepeneurs. After she completed her fellowship at Konstfack in 1933 Greta Magnusson Grossman opened a combined workshop and furniture store in Stockholm called Studio. In the 1940s she moved to the USA where she designed a series of highly acclaimed desk-, floor- and pendant lamps, Gräshoppan (Grasshopper) (1947) and Cobra (1950) being the most famous (Eklund Nyström 1992).

Another interior design firm that started in the aftermath of the Stockholm Exhibition with the ambition of creating modern and beautiful homes for the masses was Futurum. The initiative had been taken by Margareta Köhler together with the artist Marie-Louise Idestam-Blomberg (1898–1988). Their interior design style and self-designed range were described as soft and sunny, as 'a rest for the neon light tormented and colour fatigued city eyes' (Eklund Nyström 1992: 179). Köhler was a pioneer who managed to combine her profession with a husband and children, something that inspired Lena Larsson, who had practised for a time at Futurum and was in a similar situation.

Lena Larsson was one of the most influential interior designers of the 1950s and 1960s, not just in her capacity as the director of NK-bo and its successor NK-bo-nu, but as an exhibition architect for, among others, H55 and consumer advocate in magazines, books, radio and television. She is perhaps most closely associated with the notion *Köp, slit, släng* (buy, wear, throw), which was the provocative title of a debate article in *Form* in 1960. The term became a symbol of the consumer society's frivolity and rational approach. A woman who had the opportunity to realize Larsson's visions during the rational 1960s was Karin Mobring (1927–2005) who after studying at Konstfack and at Carl Malmstens Möbelskola for a time joined IKEA in 1964. There, she was approached as the first female designer to design simple but practical and cheap furniture, above all for children and adolescents (Demokratisk design 1995).

The ability to combine work and family life has been crucial to many women's career choices. Although the artistic professions, unlike many others, were without convention relatively speaking, one must not forget that even as late as the 1960s there was an attitude among many female students that considered the housewife profession as a fully legitimate and socially acceptable alternative to a career as a designer. And even in those cases where it ended in marriage with a fellow designer, which was relatively common, they generally voluntarily took a more self-sacrificing, supporting role for their soon-to-be more renowned male life companion. Olle Eksell's wife Ruthel and Carl-Arne Breger's wife Bibi are two typical examples. Many of the women that have so far emerged in this text have been emphasized in the role of driving visionaries and organizers, or have been active in the female-dominated textile arts. During the post-war period, however, there was a gradual change, partly in the form of the glass, ceramic and textile industries giving more women the chance to produce their own self-designed collections, partly that women started to come together in different groupings for certain exhibitions or later in design and producer cooperatives. Neither can the fact be ignored that women's volunteer work during the war years had an encouraging effect, and prepared the way for greater willingness among women to plan their own professional careers.

Among the more prominent female designers who were affiliated with industry was Ingeborg Lundin (1921–1992), who at H55 exhibited drinking glasses and the large green apple sculpture Äpplet, which has attained practically cult status, for Orrefors. Hertha Bengtson (1917–1993) worked at Rörstrand and made the generous, relief-patterned blue and white service Blå Eld (Blue Fire) from 1951. Karin Björquist (b. 1927) was affiliated with Gustavsberg where she designed tableware, for example, the best-selling Vardag (Everyday), but was also involved in the company's plastic production. The textile designer Viola Gråsten (1910–1994) was hired by NK's Textilkammare in 1945 and was acclaimed for her colourful abstract patterns that represented a breakthrough for textile printing in Swedish interior decorating. Hedvig Hedqvist (2002: 107) writes, 'NK's presentation of Gråstentygerna (the Gråsten fabrics) that hung over the entire lightwell aroused the same excitement as when the store first presented American jeans'. Another textile designer, Age Faith-Ell

(1912–1998), made popular curtain fabrics and soft furnishings for Kinnasand that won a gold medal at the Milan Triennials.

In 1953 two young but already acclaimed female designers debuted together at Galerie Moderne in Stockholm: the textile designer Ingrid Dessau (1923–2000) and the potter Signe Persson-Melin (b. 1925). Both had attended Konstfack and alternated, as did so many other talented designers with similar backgrounds, between the production of unique objects, public artworks and industrially manufactured consumer goods. They also created space for their own career paths even though they married equally renowned design personalities (Kaj Dessau and John Melin respectively). The exhibition was praised by Åke H. Huldt (*Form* 1953: 234), who argued that Ingrid Dessau emerged 'in the forefront of our textile artists'. She displayed carpets and drapes in discrete geometric patterns with a lot of black and grey, produced together with weavers who were affiliated with Kristianstads Läns Hemslöjdsförening (Kristianstad County Craft Association) (Plate 16). Dessau would later design large quantities of delicate Wilton carpets, Rolakan carpets and rya rugs for Kasthalls Mattfabrik (Kasthall Carpet Factory), with whom she had just started a long-term collaboration, and later also carpets and upholstery fabrics for Kinnasand.

Signe Persson-Melin had built up her own studio in Malmö and exhibited understated everyday ceramics at the exhibition, where smooth glazes contrasted with unglazed honey-yellow chamotte clay. She used a similar but more subtle contrast effect for a popular suite of rustic spice jars for H55, where she had stamped the names of the different spices in the damp clay with the help of lead type. From the mid-1960s, the business was broadened and Persson-Melin moved more and more towards various industrial commissions and new materials. There were pots and tableware for Höganäs Keramik, fire polished glass, cans, bottles and bowls for Boda Glasbruk, the majority of the well-thought-out Boda Nova range, planters for Skandinavisk Eternit in Lomma, flagstones and birdbaths made of concrete for Nordform, aluminium urns for Byarums Bruk and so on. Although her guiding principle has been practical and functional design, she has always skilfully avoided adjusting to the factory production's slightly cool and rational characteristics. As an example Kerstin Wickman (1997) highlights the arts and crafts feel of Persson-Melin's tableware, which is notable for its textured surfaces, irregularities, painstaking detail as well as a warmth and lustre in the glazing.

Illustration is an important element of graphic design and a professional field in which women with expertise in drawing could make their presence felt; with a studio set up at home it was possible to have more control over one's own working hours. Weekly magazines were full of fashion stories and illustrated ads. Gerd Miller (1925–1988) and Jane Bark (b. 1931) were among the more prominent. Gerd Miller came from a modest background and had received her basic education from Leon Welamsson, who was the head teacher at Konstfack but in addition to his regular employment ran an illustration school during the years 1933–1945. Gerd Miller was according to Lena Johannesson (1995) 'the one who drew the 1950s'. Over more than forty years she illustrated short stories and series on a freelance basis from her home studio for the successful coloured weekly magazines: *Allers*, *Husmodern*, *Vecko-Revyn*, *Året Runt*, *Min Värld* and *Damernas Värld*. She was also active as a cartoonist and fashion illustrator and had a French agent who sold her drawings to the fashion magazine *Elle* among others. Jane Bark attended Konstfack's advertising and book-craft course, where the syllabus for the final two years also included

Fig. 4.7 Katja of Sweden was an international success with its comfortable and responsive clothing that represented healthy and natural ideals. This elegant dress is a typical example of her liberated style.

fashion drawing. In the 1950s she illustrated newspaper ads for shops and department stores at *Dagens Nyheter*'s Tecknarstuga, the newspaper's advertising agency. The newcomer Hennes (later H&M), which represented a more youthful fashion and sold clothes by Kerstin Lokrantz and Gunilla Pontén, was one of the most prolific advertisers. After the company provided her with the selected garments, title, text and logo, she sketched a proposal that was presented to the director Erling Persson and which then usually resulted in a half or full page in four-colour print. The fashion illustrations were gradually supplemented by short story illustrations for *Damernas Värld* and above all *Femina* in Jane Bark's characteristic style; during the 1960s most of it took place at home in her bedroom studio (Bark 2001).

If Gerd Miller and to a certain extent Jane Bark represented a relatively anonymous group of female designers, then the silversmith and jewellery designer Vivianna Torun Bülow-Hübe (1927–2004) has been much more acclaimed. Apart from the fact that her production was considerably more exclusive, she had both a unique and remarkable career. As a student at Konstfack she had demonstrated her determination by simultaneously running a workshop in Stockholm and being a single mother, including bringing the pram to lessons, which was somewhat sensational in the late 1940s. Åke Livstedt claims that she 'is among the most prominent designers who attended Konstfack' (Livstedt 1994: 257). Bülow-Hübe was responsible for entirely new ideas in jewellery design with elegant rigid necklaces, earrings and bracelets in silver, sometimes set with polished stones that she herself found on Mediterranean beaches. She often appeared as her own model and could, through her own elegance and charisma, do the jewellery justice. In particular, the simple, stylish and elegant bracelets and gorgets inspired by the Möbius strip (symbol of eternity) have become classics and are serially produced by Georg Jensen.

Another female design pioneer who, like Bülow-Hübe created a successful international career in the 1950s and 1960s, was the fashion designer Katja Geiger (1920–2017), better known by her stage and company name Katja of Sweden. Katja was also able to wear her own-designed collections with verve and provided a foundation for a previously missing Swedish fashion tradition. She had trained with Barbro Nilsson at Konstfack and Göta Trädgårdh at Beckmans but also worked as a fashion illustrator for *Dagens Nyheter*. In 1949 she moved on to New York where she got her breakthrough when the department store chain Lord & Taylor took on her collection. The company Katja of Sweden had the advantage of being able to ride on the wave of Swedish Modern's success and the garments had associations with the practical Swedish folk tradition. In the mid-1950s, she returned to Sweden and began a twenty-year collaboration with Malmö Mekaniska Tricotfabrik (Malmö Mechanical Tricot Factory). She introduced a natural, close-fitting fashion with soft, responsive clothes and shoes that suited the modern career woman. These were elastic Jersey fabrics without accessories such as bras and girdles, which attracted attention and fuelled the image of the sinful country in the north. But 'without her there would hardly have been any shirts worn untucked, everyday jersey fabrics or low-heeled shoes in fashion history. Today, when fashion is looking back in time to move forward, she is one of the names that inspires the industry', asserted the fashion journalist Marie Birde in an interview with *Dagens Nyheter* (10/9 2007). Katja of Sweden represented a democratic fashion, something more than just highlighting a woman's beauty. 'If men had to think about how they looked all the time and have the same problems with high heels, then they would not have got as far as they have either' exclaimed Katja with some frustration in the same story.

Factory Packaging Drives out Bulk

The roughly century-old Ögonkakao (Eye-cocoa) from Mazetti was one of Sweden's first factory packaged foods. The reason for it being packaged in sealed bags was that the manufacturer could thereby ensure the precious cocoa was not mixed with cheaper substitutes. There was normally no great need for innovative packaging or branding as long as food and other basic goods were supplied over the counter. Many products were also sold in bulk. Flour was delivered from the mills to the stores in 100-kilogram sacks where it was scooped, weighed and handed to the customers in unmarked paper bags. Sugar was produced in heavy sugar-loaves, which sat on the shelves or hung from hooks in the store's ceiling and were sawed or cut into the necessary size when sold. When granulated sugar was introduced it was scooped into paper bags. Butter was ladled out of tubs and was sold in bulk, wrapped in greaseproof paper. Milk was poured into containers that customers brought with them; however, due to the risk of bacterial infection it was only sold in special milk shops. Unwieldy wooden boxes and wooden barrels were other typical traditional storage containers used by the food industry. Bulk sales had the advantage of the food colour and scent tantalizing the senses, something that has largely been lost today. However, managing it all was of course time-consuming, cumbersome and sometimes unhygienic. There was also a risk that the weight of goods sold could be tampered with – and unfortunately this was not uncommon.

The ongoing discussion about packaging took a dramatic turn with the introduction of supermarkets where the customer could control their own choice of brands. Suddenly the producer was directly confronted with the consumer while the distributor or dealers became intermediaries. The US-influenced self-service stores or supermarkets were tested by KF before the Second World War but were not adopted as a business concept until the end of the 1940s, after wartime rationing ceased. The main idea was to streamline and save labour. From KF's side it was also about being able to maintain low prices and save time for the hard-working housewife. Gradually increasing focus was put on designing shelves that were ergonomic and presented the products in the best way. When the smallest packaging had to be easily identifiable on the supermarket shelf, packages became an interesting field of work for the designer, both as a product and a carrier of visual communication (Brunnström 2004).

The first foods that had to be branded for competitive purposes were those with a long shelf life, such as canned and dry goods like biscuits and confectionery. Hard and hermetically sealed metal tins were an ideal packaging material that could survive long journeys and were also fitted with advanced colour prints as far back as the 1860s. It would take until the 1920s–1930s before locally produced staples such as flour and sugar were factory packaged. At this time the milling industry and Sockerbolaget (Sugar Company) were equipped with semi-automatic packaging machines developed by the firm Åkerlund & Rausing, and started delivering their products in consumer-friendly bleached Kraft paper bags with brands imprinted. In KF's Juvelkvarn in Gothenburg in 1937 heavy and unhygienic sacks were replaced with clean, white 2½-kilo paper bags labelled with the KF and flour brand's bright red logos.

The factory packing of foodstuffs in tin cans – so-called tinplate – has a long history. Dry goods such as biscuits and confectioneries were packed in tins with separate lids, while heat-sterilized canned foods required tins with rimmed lids. This preservation method is about 200 years old and the tin, originally handmade by

Fig. 4.8 The first plastic reinforced paper packaging, Tetra Pak, was developed in 1952, which revolutionized the sale and storage of sensitive milk products. This is how the tetrahedron-shaped packs were displayed a few years later.

skilled tinsmiths, was an indispensable element in the context of protracted warfare during the nineteenth century. The introduction in the 1850s of the Bessemer process in steel mills resulted in a more pliable light-gauge sheet metal suitable for mass production, with the first Swedish tinplate factories being founded in the 1860s. Anchovies, caviar and herring were the most common canned preserves, which towards the end of the century could also be labelled with printed text and advanced pictorial themes directly on the metal. Canned coffee, as well as beer, introduced in 1955, dominated tin can packaging from the middle of the twentieth century. Coffee had then started to be vacuum-packed in large round tins, which meant it could retain its aroma for a longer time. Co-op's Cirkelkaffe (Circle Coffee) from 1951 with graphic design by Gunnar Orrby was a pioneer in the field (Conradson 1977).

In forest-rich Sweden there is a strong tradition of using various types of paper and cardboard packaging. During the Second World War when there was a shortage of glass and steel, Åkerlund & Rausing developed the waterproof paraffin-coated cardboard container Satello, which was used extensively in the food industry. Findus used the tub for its Hushållsmarmelad (Household Marmalade), Sockerbolaget for its Bord Sirap (Table Syrup) and Kavli for the legendary Raketost (literally 'Rocket' Cheese). The last was a soft cheese that was pushed through a Satello tube and was sliced by means of an accompanying cutting string.

Cardboard packaging received a considerable boost with the introduction of flash freezing technology. Methods for freezing food had been developed in the United States as early as the 1920s and in Sweden there were attempts at freezing and storing at Münchenbryggeriet in Stockholm in the early 1940s; their products were exclusively sold at NK and marked as scientifically frozen food. Just a few years later, both KF and Findus from Bjuv in Skåne offered a frozen selection. This originally consisted of berries, spinach and peas, but was soon followed by frozen fish, ice cream and prepared foods. The ingenious and child-friendly fish fingers, which Findus introduced in 1956, inspired by American innovation, were a massive seller. Even though the frozen foods were ideal for the new supermarkets their adoption was sluggish because it was necessary to introduce freezer counters in stores. Between 1950 and 1960, however, sales of frozen food completely took off, increasing by more than fortyfold (Löndahl 1996).

The big breakthrough in packaging came in the early 1950s when liquid commodities – primarily dairy products – could for the first time be distributed in cheap, practical paper packages, laminated with a thin layer of polyethylene. Ruben Rausing, the owner of Åkerlund & Rausing, with the aid of the company's laboratory manager Erik Wallenberg, developed the new product from initial concept to the actual sealed airtight package, all made from a paper tube. The leakproof container was given a tetrahedral shape, christened the Tetra Pak and was tested for the first time in 1952 at Lundaortens Mejeri (Lundaorten's Dairy) as a one-decilitre package for cream. Tetra Pak was then quickly manufactured in other sizes, including one-litre milk cartons (Brunnström & Wagner 2015).

In 1961 the company refined the technology further. By combining a newly developed steam sterilizing technique from Switzerland with an additional thin layer of aluminium foil in the packaging, the first aseptic, that is to say bacteria-free, packaging was launched. The aluminium foil darkened the contents and ensured a more secure seal, preventing changes in taste or nutritional value. It also ensured that the contents would not be contaminated with microorganisms. The aseptic packaging soon became a worldwide success, not least in southern countries where it was now possible to stock milk and other perishable liquid foods for months on end without either refrigeration or preservatives.

With all this new factory packaging – labelled with their branding messages and slogans – coexisting on store shelves and counters as well as Swedish dining tables, interest in the importance of package design skyrocketed. Many felt package design had not kept pace with rapid technological development. The criticism was primarily led in the early 1960s by the Swedish Society of Crafts and Design, which still essentially assumed the role of the nation's aesthetic guardian. In an editorial in the Swedish Society of Crafts and Design's magazine *Form* (1963: 421) Dag Widman argued that the Swedish packaging industry might produce packages that worked at the moment of purchase but they could not replace traditional storage containers in the home environment. In a later issue in the same year Kurt Bergengren, a journalist at daily tabloid *Aftonbladet*, criticized the unreflecting visual communication:

> The freezer packaging is … a plastic-coated paper capsule without an inner bag that is automatically filled in fast machines and hermetically sealed with a paper-coated paper wafer. But the outside of this technological marvel is old fashioned. There is confusion typographically, artistically and in terms of advertising psychology. (*Form* 1963: 652)

There is no doubt that packaging was considered to be a neglected everyday product. In order to remedy this situation the Swedish Society of Crafts and Design organized a large and widely publicized packaging exhibition at a gallery in Lund (Lund Konsthall) in 1963 called Förpackningen Hemma (Packaging at Home). The initiative was taken by the local chapter for Skåne and Blekinge with Annika Heijkenskjöld as the driving force and curated by Olle Eksell. For the packaging industry, mainly represented by the dominant companies AB Plåtmanufaktur (PLM) in Malmö as well as Tetra Pak and Åkerlund & Rausing in Lund, which had not really paid much attention to the question of waste disposal, the exhibition was a rather unpleasant experience. At the exhibition a shelf displayed nothing more than white packages, serving as a stark contrast to the literal mountain of visible waste packaging, which was supposed to illustrate the waste problem. About a dozen freelance designers had also been invited to present alternative, more radical proposals for better kinds of packaging. In addition to several redesigned packages Rolf Lagerson and Stig Bark presented a container for butter and margarine that could be placed directly on the table. A few years later a similar container designed by Carl-Arne Breger went into production when Margarinbolaget introduced Flora – the first spreadable table margarine. Old-fashioned paper wrappers were now replaced by a stylish plastic reinforced cardboard box decorated with stylized yellow clover flowers.

A conference on the same theme was organized in parallel with the exhibition. Ralph E. Eckerstrom, head of design for the world's largest packaging group Container Corporation of America, which had over 130 companies in the United States, Germany and the rest of Europe, was invited to speak. Eckerstrom's main message was that the packaging industry in general had neglected design; however, he declared that his company had recognized the importance of controlling visual messages and had therefore focused more on design than technological innovation. In order to facilitate this, they placed designers in every company as well as creating six design centres in the USA and one in Germany. At these design centres – or design laboratories as Eckerstrom preferred to call them – designers and market researchers worked successfully in collaboration, undertaking advanced research in design. In addition, the head of design cooperated directly with the CEO, which he argued was crucial in terms of the design organization's development in a company. The Swedish packaging industry has hardly reached this point some fifty years later (*Form* 1963).

The rapidly growing number of packages that needed to be displayed in stores created a need for new packaging solutions and striking graphics. Design commissions, accordingly, usually ended up in the hands of advertising agencies and specifically on the graphic designer's desk; packaging design became part of product launches and advertising campaigns. Already at the first Guldägget Awards (Golden Egg) in 1961 several packages for the confectionery and food industry, including those by M&Ö, were recognized for their excellence. John Melin and Anders Österlin became known for their ability to create attractive cardboard packaging, as well as playing an important part in Kosta Boda's international sales success.

From the late 1960s typography and the graphic message was a central theme in package design, with black text on a white background tending to dominate. A typical example was advertising agency Arbmans's campaign for weapons manufacturer Bofors's toothpaste. They used a rather dry, laconic information text printed in black against the white background of the tube. The text explained that the paste counteracted cavities and reduced the risk of abrasive damage. Another example is Stig Bark's (b. 1928) powerful tin decoration for Abba's canned fish which used the large, bold Futura font.

KF used the same simple, uncompromising typeface and objective packaging communication when they launched the first Swedish series of generic products in their stores. The packages were standardized and the soap was simply called 'soap', the toothpaste 'toothpaste' and so on. The series was labelled Blåvitt (Blue-white) since the texts were all printed in blue on a white background (Plate 15). The purpose of the colour combination and the uniformity was that the packages would stand out from the rest of the selection and become easier to find in the store. The real reason for the introduction of generic or so-called white label products, however, was to, in typical KF-spirit, set up its own low-price range as an alternative to the manufacturers' brands. The experience of the French supermarket chain

Carrefour, which three years earlier had been the first to launch what they called *produits libre*, showed that through minimizing the cost of packaging, advertising and promotion, one could reduce prices by an average of 30 per cent. Blåvitt immediately surpassed expectations and new products were gradually introduced to the range for many years (documents in KF's library and archives, Stockholm).

Photographs did not, however, have the same impact on packaging as in many other forms of advertising. Packaging, often with small, irregular or seamed surfaces, demands a clearer, more concise visual effect. The communication of the key value proposition of the product must be evident on the shelf and encourage the customer to purchase and thus increase sales.

Because of this, illustration as a medium has tended to suit packaging much better than photography. Jane Bark's colourful and poignant drawings on a number of food packages stand out as excellent examples of this. Together with her husband Stig Bark, Jane illustrated Kavli's herring paste and Sockerbolaget's various cardboard boxes in collaboration with Kurt Lundkvist (b. 1921), who was art director at Arbmans in Malmö for many years. Patterns are another popular graphical packaging device. The most widespread and lasting pattern over time is without question the stripes that appear on Arla's milk packets, created in 1991 by Tom Hedqvist, later head teacher of Beckmans College of Design in Stockholm.

Rationality Shapes Everyday Life

Sweden undeniably had an automatic advantage over most other countries because both its industry and infrastructure were largely unaffected by the devastation of war. The period from the Second World War to the early 1970s was characterized in Sweden by high and continuous economic growth; in Sweden this period is usually referred to as 'the record years' or 'the golden years'. The 1960s were an exceptional decade of growth and in 1970 Sweden was the fourth richest country in the world after Switzerland, the United States and Luxembourg. The booming economy was used by the leadership of the Social Democrats to finance increasingly large-scale efforts to reduce the disparity between the living conditions of the rural and urban populace, and between the rich and poor. Building projects were intended to reduce poverty and overcrowding, bringing the population closer together, municipalities were merged and industry streamlined. The latter was achieved through a gradual structural transformation that meant concentrating on large-scale operations, corporate mergers and the closure of unprofitable activities.

The 1960s can be described as the fruition of the so-called Swedish *Folkhem* (welfare state), with a general improvement in living standards and distribution of welfare. At the same time it was also becoming increasingly clear how the ongoing efforts to promote equality and rationalization were affecting construction, industrial production and the general mood of the country. The strongest companies grew and tended to have a monopoly. This was especially noticeable in the construction industry where there were two significant changes: a focus on building houses through the so-called

Miljonprogrammet (the Million Programme) and urban transformations. Turnkey projects were in force, where a master builder took care of everything, even the projection, which in turn meant that architects had to comply with the master builder and adapt to the production chain. Almost everything was controlled by standards and regulations.

The Swedish Million Programme was a huge project that aimed to build a million new homes over ten years (1965–1974). It is associated today with the boring, standardized and large-scale high-rise estates, some distance from the major city centres; they are regarded as residential areas epitomized by violence, alienation and a host of identical grey concrete doorways where the only aesthetic approach used seemed to be the aesthetics of repetition. This is partly true, but looking at the country as a whole it in fact accounted for a significant proportion of new housing in the form of small, detached, semi-detached and terraced homes. In addition, one must not forget that Hammarkullen, Rosengård, Tensta and other similar large-scale suburban areas were safe from traffic and relatively child-friendly; in turn, the apartments were also bright, well-equipped with well-studied floor plans, largely due to the construction standards and loan terms that were in place. Skånska Cementgjuteriet (today Skanska), Gustavsberg and Electrolux were among the companies that benefited from the Million Programme's large demand for prefabricated concrete elements, sanitary-ware and white goods. It was also now that chipboard, with its standard dimensions, became widely adopted in interiors and furniture frames.

This urban transformation, which resulted in almost half of the older buildings in Swedish city centres being redeveloped away, is a sorry chapter. A lost cultural heritage is irreparable and Bengt O. H. Johansson (1997) went so far as to call the urban transformation of the 1960s a veritable cultural murder. In the general economic boom politicians and planners were struck by speed-blindness. The situation was aggravated even more by the fact that much of the new construction consisted of uniform department store boxes, windowless parking bunkers or simply traffic routes and dull parking surfaces. The urban transformation led to a clearer zoning of Swedish cities. Innovative urban centres were filled with commerce and offices, while the inhabitants of the newly built residential areas on the city outskirts had to wait for supplementary local services and depended on long commutes to work. The urban terrain was adapted to match the car's needs, although admittedly the Stockholm underground and the tram service in Gothenburg were expanded to include new suburban areas.

Swedish industry worked under immense pressure, especially the mining, steel and engineering industries, which attracted the entire available workforce – including female and foreign workers. The expansion of Sweden's uniquely powerful automotive industry was no exception. Road transport increased dramatically during the 1960s, especially long-distance haulage between Sweden and the continent. Both Volvo and Scania rapidly increased their production volumes and both would concentrate on forward control trucks without bonnets, which made better use of the cargo and road space. The enterprise was made possible by the introduction of tilt cabs, which at the same time made servicing easier than on conventional trucks with hoods.

First was Volvo with the model Raske Tiptop in 1962, closely followed by Scania-Vabis with LB76 in 1963. The forward control truck's shape became increasingly container-like and associated with the shape of buses which had long abandoned the concept of the bonnet and where Scania-Vabis with its Bulldog model was a pioneer in the 1930s (Lindh 1992 and Olsson 1987).

Standard passenger car models were clearly marketed as family cars. They were durable, safe and practical: watchwords that would distinguish Swedish-made cars for a long time but which at the same time tended to embody the concepts of 'boring' and 'uninspired'. In 1959 Saab presented its first station wagon (95), which despite its small size could load 500 kilograms or accommodate as many as seven people by folding up an additional rear-facing seat in the boot. At Volvo, Jan Wilsgaard designed the beginnings of a whole new model series (140) with a simple and angular body shape which was launched in 1966 and would continue to be refined through later models (240, 740, 940) until the 1990s. The box-like shape, which gave the cars the nickname *sossecontainer* (quite literally 'socialist container'), was naturally based on the two space-optimized box-like compartments for passengers and baggage that formed the car's main theme. Visually, the contrast could not have been greater with the ten years older and sculpturally designed Volvo Amazon, which Claes Karlsson (Stahre 2006) so aptly described as: 'Seventy-five horsepower and a Venus mound for a bonnet … Volvo's car designer Jan Wilsgaard must have caressed her out of a dream'.

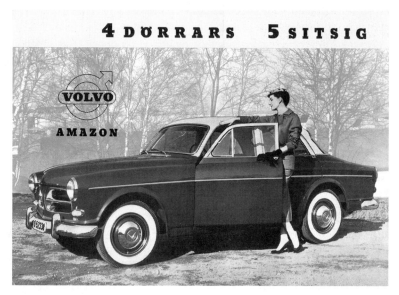

Fig. 4.9 In 1966 Volvo introduced its 140-series, which had been designed under the supervision of the design manager Jan Wilsgaard. The new models were considerably more angular and more box-like in their shape than the ten-years-old Volvo Amazon shown here. At the same time, they were considerably safer and extremely practical, making them real cars of the people. See also Fig. 4.10.

Motorized society created many new tasks for designers. It is true that before the war Sixten Sason had sketched a large number of inspired car models, round multi-storeyed car parks and a bridge across the Öresund with an integrated international casino in Saltholm but much remained to be realized. The first motorway was opened between Malmö and Lund in 1954 and more followed. The following year the first 150 parking meters were installed at Gustaf Adolfs torg in Gothenburg (Sundvall 2006). They were American but the same year Carl-Axel Andersson, founder of the company Cale, constructed the first Swedish round, yellow parking meters. The grey-coloured sequel from 1967 (Cale 67) was designed by Per Heribertson in an austere rectangular style that was closely related to his award-winning street lighting. The square, architectural and modular shapes generally replaced the post-war years' soft bulbousness during the 1960s. This was already noticeable in 1959 with the new fuel pump that Rune Monö designed for Ljungmans Verkstäder in Malmö. Standing next

Fig. 4.10 In the station wagon Volvo 145, shown here, and the successor 245, it was possible to stow most things, which gave rise to the nickname *sossecontainer* (socialist container). See also Fig. 4.9.

to its predecessor from the late 1940s it represents, in exactly the same way as car design, a completely new modernity typified by smooth, rectangular metals with large glass surfaces, a large, clear graphic visible from a distance and a rolling display instead of a clock display. Sibylle Kicherer (1990), who studied Olivetti's design history, also notes how the organic style changed during the transition from the 1950s to the 1960s towards an architectural one after Ettore Sottsass Jr and Mario Bellini took over the design work from Marcello Nizzoli. Office machinery no longer looked like sculptures by Henry Moore with a keyboard, but was divided into separate planes and volumes.

This development was an international phenomenon and must be viewed in the context of improved and streamlined production processes within industry. A major impetus for the creation of new forms has always been that they can be made. Peter Dormer (1993: 45) argues that the reason why many design classics up to the mid-1950s were so similar to each other was largely due to the fact that 'designers were stuck with the fabrication techniques of the age, which allowed manufacturers to press and bend metal sheet economically only if they allowed for shallow rather than sharp curves'. Refrigerator design was a case in point. Virtually all manufacturers utilized the Tangent Bender technique, which meant that the plate was bent in a single sweep, giving the cabinets a bowed top with large, round corners. In the late 1950s it was replaced by the Sheer Look principle, which according to the design director at Electrolux, Hugo Lindström (1997), meant that the corner radii be abolished with the sweeps in the corners cut and then the sheets welded together. This resulted in sharp corners, a thinner profile and more possibilities for installation, which soon became a dominant principle in the standard Swedish kitchen. Conditions in plastics manufacturing also changed during the 1950s, when injection-moulded thermoplastics had their breakthrough and the industry was liberated from the rounded streamlined forms of Bakelite. Knowledge of technical production limitations was important for the industrial designer, who often had to create a style based on these that could be sold to consumers.

An important source of inspiration for the more bare and square design trends of the 1960s were the ideas and products that emanated from the Bauhaus-inspired design programme operating at the Hochschule für Gestaltung (HfG) in Ulm, Germany from 1953 to 1968. Kerstin Wickman (2005) notes that although only a few Swedes studied at the school, intellectually-formed products, based on functional and methodical industrial design, quickly spread all over the world. In a couple of articles about HfG in *Form* (1958: 48) the school was presented, for example, as 'Europe's at the moment most debated educational institution for industrial design'. Furthermore, this discussion was not just taking place in design journals but also at conferences that the international industrial design organization ICSID organized, starting in Stockholm in 1959. At HfG, as opposed to Bauhaus and other design schools, there was less emphasis on art and artistry and instead emphasis on the serial production's demands for greater technical expertise, teamwork and the understanding of consumer requirements. They could also point to great successes and design awards gained from the product cooperation

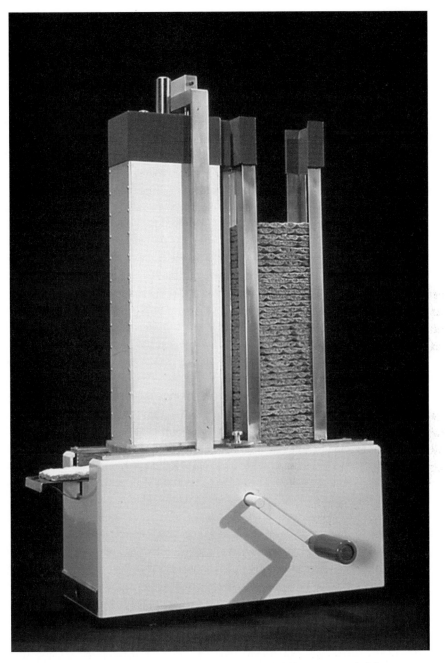

Fig. 4.11 Everything was streamlined during the rational 1960s, even sandwich production. With the help of a detailed manual the Swedish catering staff were supposed to learn how to use Wasabröd's butter spreading machine Wasanissen. The device was designed by Rune Monö 1961–1964.

that they had, in particular, with the electronics company Braun, resulting in radios and other products in refined, abstract, precise and geometric shapes.

The 1960s were marked by an unbridled optimism. Cheap oil flowed all over the world along with a belief that there was a technical solution to all problems. This concerned everything from the superpowers' investment in the space race and moon missions to means of increasing efficiency in actually quite simple activities. An example of the latter was Wasabröd's butter spreading machine, Wasanissen, with which you could crank out 2,300 pre-spread crispbreads an hour with an even layer of exactly 5 grams of butter. The machine, designed by Rune Monö, was marketed with the help of a detailed instruction manual and demonstrations for refectories, bars and canteens (Monösamlingen, Designarkivet).

In the same spirit of large-scale operations, Byggnadsstyrelsen (Board of Building) had a catering system introduced in a few newly built staff and student canteens inspired by the Ford factories' assembly lines. The food was served in the American style directly in the different compartments of white, moulded plastic trays, which travelled from the kitchen to the lunch line on a conveyor belt. On one side were the kitchen staff where everyone had their specific task, for example, adding potatoes, fish fingers, sauce and vegetables. On the other side was the winding queue with hundreds of customers who only needed to collect their tray and pay with a pre-paid coupon. It was fast and rational, just like in the case of Wasanissen. The system reached a serving speed of 30–40 portions per minute, compared with the 6–7 portions in conventional self-service (Brunnström 1997).

The post-war development of electronics – from the electron tube (1907), the transistor (1947) and the integrated circuit (1958) to the microprocessor (1971) – contributed to the miniaturization of many products, making them increasingly anonymous in form. Unlike mechanical parts the electronic components are not only small and non-moving, but also silent, more temperature-neutral and visually less spectacular.

This meant that there was no longer the same interest in exposing the technology, which in many products began to be regarded as the mechanical insides and therefore of little interest. Instead visual attention was stirred by the total shape of an object or the enveloping casing that usually gave it its shape. Whereas Ralph Lysell and his contemporary American colleagues had once begun to design something, sculpting lumps of clay, and even creating full-scale models of enormous streamlined locomotives, now they relied more on drawn, constructed models and began modelling with plastic foam, which gave the whole design a crisper impression. Soon the computer was also utilized and some of the earliest known experiments with computer-generated art and design were performed by the artist duo Holger Bäckström (1939–1997) and Bo Ljungberg (1939–2007), who worked under the name Beck & Ljung. They are above all famous for their optically confusing wall decorations for hospitals and parking garages. At the Röhsska Museum there is also an example of their design in the shape of a modular egg carton-like ashtray in cast aluminium, Ultima 15 from 1966–1969. Another pioneer in the field was Astrid Sampe who, with the help of the programming guru Sten Kallin at IBM in the late 1960s, created a number of computer designed textile patterns, which were then screen-printed at Almedahls in Gothenburg (Kallin 2007).

With the prevailing rational ideals of the 1960s and 1970s, the visual identity of many products weakened. A square box-shaped toaster might look like a radio that looked like a phone that looked like a camera and so on, which prompted Poul Ströyer to draw a classic cartoon from a design exhibition where all the included products had to be supplied with an explanation of what they represented. The smaller component sizes, however, had the advantage that home electronics in particular could be made slimmer and more elegant, which Danish designer Jacob Jensen used to perfection in his designs for Bang & Olufsen, but was also typical of Swedish manufacturers. In the 1960s, Aga and Luxor's radios underwent a remarkable shape change. The massive sideboard radio with all its piping was transformed into a transistorized, flat and angular radio that could fit on a bookshelf.

When the function required it, the geometry was varied. Ericsson's transistor-fitted speakerphone Ericovox was, for example, designed in a pyramid shape by AOS Arkitektkontor and Electrolux's first dishwasher, a table top washer from 1959, was shaped like a round tin. Carl-Arne Breger's 1969 microwave for Husqvarna was fitted with a spaceship inspired domed lid – the same year that Neil Armstrong first walked on the moon. The arrival of the space age was also reflected in furniture design: Bruno Mathsson designed the futuristic armchair Jetson with the mathematician Piet Hein in 1966, following on from the Superellips table of 1964. And Anders Pehrson's UFO-like light fixture Bumling from Ateljé Lyktan hung in many rooms from 1968.

Design Protests against a Grey and Unjust World

During the economic boom of the 1950s and 1960s design was seen almost exclusively as a tool to promote growth, but towards the end of the period the picture became more complicated. As social criticism grew, linked to issues such as over-consumption, market manipulation, environmental pollution, exploitation of the Third World and oppressive American politics, the design concept was given a more artistic and political significance. A number of important debate articles served to fuel the fire, for example: Rachel Carson's critique of environmental pollutants in *Silent Spring* 1962 (*Tyst vår* 1963), Ralph Nader's criticism of automotive safety *Unsafe at any Speed* 1965 (*Den livsfarliga bilen* 1967), Victor Papanek's calls for a socially responsible design in the book *Miljön och miljonerna* (The Environment and the Millions) 1970 and Wolfgang Fritz Haug's *Kritik der Warenästhetik* (Critique of Commodity Aesthetics) 1971 (*Kritik av varuestetiken* 1975), as well as Sven Lindqvist's aforementioned condemnation of advertising and Sara Lidman's criticism of the Vietnam War in *Samtal i Hanoi* (Conversations in Hanoi) 1966 and of the miners working conditions in *Gruva* (1968).

Criticism from the design field was expressed in many ways but it was formulated early on as a questioning of the industry's overarching profit optimization and normative modernist aesthetics, that is to say the ruling market forces' interpretative prerogative concerning good taste. Sara Kristoffersson has in her dissertation on *Memphis och den italienska antidesignrörelsen* (Memphis and the Italian anti-design movement) (2003) provided an international response to this criticism of a growing materialism. She highlights a diverse collection of avant-garde architects and designers inspired by pop art, popular culture and the hippie movement as standard-bearers; for example, the American design visionary and environmental campaigner Richard Buckminster Fuller, the Italian designer Ettore Sottsass Jr, the British group Archigram, and the Italian anti-design movements Archizoom and Superstudio. Their works were often subversive and conceptual in nature, and critical comments were directed, in particular, at the commercial dominance of public space and the furniture industry's adherence to durability.

During the 1960s there were many experiments with simpler, bolder and cheaper furniture in alternative materials. The two pop art-inspired Nordic pioneers Verner Panton and Eero Aarnio broke with all conventions and prevalent status furniture when they introduced their colourful painted fibreglass furniture in innovative shapes. In Sweden, Stephan Gip (b. 1936) attracted attention with the inflatable furniture Blås Upp (Blow Up) in blue, yellow, white or red vinyl plastic, which went on sale in 1967. Two years later, Hagaplast, who were responsible for the production, had, according to Kerstin Wickman (1991), sold as many as 250,000 inflatable armchairs, of which a good number were exported. The inflatable furniture was part of an international trend that fitted in with an emerging youth culture, and the fact that one could take everything under one's arm when moving was an obvious attraction in itself. The tough vinyl plastic could also be filled with water, which gave rise to the popular and equally spectacular waterbeds that began being imported from the United States a few years later.

Plastic furniture served as an icebreaker for the industry and was followed by a wave of experimental furniture. There were plenty of manufactured wood and corrugated cardboard factories in Sweden that mass-produced for the construction and packaging industries and young designers were not slow to test whether it was also possible to produce simple and flexible furniture from these standard materials. In 1966 Börge Lindau (1932–1999) and Bo Lindekrantz (1932–1997) designed a furniture kit in birch plywood for every housing need: the so-called Byggmöblerna (Construction Furniture). The following year Gip developed a furniture series in weaker fibreboard from Mo och Domsjö AB, which was assembled using plastic strings. And the same year Erik Karlström produced Spika-hyllan (Nail-shelf) in unpainted chipboard, which came as a kit when KF took up the production in 1968. This development came to a head when the four Konstfack students Jan Ahlin, Jan Dranger, Martin Eiserman and Johan Huldt made a whole series of corrugated cardboard furniture for Dux. The series was named Well and the armchair in this extremely lightweight but surprisingly durable material was guaranteed a one-year lifespan. Corrugated cardboard furniture was not a particularly great success, even though a star architect such as Frank Gehry continued to develop the concept into refined furniture designs. On the other hand, the chipboard was here to stay. Lena Larsson campaigned vigorously for the new material and Spika-hyllan, which was selected by the magazine *Allt i Hemmet* (Everything in the Home) as the furniture of the year in 1969, is said to have sold 1.3 million units (Wickman 1991). After IKEA embraced the idea in 1968 and the material

Fig. 4.12 The clothes label Mah-Jong stood for political awareness, gender equality and sexual liberation. It manifested itself in a unisex fashion that followed the body's contours and a limited number of models that could be combined for different occasions. Typical features of the range were the comfortable so-called *mysdressar* (cosy dresses) or *mjukiskläder* (soft clothes) in cotton plush velour for both women and men. The picture shows the cover of Mah-Jong's 1972 catalogue, which had been illustrated by the artist Gittan Jönsson.

was gradually improved, chipboard gained an increasingly strong position during the 1970s, but mainly as a frame and shelf material.

The rebellion against materialism and a uniform, patriarchal lifestyle was depicted early on in the more ephemeral fashion industry. Such repudiation was clearly observable in the clothes worn by youth culture's pop musicians and in the hippie movement's bohemian anti-design fashion; it was also quickly picked up by the big fashion houses. Designer Sighsten Herrgård (1945–1989), who studied at Beckmans in Stockholm, arrived in the spotlight when in 1966 he won the Courtauld International Design Competition with a collection of gender-neutral unisex clothes. By the following year his unisex overalls were available from the British fashion house House of Worth, and Herrgård's gender-equal collections in a slim and slightly relaxed style were soon an international success.

1966 was also the year that the left-wing radical clothing brand Mah-Jong was created by three Konstfack-educated friends: Helena Henschen (1940–2011), Veronica Nygren (1940–2006) and Kristina Torsson (b. 1940). They had grown tired of the clothing industry's conservatism, writes Carolina Söderholm (2008), and of the fact that Swedish-made clothes were being driven out by cheap imports. With the help of bank loans and good contacts with Borås Trikåfabrik the trading company Mah-Jong was started, named after the Chinese board game. Their inspirations were Katja of Sweden, Mary Quant with her British poppy youth fashion and Marimekko's bold designs. A sample sale of their first collection at NK showed that they were on the right track with their colourful, patterned and figure-hugging fashion; the clothes sold out in a few days and six months later the order backlog had reached 5,000 pieces. There were minidresses, long-sleeved jumpers and trousers, for the most part knitted in neon-coloured acrylic yarn. The circle of friends and the designers themselves served as models and Carl Johan De Geer was responsible for the bold advertising images. In later collections the innovative process slowed as the political work became increasingly time-consuming. Anti-fashion in the form of basic clothes in natural materials such as balbriggan, silk and plush was now top of the agenda, along with maternity wear, comfortable casual wear for men and unisex suits in corduroy. Before Mah-Jong closed shop in 1976 they had time to shape a completely new reversed male ideal: the velour man of the 1970s.

Mah-Jong's creative stagnation was far from unique. The growing protests against the Vietnam War, channelled primarily through the FNL-movement, an ongoing cultural revolution in China and the protests of May 1968 in Paris led to a general radicalization of large groups of young people. Few could feel unaffected in the period that followed, where the political conversation often left its mark on everyday life. In the schools, traditional professional knowledge was challenged and 'lost years' is not an unusual retrospective reflection from the teachers at Konstfack, while students who graduated before 1968 could express their satisfaction that they 'got out in time'. Those who were closely affected by the leftist wave generally express themselves more cautiously and might think that it was a necessary cleansing for democracy. After years of political complacency, many new voices emerged in the public debate and new laws were created that gave workers more power to influence their employers. As a clear message against oppression and material imbalance, the designer's loyalty now shifted from the producer to the user. At Konstfack this was especially noticeable in the project work and the focus of the master's dissertations. Under the direction of among others the guest lecturer Victor Papanek projects were developed around muscle-powered means of transport for the Third World, playrooms for children with prosthetic arms and boiler suits that were going to be produced by the seamstresses at Algots Nord in Västerbotten. New urgent fields of work were opened where the growing industrial design corps could really feel that their efforts were needed (Wickman 1994).

The collective and group work became the buzzwords of the time; loose or more fixed groupings of like-minded people with idealistic intentions. One of the main groups on the design side was the textile collective 10-gruppen (Ten Swedish Designers), which was formed in 1970. Like Mah-Jong the group was started as a reaction against structural reorganizations and closures in the textile and clothing industry. There was also a desire to have control over their patterns by participating in the entire manufacturing process, as they argued that the manufacturers and supermarket chains usually refused the most interesting and innovative patterns. At the heart of the group, in which almost everyone had attended Konstfack or Beckmans, was the slightly older Inez Svensson (1932–2005). She had just left a long-term role as the artistic director of Borås Wäfveri. It was also there that the collective's fabrics were printed while Duro Tapet developed the wallpaper collections. The group's patterns were colourful and graphically powerful, ranging from simple stripes and checks to more naive animal and plant motifs. There was no problem with the coverage, either internationally or domestically but sales did not go so well. A collaboration with IKEA in 1974 resulted in a wider distribution of their products, although it hardly resulted in any earnings. Carl Johan De Geer, who was one of the members, claimed that he earned more as a tone-deaf trombonist in the band Blå Tåget (Blue Train) than from the textile patterns. The group was gradually thinned out and latterly 10-gruppen has been run by three of the original members: Birgitta Hahn (b.1938), Ingela Håkansson (b.1944) and Tom Hedqvist (b.1948) with the goal of designing at least one new pattern each per year (Söderholm 2008).

Another, albeit looser collective, but one that definitely fuelled the political debate, was the challenging, anarchistic magazine *Puss* (Kiss), which was published from January 1968 until the autumn of 1973. The contents consisted of satirical images and texts, sometimes described as political pornography and the distribution was handled by street vendors.

The core group on the graphic side were Lena Svedberg, Ulf Rahmberg and the editor Lars Hillersberg, but Monica Sjöö and Marie-Louise Ekman also submitted significant contributions with a strong feminist perspective. *Puss* was a product of its time and, according to Lars Bang Larsen (2007), was in keeping with other contemporary underground literature, such as the Dutch *Provo*-magazine, the psychedelic *Superlove* in Copenhagen, *Oz* in London and *Agit 883* in West Berlin. Carl Johan De Geer, who took photographs and drew speech bubbles, has described *Puss* as far too rampant for the left, far too radical for the right and far too obscene for all forms of public discussion (Lennermo 2007).

America's war in Vietnam influenced much of the political agenda during the late 1960s and early 1970s and factional thinking was widespread. In a polarized and, after all, fairly grey concrete society characterized by great seriousness, graphic communication was a haven for the freedom of thought. The group around *Puss* was far from alone in being provocative, through sometimes uninhibited caricatures in which their satirical dig could be aimed at anyone and anything. Much contemporary poster art also existed in a no-man's-land between left-wing agitation and crass goofiness. One of the period's most controversial works was Sture Johannesson's confiscated underground poster for Lunds Konsthall (Plate 17).

Design with a User Focus Becomes a Speciality

Sweden's economic development lost momentum during the 1970s after having gone from being one of the world's poorest countries to one of the richest in the world, and also perhaps the most egalitarian, in less than one hundred years. Political economists and economic historians emphasize different causal factors for the subsequent recession, partly due to their political sympathies. Increased competitive pressure from the outside world, high and rising labour costs, inadequate and poorly utilized innovation, high inflation with unpredictable currency devaluations, direct subsidy of troubled companies and inappropriately designed tax and benefit systems, all spurred on by the international oil crises, are some of the reasons that are usually highlighted.

Although a number of design consultants had to cut back on operations, and some of the major offices were even forced to close, there were still many positive glimmers amid the economic darkness. The simple, objective design, which had blossomed during the 1960s, proved very suitable during the prevailing economic situation, and could now be reinforced with an emphasis on durability. Within commerce, the range was extended with various types of well-designed basic goods. There were functional basic clothes that were designed to resist changes in fashion, inspired by work clothes and uniform fashions, there was basic furniture made of pine and chipboard that would meet people's basic needs, and there was not least KF's generic low-priced range Blåvitt, where everything but the most essential had been peeled away from the uniform packaging. Solidarity with weaker groups in society was also strengthened, and design issues very much revolved around solving practical problems that made life easier for children, the elderly and the disabled. The last area was not new but had long been undermined as aids for the disabled were generally regarded as a failure of medical science. The work environment also came into focus: serving the public became for many young designers more important than serving the companies.

Many other smart products for children came into production. Carl-Arne Breger designed an innovative child's bicycle seat in plastic for Rex in 1975. The principle was similar to the one used by Bertil Aldman for his aforementioned child seat, with a moulded seat that provided support for the entire body. As the seat was facing in the direction of travel, the child was secured with a harness belt, as opposed to the rear-facing child seat where a two-point belt was enough. The foot protectors, which were an extension of the seat and came down on either side of the rear wheel, were an important detail. They effectively prevented a common cause of accidents, which existed with older seats, that the children's feet or toes got stuck in the bicycle's spokes. The seat was given an orange colour that became typical of the 1970s, and that had been introduced by Televerket as a warning colour (teleorange) on cars and telephone booths as early as 1959. Other child-related products from this period were a series of singularly practical, double-walled mugs, cups, jugs, plates and bowls that Sven-Eric Juhlin designed for Gustavsberg. They were stable, strong and retained both heat and cold better than other products.

However, perhaps the most revolutionary was the baby carrier launched under the name Hjärtenära (Close to the heart) in 1973 by the company BabyBjörn. It had been designed by the father of four Björn Jakobson and his wife, the textile designer Lillemor Jakobson. The family was used as a test group and the basic idea was based on new medical evidence from the USA, which indicated the importance of a close connection between child and parents during the child's first year. The harness's position against

Fig. 4.13 BabyBjörn's baby carrier, launched in 1973, was one example of a number of Swedish products that at this time were designed to create security and safety for the weak and vulnerable in society. Baby carriers also gave men the opportunity to increase their closeness to their children. The picture of the baby carrier shows the 1983 model.

the chest and stomach gave maximum body contact and eye contact. The body heat and close fit meant that the child could feel as one with the parent, which helped in the adjustment to life outside the womb. Supported by the recommendations of paediatricians, BabyBjörn's baby carriers quickly became a hit and the models, fabrics, patterns and colours were updated over time. Even in the early advertising images one can see that fathers were also encouraged to wear the harness, which was perhaps not so revolutionary for the soft Swedish fathers of the 1970s. However, it would take until 1996 before it became common practice on the international market. That is when the pastel-coloured models and the models adapted to babies were supplemented with a black gender-neutral and suit-matching variant, which practically turned the carrier into a fashion accessory (www.babybjorn.com).

There were development funds available for aids for the elderly, disabled and the improvement of the working environment, which could be applied for through, for example, the state Handikappinstitutet (Swedish Handicap Institute) and Arbetarskyddsfonden (Swedish Work Environment Fund). This gave young designers unique opportunities for more systematic development work within several areas. A long and severe mining strike in Malmfälten (the great mining fields in the far north of Sweden) in the final months of 1969 had put the focus on work environment issues. At the same time there was an increasing need for various aids as a result of the de-institutionalization that was taking place in Sweden, where more and more disabled people sought out independent housing and a life in society. The traditional debate on braces and prostheses was now abandoned in favour of more rational reasoning on aid support and the place of disabled people in society. They began to be seen as a resource and not a burden, something Henry Ford had recognized as early as the 1920s when he employed nearly 10,000 workers with different disabilities on the same conditions as those who were 'healthy and ready' (Brunnström 1997).

Technically sophisticated projects were held in high regard and among the more high-profile pioneering projects were Dagmar and Henrik Wahlforss's attempts during the late 1960s to make the battery-powered four-wheeled Permobil wheelchair more manageable and manoeuvrable. Carl-Göran Craoford and Torsten Dahlin, who had received their basic training through ASEA commissions with Rune Zernell, broke away and started their own company. Among their first joint assignments was a comprehensive and ergonomically thorough project developing several generations of printing presses for Solna Offset, which were tested by printing workers with full-scale models. In fact, many ergonomic studies were carried out at various workplaces with support from the user groups. This included operating theatres (Mike Stott & Henrik Wahlforss 1974), welding workplaces (Bengt Palmgren & Henrik Wahlforss 1975), stretchers for ambulance staff (Per Lindahl & Bengt Palmgren 1983) and Roland Lindhé Design's (RLD) long-term work with Ericsson's terminals. The projects were time-consuming and extensive, which is why there were many group projects.

The most extensive work environment project, however, concerned ergonomic hand tools for Bahco. It started with a series of revolutionary ergonomic screwdrivers by Ergoskruvmejslar (Håkan Bergkvist, Hans Himbert & Bengt Palmgren 1978–1982) and had in 2006 generated about 30 patents or pattern patents, 400 new professional tools and a turnover of about two billion Swedish kronor (Pagold 2006). The painstaking work on the screwdriver led this centuries-old tool into a new era.

Instead of judging the screwdriver by the quality of the steel as the starting point, now all the attention was focused on the design of the handle. Many models of handle were developed, which various professionals were able to try out while people studied, interviewed, measured torque and photographed. What they arrived at was a thick and round but at the same time somewhat striated handle in black polypropylene that filled the whole hand and thus gave the maximum contact and frictional surface. Compared with traditional grips, the new grips improved torque by 30 per cent when the hands were dry and a full 100 per cent when the hands were sweaty or covered in oil. The screwdriver with a two-hand grip was particularly innovative, and was also fitted with an inbuilt nut socket that made it possible to get extra torque with a spanner. There was really only one miscalculation: the new screwdriver would have had a greater impact if it had not coincided with the introduction of electric screwdrivers.

The projects were often concerned with the development of relatively simple and obvious everyday aids. Some examples were the curvy rheumatic pen that could be used with a thumb web grip and could be weighted if necessary by filling it with sand or lead pellets (Hans Tollin in the Gothenburg-based Designkonsulterna in 1978), an anatomically designed lift chair for lifting the disabled (A&E Design 1975) and the foldable lightweight wheelchair Swede 24 Champ, which was developed in collaboration with the successful wheelchair racing athlete Bo Lindkvist (Carl-Axel Andersson and Morgan Ferm in the Malmö-based 3D Industridesign in 1984). Another innovative wheelchair from the same time was the band-wheel fitted shower and toilet chair Mobil for patients who wanted to take care of their own needs (A&E Design).

At Gustavsberg's plastics factory they focused persistently and systematically on developing simpler hand tools. Jan-Olof Landqvist realized his thesis on large handicap-friendly easy-grip levers for mixing taps, while Sven-Eric Juhlin began a collaboration with Henrik Wahlforss and Maria Benktzon that resulted in two well-known products: a gripping device for the disabled in 1973 and a bread saw for rheumatics in 1974. Experiences from woodworking were applied to the bread saw, resulting in the bread knife, which had been standardized in the 1940s, getting a saw-like character. A high knife blade for stability was combined with a saw handle, which reduced the involvement of several muscle groups. A cutting aid in the form of a plastic mitre block was manufactured as an accessory, which facilitated the cutting process for the visually impaired by holding the knife and bread in place. The bread knife project has resulted in various spin-offs in the form of, for example, knife series from both the American firm Tupperware (1998) and IKEA (David Crafoord and Ulrika Vejbrink, Ergonomidesign 2002).

The collaboration between Sven-Eric Juhlin and Maria Benktzon turned out to be particularly fruitful and resulted in numerous studies on grips and aids. After 1979 they were included together with many of the above-mentioned Stockholm-based

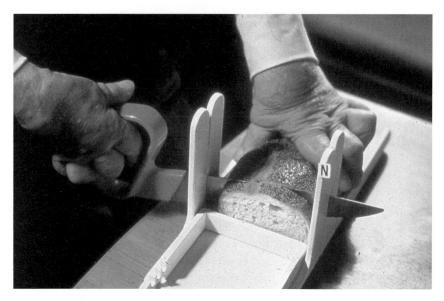

Fig. 4.14 Sweden's most prominent design consultancy Veryday (formerly Ergonomidesign) had its breakthrough in the 1970s with practical aids that were based on extensive research relating primarily to handles and grips. The bread saw in the picture was developed in 1974 to facilitate the cutting ability for rheumatics but was also significant in the development of ergonomically optimal grips for a number of later products for people without disabilities. A special plastic cutting aid gave extra support to the knife blade.

designers in the collectively owned enterprise Ergonomi Design Gruppen (a merger of Designgruppen from 1969 and Wahlforss's company Ergonomidesign from 1970), a limited liability company since 2001 and once again named Ergonomidesign, (now Veryday). One of their most famous projects, which most people will have come into contact with at some point, is the so-called SAS-kannan (SAS coffee pot), which not only SAS but about thirty airlines all over the world use to serve hot drinks on board. Since the 1950s, SAS had the elegant stainless steel coffee pot that Folke Arström had designed but it was neither comfortable to grip nor pour from. Cabin crews also complained that it was easy to burn oneself on and resulted in overload injuries of the hands, shoulders and forearms. Particularly straining was when crew were serving window seat passengers and had to stretch the several-kilograms-heavy coffee pot over people's heads. Maria Benktzon and Sven-Eric Juhlin were therefore tasked with developing a completely new coffee pot with the cabin crews. The work was carried out between 1984 and 1987 and a large number of handles, coffee pot shapes and spout designs were tested in different work situations, at the same time as the loads on different muscle groups were measured and evaluated. There were numerous specifications required. The coffee pot should be drip-free, able to withstand rough treatment, fit in the storage lockers and withstand temperature differences from sub-zero up to 120 degrees (Pagold 2006).

Fig. 4.15 The Scandinavian airline SAS has since the beginning in 1946 always collaborated with talented designers. In the mid-1980s, the company Ergonomidesign's work allowed the cabin crews to participate in the design process of developing an optimally user-friendly plastic serving jug that was supposed to replace the old stainless one (shown in this photo) designed by Folke Arström in the 1950s. See also Fig. 4.16.

Fig. 4.16 Plastic serving jug designed for Scandinavian airline SAS. See also Fig. 4.15.

The new pot was made of polycarbonate plastic in a, what may seem in retrospect obvious, elliptical shape with a separate spout and a long curved handle that began almost down by the baseplate. The elliptical shape made it easier to reach in pouring situations. With a separate spout, one can control the flow when serving and since the end of the spout consists of an inserted stainless steel tube, the coffee pot is able to cut the stream without subsequent dripping.

The design of the handle means that one always finds the right balance point regardless of the amount of coffee in the pot. The grooved surface on the inside of the handle also increases friction. Opening the lid of the old coffee pot required two hands. The new coffee pot had a foldable lid that by means of a small lip could be opened with the thumb, which in turn facilitates refilling. Lastly, the spout's slant, together with a concave chamfering of the pot's body, gives the whole pot an active, attractive and resilient shape.

Several of Ergonomidesign's projects, not only the SAS coffee pot, have been groundbreaking, even seen from an international perspective. It is true that some of HFI's consumer-oriented projects from the 1940s and 1950s have been fundamental within the applied product areas, but on the other hand they lacked Ergonomidesign's aesthetic refinement and almost scientific precision in the design process. In particular, the attractive tools for the disabled, which they developed in the 1970s and 1980s with public funding, were pioneering works in a field that would later become internationally known as Universal Design or Inclusive Design, in Swedish often called *Design för alla* (Design for Everyone). Some fundamental considerations here are that the product should be usable by everyone and satisfy many different needs, should be easy to understand and should be possible to handle with minimal effort. Ergonomidesign's structured and user-adapted design methodology has also been fundamental, both in the design schools' teaching and for many Swedish design firms focused on industrial design.

5   The Limitless Design, 1980s to 2000s

The Visual Values Are Upgraded

Postmodernism's breakthrough in design arrived with a bang at the Milan Exhibition in September 1981. Under the direction of Olivetti's former chief designer Ettore Sottsass Jr the Italian Memphis group with its twenty-odd members showed a series of furniture and other household goods that provoked the public by breaking down hierarchies and challenging so-called good taste. There were colourful and decorated objects with a lot of pink and dots. There was flirting with both pop art and high culture, where precious materials were combined with cheap and the authentic met the imitation. The favourite material was the MDF board, which was painted in glossy colours or covered with veneer or plastic laminate. A common feature of the collection was that the traditional concept of function had often been deliberately set aside. The communicative function was as important as the practical. One of the most significant objects was Sottsass's large bookcase or rather the room sculpture Carlton, which was playfully structured with both straight and crooked shelves as well as a couple of drawers, all painted in a whole palette of colours. For this piece its function as a bookcase was secondary. It was more important to show off the books than to accommodate them and Carlton should be experienced, not just serve a functional purpose.

Memphis garnered considerable media interest and new designers gradually attached themselves. In annual collections more than 300 objects altogether were exhibited all over the world until the group disbanded in 1988. Memphis came to inspire many young designers by emphasizing the conceptual and the spectacular as an alternative to the eminently practical. Its legacy among critics was mixed. Some argued that Memphis was just another fad, but hardly anyone could deny the movement's significance for the widening of both sensory experiences and design concepts. Interest in visual communication, semiotics, metaphors and art history took off. At the same time, the movement gave the atrophied modernists an excuse to finally get to play with some colours and shapes or, as Stephen Bayley put it in 1991, Memphis 'became quite appropriately the most celebrated cliché of recent years' (Kristoffersson 2003: 32).

A Swedish provocation almost on a par with Memphis was the chair Concrete, which was exhibited at the Stockholm Furniture Fair a few months later. The chair, which was a degree project from Konstfack by Jonas Bohlin (b. 1953), consisted of untreated steel tubes with seat and backrest made of raw concrete. One person very affected by this strange experience was the art-interested furniture manufacturer Sven Lundh from Källemo, who decided to take it into production. Even though it was only produced in a limited edition, it was a daring project, not least for the company's good reputation. Concrete was in fact no ordinary chair, intended for sitting on. Instead, it was considered to be a modern conversation piece or an early example of concept design. It was, in its heavy, cold and inflexible structure a comment on all the 1970s-magnificence in design. Concrete created a justified excitement, and among the proponents of functionalism also a great deal of annoyance.

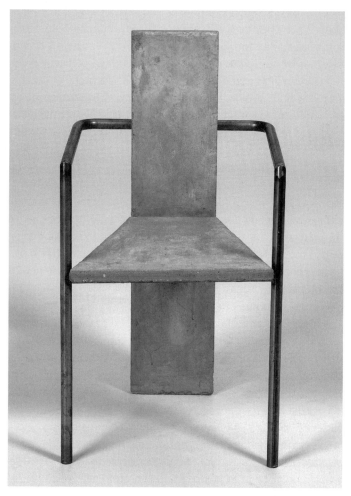

Fig. 5.1 Jonas Bohlin shocked many when he in 1981 exhibited Concrete, a chair made of steel tubes and rough concrete. It broke completely with the Swedish thinking of the 1960s and 1970s about how a functional chair with a product declaration should be constituted. In the same way that the Memphis group's exhibition that year marked a breakthrough for postmodernist design, Concrete came to embody the Swedish version of the same movement.

While the concrete chair was of limited interest to the average Swede, it was defi-nitely an eye-opener for the furniture industry and the household goods sector as a whole. It represented a different perspective from the one that the Swedish Society of Crafts and Design and Möbelinstitutet (Furniture Institute) had long enforced. Old values that had been the norm until the early 1900s were restored, such as that, in addition to purely functional, rational requirements there were other legitimate experience values; not to mention that economic conditions had also improved. While Arne Jacobsen's three-legged Myranstol (Ant chair) was fitted with a fourth leg and the office's swivel chairs were for safety reasons fitted with a fifth, John Kandell (1925–1991) instead designed an elegant little three-legged chair Camilla (1982) inspired by the Swedish milking-stool; at the same time his furniture role model Philippe Starck designed his famous three-legged chair Costes for a famous Paris café of the same name. In 1985 Kandell emphasized the chair's ceremonial values with his powerful chieftains chair Solitär and its symbolic values in the chair Victory in 1990, which had Churchill's V-sign in the back-piece. Mats Theselius's (b. 1956) impressive elk-skin armchair from 1985 also evoked the feeling of sitting on a throne, but a robust one with something of a Wild West feel. The same year, Börge Lindau and Bo Lindekrantz's playful but extremely ascetic chair Planka was released. It was a tribute to the Dutch master Gerrit Rietveld and his simple plywood chairs from the 1910s, and appeared to be a stylized image of 'the man on the beach, who has stuck a plank in the sand and rolled a newspaper to support the neck' (Gordan 2005: 252).

In the standard work on Swedish furniture (Boman 1991) Jill Dufwa highlights the Gothenburg designer Olle Anderson (b. 1939) as someone who has perhaps most cleverly and humorously interpreted the Memphis group's intentions. The pendulum fitting Halo There for Boréns from 1982–1983 and Stol 590 for Klaessons from 1988 are two excellent examples from that period of this jack-of-all-trades' rich produc-tion. In 1983 A&E Design made the advanced five-legged floor lamp Stella Polaris for Yamagiwa from Japan in the same playful spirit. Creativity translated into a more laid-back style also characterized many other design areas during the 1980s. Sara Kristoffersson (2003) particularly emphasizes 10-gruppen's patterns, which she believes are very reminiscent of Memphis's; for example, Birgitta Hahn's Buenos-Aires from 1986. Ulf Hanses' conical thermos jug with a clever swivel spout from 1987 for Boda Nova International has a playfulness very much in the spirit of Memphis, as does H. C. Ericson's poster for Lammhults from 1985 where he wreaks havoc across the black type area with the names Lindau, Lindekrantz and Lammhults set in upper-case type and printed in a dozen different colours. Colours also exploded among IKEA's new ventures in their strictly production technology controlled manufacturing. The armchair Tärnaby by Jan Dranger in red, yellow and green from 1983 as well as Knut and Marianne Hagberg's equally colourful children's furniture Puzzel from 1988 are good examples (Demokratisk design 1995).

At the same time we have to understand that postmodernist ideas in general were relatively unenthusiastically received in Sweden, where functional fundamentalism was deeply rooted. The textile designer Inez Svensson interpreted the zeitgeist in her own ingenious way in an ad campaign for Industriförbundet in 1985:

> In Sweden, we often want to solve the function in a good way, but then we think it is embarrassing to do more. Great design, great colours – that is verging on the immoral. Look around you. Look at Swedish phones, hobs, shoes, flower-pots, whatever you want. It is so Swedish it brings tears to your eyes. Swedish, solid, splendid – and boring. I long for a better balance between reason and imagination. I think it would be reasonable if Swedish industry gave way to more imagination. Those who have are actually doing well. (Hald 1985: 72)

During the 1980s the major deregulation of many traditionally public services began, including telecommunications. Privatization meant that activities were subjected to increased competitive pressures and the telephone in many countries went from being a leased product to a consumer product. This change meant that not only the operators but also the phone manufacturers found themselves in a completely new situation. Previously they had dealt business-to-business, that is to say they sold large items to professional buyers with a high degree of technical understanding; now they were going to sell their devices to the ordinary consumer, who was only moderately interested in technology. This conversion resulted in a changed view of the telephone as an artefact in which visual values were re-eval-uated. That the phone had to work was obvious; however, there were individual preferences, which mostly concerned the enveloping casing's shape and colour, which now had to be met.

The Swedish Televerket had, since the telephone's infancy, existed in a world in which priority was given to major standardized models to simplify service and keep prices down. That was true for the black Bakelite telephones from the 1930s until the 1950s and the standard grey Dialog telephones in the 1960s and 1970s (in former Eastern Germany it was called Die Graue Maus). As a reaction to the domi-nance of black as a colour, colourful plastic phone covers started appearing after the Second World War. These styling initiatives were, however, halted at an early stage with various justifications: they had a disruptive influence on the function, increased the workload for the office's maintenance staff and could give rise to requirements for cord colours in the same shades.

In the 1980s, when the responsibility for the telephone's handling and care was placed on the subscriber, this kind of evasion was no longer good enough. At the same time Televerket noticed that there was not much demand for the regular range, but instead consumers bought cheap imported telephones from Asia of sometimes dubious quality. In response they turned to three industrial designers: Lars Lallerstedt (b. 1938) in Stockholm, Jan Hampf in Gothenburg and Richard Lindahl in Malmö; tasking them with designing something that 'titillates slightly and pushes the bounda-ries'. The goal was a completely new Televerket family consisting of what they called 'Designtelefoner (Design telephones)'. Production proceeded quickly thanks to the new approach of outsourcing both construction and manufacturing to China; it took

Fig. 5.2 The plastic bicycle is in many contexts considered one of Sweden's most failed industrial projects. Despite interesting design efforts, spectacular marketing and many millions spent in local grants, the world proved not to be ready for the odd creation.

only about a year from the sketchbook to the sales counter. The initiative was a success in the sense that they produced a suite of new, fresh models at acceptable prices, which should have pleased Inez Svensson and definitely increased the market potential (Brunnström 2006: 23–24).

One of the 1980s most spectacular and publicized Swedish industrial projects was the Itera bicycle, designed primarily by the Gothenburg designer Claes Nordenstam (b. 1943). It had a frame, fork, wheel and crank set in moulded fibre-glass reinforced plastic composite, and the hope was that the revolutionary plastic bicycle with the help of a massive advertising campaign would conquer the world market. It was an excellent idea and a product that with local grants was expected to provide many jobs at Wilhelmina Plast in remote northern Sweden. Since the bicycle was stainless it was named Evighetsmaskinen (Perpetual Motion Machine), even though some journalists chose instead to call it Anacondan (the Anaconda) as the sprung design caused the bike occasionally to slither like a snake between one's legs. But it was not the only reason the project failed, in 1985, after just about three years in production. The technology historian Jan Hult points to several factors: the bicycle boom that had come after the oil crises had begun to die down, the weight was too heavy due to the extra material that was needed to compensate for the limitation on its thickness in the manufacturing process, which in turn gave this extremely functional conveyance a robust and odd, almost postmodern character.

Furthermore, the price was yuppie-related and was set far too high when it became apparent that the bicycle did not appeal to trend-setting urbanites (Hult 1992).

Design Is Recognized as an Economic Success Factor

Televerket's (from 1993 Telia and 2002 Telia Sonera; since 2016 Telia Company AB) use of design as a competitive weapon was a prescient response to the wave of cheap imports from mainly Japan, Singapore, Hong Kong and Taiwan that swept over the Western world. The imports turned out to be not only cheaper but also began to compete in terms of quality, which was a major problem for Swedish industry, which was used to being able to refer to 'Made in Sweden' as an indicator of quality. In particular, Japanese industry was far advanced with high quality assurance in car manufacturing and advanced technology in the consumer electronics area, along with excellent market-driven design. Governments in Japan and in many European countries had long been pursuing an active design policy with the intention of increasing their export earnings. Back in Sweden, many tradition-rich and labour-intensive business categories were already ruined, such as shipbuilding, the textile and clothing industry and parts of the precision mechanical industry. In order not to fall even further behind, there was therefore every reason to push forward even in Sweden.

It was the non-profit organization Svensk Form (Swedish Society of Crafts and Design, before 1976 Svenska Slöjdföreningen) who, with a small state subsidy, had borne a large share of responsibility over the years when it came to asserting the interests of contemporary Swedish design. This had mainly been done through the Stockholm Exhibition of 1930 and H55, where it was a major attraction. The publication of an ambitious design journal (*Form*) also played a significant role. During a period in the 1960s they also ran a permanent exhibition venue in the form of a Design Center in Stockholm and, through their local chapter, a similar venue in Malmö from 1964, which still exists today under the name Form/Design Center. Successful design centres existed in many industrialized countries, so it therefore came as no surprise that the government, as an offensive measure, granted funds to the Swedish Society of Crafts and Design together with SIND (now Nutek) to reopen and run a Design Center Stockholm in 1985 (Mötesplats för form och design 1999).

Two years earlier the association had instituted an annual jury award, Utmärkt Svensk Form (Excellent Swedish Design), to highlight good efforts in the various design disciplines. The proposal came from the then president of the design section H. C. Ericson, who also designed the punchy logo. The jury, consisting of representatives from the professional design associations, weighed a variety of assessment criteria in the same way as the ecolabel Svanen. As it was design that was supposed to be the focus, however, the design criteria were prioritized. The award was to be considered a mark of quality and was aimed primarily at producers who could use it in their marketing. The selected products were made into travelling exhibitions, which were exhibited at venues around the country and came to be very significant in raising both the industry's and public's awareness of design (Robach 1995). Utmärkt

Svensk Form survived until 2002 and was replaced four years later by the new award Design S, which puts more emphasis on the problem-solving function of design.

Towards the end of the 1980s national design ambitions became increasingly clear. Design was necessary to stimulate growth in Swedish industry and it was important to conquer new industries in addition to the already design-intensive furniture industry. Increasing focus was directed towards product-oriented industrial design. Stiftelsen Svensk Industridesign (Swedish Industrial Design Foundation or SVID) was formed in 1989 with responsibility for the state's promotion of design within commercial policy. Torsten Dahlin, from Ergonomi Design Gruppen (now called Veryday), was hired as the CEO. SVID took over the entire operation of Design Center Stockholm but shut down the exhibition and vacated the premises in 1991. Instead, they specialized more in giving design advice to industry, initiated education and research efforts, and actively agitated for an increased use of design. Exemplary design projects were highlighted and presented in a persuasive way in, among other things, a number of films on the theme 'Design är lönsamt (Design is profitable)'. Regional offices were gradually opened across the country and, in the spirit of Förmedlingsbyrån (The Mediation agency) from the 1910s, they attempted to link designers with industry. However, now they had a little more financial muscle and could, for about a decade, hand out so-called design-cheques for 25,000 Swedish kronor so that small and mid-sized companies could for the first time have the opportunity to work with a designer. During the 1990s a total of almost 17 million kronor was appropriated for such projects (Kolmodin & Pelli 2005).

Parallel to and in close cooperation with the emerging SVID, a new Swedish design college was born in 1989. It was the first since the establishment of Konstfack and HDK in the 1840s. Located at Umeå University, and created alongside a new art college, it was initially attached to the Faculty of Humanities and later to the Faculty of Natural Science and Technology. The need for artistic higher education in Norrland – the north of Sweden – had been discussed since the 1970s and after a good deal of lobbying, the university could boast that it had both an art college and an adjacent design college (since 2009 also a school of architecture). The latter would, as stated in the initial planning stages, focus on 'product and environmental design' with healthcare as the main focus. This was gradually changed to a more general industrial profile. Bengt Palmgren, who was also recruited from Ergonomi Design Gruppen, was appointed as head teacher. New purpose-built premises were arranged in cooperation with the municipality in a beautiful signal tower by the Umeå River. An annex building housed a magnificent full-scale laboratory with workshops and a machine park with powerful computer support.

The Umeå Institute of Design's (UID) determined management quickly profiled its curriculum after German models (Ulm and Bauhaus schools) as a demanding elite school. This was signalled through a large international element, a close cooperation with industry, a high degree of realism in the presentations as well as, by Swedish standards, unusually heavy demands on teachers and students. The unique industrial design profile and the close cooperation with SVID immediately gave the school a national status. This reputation was reinforced when some of Sweden's finest indus-trial designers were attached to the school as professors and mentors, such as Rune Monö, Sven-Eric Juhlin, Mike Stott, Hans Philip Zachau, Aina Nilsson and Roland Lindhé. The investment has paid off in the sense that a completed education there has almost always qualified students for a job after graduation. This level of efficiency, however, has, according to critics, been achieved at the expense of a sometimes overly conventional profile, lacking artistic and creative innovation. Nevertheless, the UID has in recent years been ranked as one of the best design schools in the world.

The Umeå Institute of Design's location was an important regional policy initiative which the school implemented by creating a series of collaborative projects with companies and institutions in Upper Norrland. As soon as 1994, the first design company from Norrland was started, Struktur Design, by some recent graduates. The company had a successful beginning with a project for Konftel in the form of an elegant loud-speaking conference phone (Plate 18). In recent years they have also distinguished themselves through a user-friendly, IT-based service design project called Tillit (Trust), which simplifies and streamlines communications between patients, municipalities and counties in Västerbotten. With its headquarters in Umeå, Struktur Design quickly expanded: in 2009 they had offices in Skellefteå, Härnösand and Stockholm, with about ten employees in total.

Swedish pioneers in manufacturing also increased their efforts to obtain a more market-oriented design profile and often looked for international inspiration. Electrolux had a large international network of contacts, even before the dynamic Hugo Lindström's (1920–2009) time as head of design, 1963–1985, particularly among American designers. The renowned Raymond Loewy helped the company with refrigerator sketches in 1939, while another famous American industrial designer, Lurelle Guild, had designed the vacuum cleaner Z30 the year before. In the 1950s several design commissions such as washing machines, vacuum cleaners and refrigerators went to Carl Otto, but also to Don Dailey & Associates and Chuck Waltman. In order to further cultivate the American market, Lindström took on Bob Bourke, best known as the man responsible for the successful design of Studebaker, at Loewy's office, as well as hiring the British firm Ogle Design for many commissions. In particular, the design of vacuum cleaners was often closely linked to contempo-rary automotive design. During the early 1980s, even before the acquisition of their competitor Zanussi in 1984, Electrolux had turned to Italian car designers in order to offer consumers more challenging designs. The design house Bertone made some elegant car design-inspired proposals with slender, slightly uneven designs while Coggiola was responsible for a more playful vacuum cleaner design in a typically postmodern spirit (sketches at Centrum för Näringslivshistoria [Centre for Business History]).

Coggiola and Bertone had both helped the Swedish car industry to upgrade the designs of their models in the 1970s, but only when it concerned small special projects; Sergio Coggiola had designed the Saab Sonett III and made a few vari-ations on Pelle Petterson's Volvo P1800, while Nuccio Bertone had sold services to Saab in connection with the Sonett project and designed the Volvo 262 coupe and later also the 780. When Saab in the beginning of the 1980s considered itself ready to develop, in collaboration with Fiat/Lancia, a new, more exclusive and larger standard model to succeed the successful 900 series, they turned to these two Italian design houses and also to a third: Italdesign. Italdesign won an invited competition through the car design guru Giorgio Giugiaro. Saab's design team, led by Björn Envall, would be responsible for the interior design while responsibility for the exterior was handed over to Giugiaro; a far from simple division of labour. The model that came into production in 1984 was called Saab 9000 but in spite of their best efforts the design was met with a relatively unenthusiastic response. 'Another euro box' and 'whatever became of weird' were two typical American comments (Tunberg 1997).

All the more interesting was Saab's investment in the dream car project EV1 (Experimental Vehicle), which was presented in the following year. The sleek, wedge-shaped experimental car with a Targa top exhibited many interesting solutions that pointed to the future. The upper part was completely glazed and fitted with solar cells, which powered a fan that ventilated the coupe, the front and rear sections were made of tough but malleable aramid fibre-reinforced composites and the dashboard was a black panel. The EV1 capped Envall's time as chief designer, 1969–1992. The only copy is now in the Saab Museum in Trollhättan (Plate 19). If it had gone into production Saab's recent history could have been completely different.

Fig. 5.3 Saab EV1. This sketch is a draft from 1984 from Björn Envall's sketchbook.

After Jan Wilsgaard's long stint as head of design at Volvo, 1950–1990, the British designer Peter Horbury was recruited. His arrival was a breath of fresh air, accompanied by the typical post-war British fascination with the somewhat exotic Swedish welfare state with its well-established design reputation. Volvo, who for several decades had been refining and profiting from the functional box-like design, was beginning to enter an identity crisis.

With an outsider's perspective and convincing rhetoric, Horbury began by speaking enthusiastically, like no one before, about Volvo's roots, its very DNA; a similar revitalization effort was also taking place at Volkswagen. Volvo's unique story would be emphasized and communicated; a story that captured the values the consumer had learned to appreciate in the Swedish car brand: quality, safety and consideration for the environment (Zetterlund 2002).

Horbury claimed that a designer must know and even appreciate design history to find a brand identity. Among the older Volvo models he particularly highlighted the Duett, Amazon and P1800s of the 1950s and 1960s. There was a rich supply of designs to dip into here. At the same time, he argued in a later interview, as an actor in a global market you have to be able to look beyond the traditionally narrow national (Birch 2000):

> Function is everything – historically. Volvo is Swedish, and Swedish equates to function. Previously, that 'drove' everything at Volvo. If a farmer working in northern Sweden in an outside temperature of –40°C (–40°F) wearing gloves could climb into a Volvo and operate switches and those switches never failed, that was primarily what was wanted. Volvo was – and is – all about safety, too. From pioneering three-point seat belts in the Amazon of 1959, we now have comprehensive systems, including airbag side curtains and anti-whiplash seats. However, we are selling cars to businessmen in Frankfurt, film directors in L.A., and lady drivers in Tokyo. They have a different set of rules, and to them, function and safety are not enough. They want style. And although switches still need to work in –40°C (–40°F) temperatures, they also need the right sort of tactility to be acceptable to customers other than just Swedish farmers.

Many of Horbury's ideas were already realized in the concept car ECC, which was unveiled in 1992 and would affect a number of later Volvo models. Here was a considerably softer, rounder design language and a more luxurious interior than in previous models. There were also clear retro features in the form of a V-shaped hood and accentuated shoulders running along the sides of the car. The reinvented designs were repeated above all in the coupe and convertible model C70 (1996), the sedan models S80 (1998) and S60 (2000) as well as the SUV XC90 (2002), but also included in the face-lift of the best-selling station wagon V70 (2000). Increasingly, non-visual experiences such as the sound of the car door when it was shut were taken into account.

With the concept cars they certainly took a gamble, the design partly inspired by sports cars, but only a few fine details usually made it into the final production. On the other hand, no fewer than three brand new sports car brands were launched in Sweden during the 1990s, without help from Italian design houses. The first project

Solon 2000 from 1992 was not completely thought through. The car did have gull-wing doors and a Ferrari-shape but it lacked essential sports car attributes: speed and sound. Solon 2000 was in fact a small hybrid electric vehicle of the plug-in type, which could reach up to 150 kilometres per hour and sounded like a sewing machine. The result was that only five complete cars are said to have been built (Tekniska museet).

The second project was launched in 1994 in the form of the small challenger Jösse Car from Värmland. The initiator Bengt Lidmalm, with the help of Hans Philip Zachau from the design company New Perspectives in Gothenburg, concentrated on classic sports car design with a touch of Pininfarinas Cisitalia. The car was called Indigo and was based on Volvo parts, had fibreglass bodywork, the engine placed centrally and a heavy-duty exhaust system with an appealing sound. At the start there were plans for a production of 500 cars a year but after only 40 had been completed the company had to close down for economic reasons four years later.

The third project was Koenigsegg from Skåne, an even more comprehensive sports car project led by Christian Von Koenigsegg. When in 1995 Ergonomidesign was involved in the design the decision was made not to try to compete with the sector that Jösse Car had got involved in. Instead they thought big and set out to build the world's best sports car. It was a goal that was partly realized when in 2005 they broke the Guinness World Record for the fastest production car by reaching a speed of 388 kilometres per hour.

Design had long played a self-evident role within Swedish car production with increasingly large teams and an increasing number of competencies involved. Within Ericsson's mobile phone division, on the other hand, it was not until the 1990s that they realized the impact of design. The technologically strong Ericsson was permeated by an engineer culture that was resistant to change, believing they knew what the customer wanted. It worked when they were making their switchboard systems, but faired much worse in terms of consumer products for an unregulated telecommunications market. Ever since Ralph Lysell left the company in 1945, Ericsson had contented itself with external design consultants whose primary role was to satisfy the engineers' requests. In the 1990s, cell phones became smaller and lighter with a weight that was measured in grams rather than hectograms and kilograms as before. Gradually the realization came that mobile phones were not just used for work, but were becoming common consumer items; however, in the mid-1990s there were still a series of fixed ideas among Ericsson's engineers about what a mobile phone should look like.

In particular, there should be a large antenna that signalled power, so that the phone really communicated its message, a perhaps mixed message at a time when radiation risks began to be discussed. And when they reinforced this with their slogan 'Make Yourself Heard' it was very much out of step at a time when the emphasis turned to everything you could do with your mobile phone in addition to talking into it.

In 1998, the Finnish company Nokia emerged as the world leader in the mobile phone market with its more consumer-oriented design strategy. The same year it launched the first phone with a built-in antenna: the spectacular, silvery Nokia 8810. It confirmed that it was no longer just a matter of satisfying a communication need but must also appeal to a desire for style. While Nokia was focusing on a design-intensive, segmented production with close connections to the fashion industry, Ericsson's mobile phones were as black and square as the landlines before the Cobra phone in the 1950s. And while Ericsson launched one or maybe two models a year, Nokia released around twenty. Ericsson's mobile phones certainly sold well enough for a long time and just keeping up with deliveries was a big job. But when one model started resembling another, the company's design consultants, headed by Richard Lindahl, started to worry; it was obvious that the senior engineers who led product development had got stuck in a rut. Salvation came in 2001 when the mobile phone division was merged with Sony in the new company, Sony Ericsson, and they could take advantage of the Japanese company's long experience in consumer-driven design and marketing (Brunnström 2006). New concepts such as design management, design as competitiveness and strategic design now started to become part of Swedish design vocabulary. Ten years later Sony bought the whole mobile phone division while Ericsson concentrated on system solutions.

The Personal Signature Becomes Increasingly Important

There were very few Swedish designers who before the yuppie era of the 1980s had been able to make a name for themselves through their work. The general feeling was that design work was a team effort and therefore the designer's signature was usually hidden behind the company name or possibly one designer's name. Ralph Lysell, for example, was virtually unknown before the 1990s and it was almost impossible to find out who had designed Ericsson's various mobile phones as recently as the 2000s. Highlighting individual designers in a collegial activity was considered disloyal and un-Swedish, which in turn has made Swedish designers unnecessarily anonymous and disproportionally absent from international surveys. The big exception has been the art industry that has almost always proudly highlighted its designers as an integral part of its business history.

The attitude was different in southern Europe where the designer more often had an architectural background with an artistic status that, as Kersti Sandin Bülow (2007) points out, has made 'the design more grandiose and public in its expression while the one in the Nordic countries is colloquially toned down through its association to serviceability and craft'. In America, on the other hand, where the designer had long had their background in fashion, advertising and set design, the mercantile qualities of the profession were often highlighted. There are plenty of examples that demonstrate these fundamental cultural differences. In 1959, for example, the

technical manager for Husqvarna lamented that teamwork could not be appreciated at all at the Milan Triennial after their designer, Sixten Sason, was denied the
opportunity to exhibit his products on the grounds that the work must be completely
independent.

A famous American example of the miraculous powers of the magicians of
streamlined design is Kemp Starrett's caricature in *The New Yorker* from the 1930s
where the chairman of a cookie company stands up in a board meeting and names
one of the most celebrated contemporary designers: 'Gentlemen – I Am Convinced
That Our Next New biscuit Must Be Styled by Norman Bel Geddes' (Brunnström
1997).

During the 1980s and 1990s there was a gradual change in attitude due to
several interacting factors that increased the interest in design issues. Within
graphic design traditional hot metal typesetting had been replaced by simplified
phototypesetting during the 1970s. A lot of the practical typography experience
consequently disappeared and was instead, through computerization and digitized

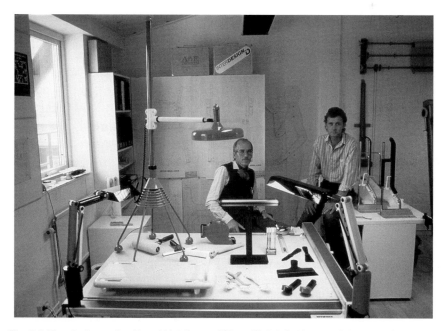

Fig. 5.4 The designer duo Tom Ahlström and Hans Ehrich (left) started the consulting firm
A & E Design in 1968. They have over the years in a somewhat un-Swedish way always
been very careful to make the company's logo visible on their designed products. In this
picture from 1987 they have arranged a selection of their homogeneous production, from
left, the desk lamp Lucifer for Fagerhult from 1975, the floor lamp Stella Polaris from 1983,
painting tools for Anza, Turn-O-Matic's queue ticket dispenser from 1974, toothbrushes
for Colgate, washing up brushes for Jordan and the bath board Rufus. Their later products
include the popular foldable museum stool Stockholm, which is used by more than 1,700
museums worldwide.

imaging, replaced by a general desire to experiment with layouts and typefaces; suddenly it became possible for everyone to be their own creator. As a result book-printing, for example, could experience problems with uneven blackness, inappropriate choices of paper, incorrect fibre direction, inadequate adhesive bindings, etc. At times texts were treated as decorative elements. One person who reacted to the frequent loss of functional legibility was the polemical typographer Carl Fredrik Hultenheim (1928–2010), who during the 1980s started his own popular seminar activity in protest. In a retrospective interview with Gunnar Ohrlander in the journal *Biblis* in 2003, he complained that everything had become design and argued that:

> It is not enjoyability, but serviceability that creates good everyday typography. Today, most believe that aesthetics precede function … a newspaper page is not interesting because it looks nice from distance, like a painting, but because it is readable. (Ohrlander 2003:9, 14)

This amateurism, however, had the advantage that it resulted in an increased interest in typography and book art in society, at the same time as the designer's role expanded. The prestigious annual quality award Svensk Bokkonst (Swedish Book Art), which had been suspended during the period 1978–1982, was now resumed with renewed vigour. New generations of book designers followed on from giants such as the brothers Karl-Erik and Vidar Forsberg. When Svensk Bokkonst in 1995 reviewed its activities, it was found that an increasing number of fonts were being used and that font preferences had changed. The once-popular sans serifs Univers and Helvetica had been replaced by the typical 1980s font Palatino, while Sabon, which worked equally well for both hot metal typesetting and phototypesetting, became increasingly important from the beginning of the 1990s. Garamond, Baskerville and Bodoni, however, were typefaces that had survived the changes in taste. Bo Berndal (1924–2013) emerged as one of the more productive typeface designers and has over the years designed hundreds of new typefaces. It was also no coincidence that he became the first recipient when the newly established Berling Prize was awarded in 1991.

New publishing houses entered the business with a greater emphasis on typographical quality. Biographies as well as art books in a broader sense became fashionable when the graphic designer was able to play a central role. Per Werme (b. 1939) made a suite of powerful architectural books for Byggförlaget, while Christer Jonson (b.1937) and Lars E. Pettersson (b. 1937) gained firm graphic control over production at the publishers Atlantis and Raster respectively; all three were also awarded the Berling Prize. In recent decades, interest in two-dimensional design has only increased and books and other printed media have especially appealed to female designers. The expression may vary but the individual style is usually discernible with designers such as Lotta Kühlhorn (b. 1963), Anna Larsson (b. 1963), Nina Ulmaja (b. 1967) and the group Hjärta Smärta with Angela Tillman Sperandio (b.1975) and Samira Bouabana (b. 1975).

As visual values were upgraded design began to be increasingly viewed as an economic success factor. A measure of this was the reawakened interest in housing exhibitions. A series of municipal and regional housing fairs started across the country, beginning with Upplands Väsby in 1985 (Bo 85). The fairs benefited the furniture and household goods sector, which gained new, popular venues to exhibit their latest collections. Not least, they came to mean a great deal in terms of opening the public's eyes to architecture, design and issues of taste and quality. Interest in Swedish design abroad also increased, which was reflected in a growing demand for Swedish design exhibitions. The first Western design exhibition ever held in China took place in 1976 on the theme Swedish Interior Design and drew over 3,000 visitors a day; interest was so great that the furniture had to be cordoned off with ropes so as not to be completely dismantled into its component parts. In the 1980s alone successful exhibitions followed in forty-odd countries, including in Latin America, Africa, Canada, Australia, the USA and India, and during the 1990s serious interest in Swedish design developed in Japan. Enquiries usually came through embassies and museums, while the Swedish Institute contributed financially and the Swedish Society of Crafts and Design produced. The items shown were largely products with the stamp 'Utmärkt Svensk Form (Excellent Swedish Design)' (Robach 1995).

Even though the exhibitions displayed a relatively wide range of consumer goods, furniture constituted a key element. The furniture industry had been both rationalized and toughened up by low-cost competition from domestic furniture giant IKEA. This development had been towards fewer and larger companies, production had been simplified as had the materials; chipboard and polyurethane plastic (plastic foam) facilitated serial production. The Million Programme, public space and fast-growing exports paved the way for larger volumes during the 1970s, but at the same time they were very much living off former glories. There was a good deal of beige and brown and elements of renewal were scarce. One of the exceptions was the design-driven furniture company Innovator Design with Jan Dranger and Johan Huldt, who used modern technology to create cheap furniture in new designs. The target group was mainly young people and the furniture, which was easy to stow away and came with washable, colourful covers, quickly became an export success, not least in Japan where Swedish and Nordic design was gaining a unique reputation. Another successful example was Lammhults, which had already hired the designers Börge Lindau and Bo Lindekrantz in the mid-1960s. Twenty years later, they accounted for 98 per cent of the company's extensive operations, of which about half was exported (Söderholm 2008).

New opportunities for awards celebrating quality, display possibilities in representative contexts, Swedish export successes, and media attention combined to stimulate furniture producers to innovate during the 1980s. Companies increasingly took on promising young designers with strong personal styles. Källemo in Värnamo was a front runner with a unique concept, thought up by the art-interested factory owner Sven Lundh. After having produced traditional upholstered furniture for about ten years, he started producing furniture as art in numbered editions. Through his art he created added value for the product, which built up an aura around the whole company, claims Ivar Björkman (1998), who has called Sven Lundh an expert on the production of auras. He received an extra boost from auction houses and the antique trade's growing interest in contemporary design with a personal signature.

For Lundh it all started with Johan Bohlin's concrete chair, which was produced in 100 copies (as well as ten copies equivalent to the graphical Épreuve d'artiste [artist proof]). This production of the genuinely different concrete chair was the beginning of a collaboration with a number of young Nordic designers, who all crossed the boundaries between art and design in their work. Production was passed on to subcontractors (in 2009 there were 120) and Lundh with his Källemo was thus behaving more like a modern furniture manufacturer. The result has been a long series of odd and spectacular furniture types, usually manufactured in small batches. In 1990 came a glaring yellow eye-catching cabinet named National Geographic, which celebrated twenty-five years of the renowned journal and its yellow cover (Plate 20). The cabinet was designed by Mats Theselius (b.1956), who also made several other high-profile, but not always so easily constructed pieces of furniture, which flirted with the American market.

Lundh's collaboration with his friend, the furniture designer and architect John Kandell (1925–1991), resulted in, for example, the development of a smart and minimalist bookshelf called Pilaster in 1989. The pillar-thin shelf was meant to be integrated into the architecture of difficult-to-use wall spaces. Pilaster quickly became popular when it became apparent that you could attractively pile up the books. Accordingly, it also became a frequently copied object. Among the newer works with a calculated classic status is the architectural theorist Johan Linton's recliner Caravaggio from 2002, designed with inspiration from the Italian Baroque artist's four hundred years older masterpiece *Entombment*. Precisely this kind of elegant narrative packaging with clear intellectual meta-values epitomized Lundh's thesis that furniture should have a strong effect but also be easy on the eye; quality is in the eye of the beholder rather than in the furniture's material durability. On Källemo's website the music fades out in a perpetual loop: 'It shall stand the wear of the eye' (Nordgren 2007).

Individualism, grandiosity and brand hysteria characterized the 1980s and 1990s. Surface and superficiality were in the foreground. Traditional gender barriers were crossed; Angela Partington (1996) described it as women becoming more voyeuristic and becoming interested in pornography and striptease, while men became more narcissistic and focused on fashion and body care. The period also meant that creators of the most varied kinds were transformed into superstars and became their own brands, hyped by the companies that they were allied with. Everything from reality show stars and super models to designers could surprisingly quickly attain a star status previously reserved for a select few within well-established art forms such as music, art, architecture, film and dance. The

IT boom and the internet helped to create individual brands. This applied to, for example, the Madonna phenomenon and fashion industry superstars, such as Cindy Crawford, Kate Moss and Naomi Campbell, but also the increasingly international design scene's cherished heroes: Philippe Starck, Ron Arad, Marc Newson, Ross Lovegrove, Tom Dixon, Patricia Urquiola, Jasper Morrison and others. Like Raymond Loewy, the greatest symbol of individual design success, they attained a status as iconic designers and their products were often design icons. Typical of many of them and something that contributed to their fame is that they have had a wide range of activities.

Fig. 5.5 A lot of Swedish interior design around the turn of the millennium was characterized by a minimalist, almost ascetic approach. White was often dominant as were references to Japanese interior design. A typical example is Gunilla Allard's neofunctionalist chair Cinema for Lammhults that was released in 1993.

Sweden has not had the same tradition of large individually centred design consultancy firms like America, nor has it had the same tradition of creating uniquely modern items, except possibly in the 1990s. Most successful Swedish design was dominated by traditional ideals, with a simple, stripped, blonde and natural functionalism; during the 1990s it was upgraded to a slightly more luxurious and minimalist neomodernism. Designs should be low, wide, white, clean, delicate and very sparing: a Mies van der Rohe aesthetic mixed with influences from traditional Japanese architecture. These were the ideals that were rewarded by the design establishment, espoused by the likes of Jasper Morrison, and were held in high regard internationally. When Stockholm was the European City of Culture in 1998, the influential interior design magazine *Wallpaper* portrayed 'Designstockholm' in very positive terms; in fact, they even felt that Stockholm should be declared the world's design capital. In addition to the dominant figures on the design scene, who all more or less worked in the neo-modernist tradition, a young and new generation of producers developed: Asplunds, Cbi/Klara and Box Design, who along with David Design in Malmö attracted international attention to Swedish design and contributed to a temporary increase in sales abroad (Zetterlund 2005).

More female designers started to attract attention in the 1990s. Among those with a strong personal style was the potter and glass designer Ingegerd Råman (b. 1943). Her work for Skrufs Glasbruk in the period 1981–1998 comprised an entire suite of practical drinking vessels in simple, well-balanced designs.

There were elegant thin-walled carafes that accentuated the contents and there were robust drinking glasses in the Bellman series, where a person's lips could enjoyably caress the soft edges of the glass. There was also the work of Gunnel Sahlin (b. 1954) and Lena Bergström (b. 1961), both of whom grew up in Umeå, received an education in textile arts at Konstfack but then worked just as much as glass designers. Sahlin's sensual, colourful glass collections for Kosta Boda and Bergström's more severe black and white works for Orrefors are among the highlights of the 1990s, as are Gunilla Lagerhem Ullberg's (b. 1955) carpets in austere patterns for Kasthall.

On the fashion side, Anna Holtblad (b. 1969) excelled when, following Katja of Sweden's example, she managed to turn 'pure Swedish wool into something stylish and modern', as the jury of Stockholm Fashion Week 2008 put it when she was awarded Årets Hederspris (the honorary award of the year). The furniture and set designer Gunilla Allard (b. 1957) helped to shape contemporary interior design ideals in white and beech, and designed sleek, chromed tubular steel furniture in the spirit of 1930s functionalism for Lammhults, such as the armchair Cinema from 1993 and the chair Cosmos from 2000. The architect and furniture designer Thomas Sandell (b. 1959) worked in the same ascetic spirit, as did the trio Mårten Claesson, Eero Koivisto and Ola Rune, who in 1995 founded a joint architect office, while the designer Björn Dahlström (b. 1957) established himself early on as a multi-designer. Dahlström trained as a graphic designer but quickly got into the furniture and product design field. Several of his works are also notable for their unusual graphic sharpness, such as the armchairs BD1 (1996) (Plate 21) and Superstructure (2003) for David Design, as well as Z-cykeln (the Z-bicycle) (1998) with a completely new frame for Skeppshult.

The Budget Giants Step into the Salon of Design

Companies with a pronounced low-cost profile are seldom associated with design-intensive activities, but that does not apply to the two large Swedish companies IKEA and Hennes & Mauritz (H&M). The retail chain IKEA and the clothing giant H&M were founded in the 1940s by the market geniuses Ingvar Kamprad and Erling Persson respectively. Together with Rausing's Tetra Pak, they can be considered Sweden's foremost post-war entrepreneurial companies. Their success is built on the concept of rationalized distribution aimed at a mass market. These are two top-down companies that are distinguished by a family business spirit whose skill on the design side lay for a long time in the ability to capture new trends, not create them. There the similarity ends. Sweden has no tradition as a major fashion country and that is certainly one reason why H&M has, unlike IKEA, consistently denied its Swedish origin.

The foundation of H&M's (before 1968 just Hennes [Hers]) success became selling a lot, selling cheap and selling fast according to the supermarket principle. The collections were brought home with the help of a team of, for a long time relatively fashion-unconscious buyers, who travelled the world to find the cheapest suppliers. The clothes were then sold with a great deal of help from illustrated advertisements in the major newspapers. This fashion mindset was reinforced during the 1970s. The former advertising and marketing manager Carin Steinwall (1989) explains that several talented fashion illustrators were attached to H&M on her initiative, including Mats Gustafson, while she herself walked around the fashion boutiques on the Rue de Rennes and Champs-Elysées in Paris and reproduced models that where then copied. She also attended all the most fashionable shows and then the morning after took the flight back to London and 'walked into the supplier with a quickly jotted down drawing in her hand'. The conclusion of her story is remarkable:

> Before the first pictures from the show were premiered in the world press, ten thousand Swedish women could strut around in Yves Saint Laurent's latest dress for a price of 49:90. (Steinwall and Crona 1989: 100)

In view of the overall design climate in the 1990s, it was no coincidence that both H&M and IKEA clearly stepped into the arena of design during this period. In 1987 H&M hired the experienced Margareta van den Bosch (b. 1942) as chief designer. She had worked in the Italian fashion industry for twelve years and also taught at Beckmans for several years, which meant that she knew how young designers thought and worked. Although sales were still the engine that drove the company,

Fig. 5.6 Fashion advertising received a boost in the 1950s with lots of colourful ads in newspapers and weeklies. Hennes, later the global company H&M, quickly found its business idea of latching onto the current fashion trends and selling clothes with the help of intensive advertising campaigns. This Hennes advertisement, which was illustrated by Jane Bark for advertising in *Dagens Nyheter* in 1956–1957, shows Swedish fashion design before H&M initiates its international expansion. What we see is the fashion designer Kerstin Lokrantz's youthful dresses sewn from Viola Gråsten's fabrics.

design and advertising became an increasingly important cog in the machine. The design workshop Vita Rummet (The White Room) was created to inspire buyers before they embarked on their buying trips. 'The competence that caused the company in 2000 to dare to print the text "Design by H&M" on all their carrier bags in America and Europe was built on the quiet', writes Bo Pettersson (2003). At the same time he is careful to point out that the foundation for H&M's business strategy was to allow designers and buyers to adapt to trends, 'but not embark on the risky enterprise of taking the lead in something totally new. Somewhere there is the, sometimes subtle, difference between H&M and a classic fashion house' (Pettersson 2003: 278).

H&M has become famous for its highly innovative marketing. For a number of years since 1990, the company's underwear has been introduced in Christmas campaigns with the help of attractive supermodels and actresses. The delicate balance between exclusive marketing and the sexist debasement of women has led to the company receiving both criticism and attention. Since strong marketing and low prices have not been sufficient incentives for expansion, H&M developed its design strategy in 2004 by launching annual one-off collections by selected top designers. The collections, which were only released in the urban stores, sold like hotcakes and customers queued all night waiting for the doors to open. These collaborations were launched under the leadership of Margareta van den Bosch, at the time considered by the media to be Sweden's most powerful woman in fashion. Long established fashion designers such as Karl Lagerfeld and Roberto Cavalli were invited, interspersed with younger, then less established names such as Stella McCartney, the Dutch designer duo Viktor & Rolf and Jimmy Choo. Even pop celebrities such as Madonna and Kylie Minogue have added a touch of glamour to some collections.

Inviting catwalk fashionistas has helped raise the status of the brand and attracted new consumer groups. And it has certainly been a contributing factor to H&M being able to seriously compete with Zara and Gap as the world's leading fashion chain since 2008, at least in terms of number of stores. That year about a hundred designers worked in the design department to identify trends and translate them into fashions that would be accessible to all. The trend managers worked with a number of trends in parallel, with a tailored, sporty, ethnic, romantic and futuristic trend being included in the collections of all departments. Internationally, there are perhaps not that many people who associate H&M with Sweden these days. In keeping with its rapid expansion and internationalization H&M has chosen to brand itself as a chameleon company that would rather associate itself with the fashion metropolises than convey any Swedish connotations. Not committing to ownership, either of factories or shops, is included as part of the strategy (H&M's annual report 2008).

IKEA, on the other hand, has made Swedishness a virtue and an increasingly essential part of its branding strategy. In vast, blue and yellow, box-like retail complexes and in the world's most widely distributed free brochure they present their household goods under genuinely Swedish names. Their extensive range is complemented by an increasingly large and wide assortment of traditional Swedish food. The company has also become one of the best advertisements for Swedish design abroad. Their design strategy rests on a roughly century-old conception of what constitutes Swedish design. In the spirit of Ellen Keys, the Larssons and the Swedish Society of Crafts and Design, it should be simple and efficient, bright, airy and solid with plenty of wood; about 70 per cent of IKEA's production is wood based. The founder from Småland has also added the concept of 'sparing' as an irrefutable foundation in IKEA's brand, which the company's strategists have cleverly reinterpreted as the vision of a good design for all and the slogan 'Democratic design'.

IKEA must now be regarded as a battering ram for many smaller Swedish furniture companies in terms of succeeding internationally. But that has not always been the case. Ingvar Kamprad's consistent focus on volume and low cost led, early on, to serious conflict with the established furniture industry in the form of refusal to supply and boycotts at the trade fairs. But this adversity strengthened him. When supplies were not forthcoming, he developed his own product range in the mid-1950s with the help of four architects from Denmark, which at that time was the leading country in furniture design. The mail order collection could now be supplemented by a number of original models, although for a long time they borrowed heavily from established concepts, especially from giants such as NK and KF. The architect Erik Wørts had previously been involved in the development of easy-to-assemble furniture packed in flat boxes with corrugated cardboard and string for NK, and from 1956 he did the same thing for IKEA. The strategy of naming its products, with, for example, beds being named after cities, bookshelves and desks having boy's names and textiles girl's names, also has an antecedent in NK; there the standard furniture was given everyday names such as Börje, Sven, Blenda and Torsten. For its part, KF had long before IKEA based its entire business concept on creating good and inexpensive design for the public. Kamprad acquired his own exhibition venues by starting to build department stores; the first opened in 1958 at home in Älmhult, Småland (Torekull 1998 and IKEA's museum).

Up to 1995 more than 230 designers, architects and artists had contributed to IKEA's success. Among the contractors one encounters many famous names from the 1950s and 1960s such as Viola Gråsten, Göta Trädgårdh, G. A. Berg, Sigvard Bernadotte, Verner Panton and Tapio Wirkkala. Their detractors' criticisms of deficiencies in quality could be brushed aside as early as 1964, when a large unbiased furniture test, arranged by the magazine *Allt i Hemmet* with the help of the Swedish Society of Crafts and Design's furniture testing lab, showed that this was not the case. On the contrary, their cheap furniture often held up better than their more expensive counterparts, 'the IKEA furniture proved not only to be very strong but also well executed, aesthetically pleasing', stated the magazine (Arwidson 2006: 104–105). IKEA subsequently became one of the biggest backers for the use of the Möbelfakta (Furniture facts) system and built its own testing laboratory following Möbelinstitutet's designs (Berglund 1997).

IKEA's inventiveness in terms of rationalizing and cheapening production is widely attested. For Ögla from 1964, which was a copy of Thonet's classic café chair, they struggled for many years to find a material that was durable enough for the seat to be packed in a flat package. For the production of the round plastic chair Skopa from 1974 they employed the services of a bucket manufacturer, while they contracted a manufacturer of supermarket trolleys for the slim and elegant steel base of the 1980s couch and table Moment. The table top Bra, as well as the coffee table and shelf Lack, was in turn manufactured from interior door leaf (Demokratisk design 1995). The really big seller is the bookshelf Billy from 1978, which is still sold in about four million copies every year. The spring-loaded, laminated Poem (later Poäng) from 1976 is the best-selling armchair, while Klippan from 1980 is said to be the best-selling sofa in the company's history. This is what IKEA's designers have really been good at: making millimetre adjustments to their products together with logisticians to lower production costs. To help them they have, according to the former design manager Lars Engman, the world's leading model workshop. The table lamp Lampan in plastic designed by Carl Öjerstam (b. 1971) is a good example, where the final price for the customer (2.5 euros) was set before the design work began and where the screen could be used as packaging. These are the kind of constraints that challenge creativity.

In 1995, the extensive but sometimes slightly undistinguished basic range was complemented. A timely design effort, the supplementary collection 'PS' (Post Scriptum) was launched with the aid of the design strategist Stefan Ytterborn. It consisted of forty-odd characteristically cutting-edge products, and was first exhibited at the annual furniture fair in Milan. The collection had been developed by 19 established young designers, who had been successful in a competition with 220 participants which had the theme 'Democratic design'. 'IKEA was the most Swedish of all in Milan … IKEA has now after many years of being accused of plagiarising responded through PS', reported Lis Hogdal in the journal *Arkitektur* (1995/4: 65). The PS collection was a successful approach that has subsequently had several sequels: 1999 ('High design value'), 2002 ('Inside out, outside in'), 2004 ('Unlimited play'), 2006 ('What if') and 2009 ('Designberättelser utan slut [Design stories without end]'). Some of the products disappeared from the range quite quickly while others have persisted, such as Maria Vinka's low, skilfully accomplished rocking chair Gullholmen of plaited banana leaves from 2002, which with its associations to both ptarmigan and guksi hint at the designer's Sami roots, and Monika Mulder's stackable watering can Vållö from the same year, which with its organically flowing shape harmonizes with both plants and running water.

In the spring of 2009, IKEA's product range consisted of four divisions: Textile, Work IKEA, Children's IKEA and Kitchen & Dining. The development was controlled from IKEA of Sweden in Älmhult where the ideas were taken care of by about fifty product developers, who with their teams decided on product types, materials and so on. They then formulated design briefs for their twelve in-house designers and sixty-odd design consultants in a matrix comprising four style divisions (Modern, Scandinavian, Country and Young Swede) and four price segments (High, Medium, Low and BTI, where the last is recognizable by a price that should practically take the customers' breath away).

When the product developers had approved the design, it was their task to convince the sales team of the design proposal's strength, after which it would take about two years for a product to go from sketch to shelf. For children's products, it could take an additional year before it passed all the tests.

Fig. 5.7 Maria Vinka's weather-resistant small rocking chair 'Gullholmen' was included in IKEA's PS collection from 2002, where the theme concerned the space between indoors and outdoors. Her Sami background was the inspiration for the shape, which is reminiscent of a ptarmigan or guksi. The material is plaited banana leaf, normally a waste product.

In addition to price and style, it is the pallet that more than anything controls IKEA's design. Previously all the company's products were packed on a standardized EU pallet with the dimensions 80–120 centimetres and a maximum height of 1 metre. As many copies of the product as possible were supposed to fit within this space, which made extraordinary demands on IKEA designers. In order to avoid the transportation of too many empty wooden pallets in their formidable logistics chain, which included thousands of suppliers and more than 350 stores worldwide, IKEA has now developed its own disposable plastic pallet, which can be ground down after use and recycled. It used to be said that IKEA furnished the Folkhem (welfare state) and that is even truer today. In recent years they have also understood the importance of designing various storage solutions; it is important to be able to provide storage facilities for all the stuff that Swedish people fill their homes with.

The Need for Strategic Brand Design Increases

During the 1990s, design became an increasingly important means of competition for companies. In the global economy, where products could be manufactured equally as well in Vietnam or China as in Kista, traditional means of competition such as price and quality no longer play the same crucial role. The product as a functional, instrumental phenomenon dropped in value and in some cases was not even the most important reason to purchase it. Instead, the importance of the consumption of the experience itself increased along with the immaterial, emotional values that were linked to the product. The physical product and the immaterial could in this way be regarded as a composite and indivisible whole. Christina Zetterlund (2002) exemplifies this with what she calls the information age's *neoluxury*, where the exclusive became comprised of things and experiences that could only be distinguished through knowledge. This could be tomatoes with pedigree or tea that had been cultivated on thousand-year-old tea trees from the Song Dynasty.

As design institutions took up more space in the public debate, Swedish industry began to slowly take in what, for example, the Japanese had realized much earlier, that it is possible to calculate constructions but not the experience of them; research reports from this time showed that Japanese companies invested on average four times more on design than the Swedish (Svengren 1995). It became increasingly obvious that logical product development calculations had to be supplemented by a humanistic dimension and an artistic, holistic thinking, and to be able to utilize the potential of this skill the design must be handled at the management level, where strategic decisions are made.

The power of consumers has also gradually increased, largely thanks to the internet's rapid search engines and its possibilities for product comparisons and exchange of ideas. Simple advertising messages were met with suspicion and were no longer effective among ordinary people. The brands, which previously had usually been expressed in the form of simple company logos, now needed to be filled with a deeper content. It became increasingly clear that they had to be bearers of a message that reflected the company's core values. Here the products or services interacted with the company's architectural profile, visual identity, and corporate culture. Per Mollerup's (2002) studies showed that investing in the brand was profitable:

> The directors of the largest manufacturers of brand products compete to explain that their brand is worth more than the whole physical production facility that manufactures the product. Recent company acquisitions in the consumer sector confirm this assertion.

Trademarks have been around for thousands of years and there were two fundamental reasons why they became an issue as soon as production was for a broad market: that you were proud of your product and wanted to guarantee its quality. For example, brick mills and manufacturers of oil lamps in antiquity branded their products, which were distributed over the vast Roman Empire, brands that consisted of a simple logo with letters and/or a symbol. Marks, crests, monograms and bookplates are all a kind of brand. A good deal of emotion is attached to a brand, but not always legal protection. Therefore, the English language conveniently has two terms: trademark signifies the protection and brand the possession itself, the 'branding' of the product (Mollerup 2002). The meaning of the term brand and branding has broadened, however, as brands have evolved into something more than just the sum of the product's actual utility; it is no longer just a symbol or a mark of ownership, but in extreme cases also a promise to satisfy both worldly and spiritual needs.

Architecture has been important in the manifestation of a company's operations. The ability to convey values and other symbolic images increased dramatically during the nineteenth and twentieth centuries. Anyone who has ever studied, for example, incoming letters in old company archives will not have been able to miss all the stylish letterheads, especially on stationery from the late nineteenth century and the early twentieth century. Often they depict a magnificently portrayed view of the factory buildings themselves. At that time companies did not have many opportunities to visually communicate their identity, except when they sent an invoice, responded to an offer or made an order. The factory images in these logos were often created with an exaggerated perspective of value with tall, smoking chimneys, which emphasized stability and confidence in the future. Brand building took off with the packaged product, becoming more commonly expressed in the form of a single, clear visual identity in the 1950s and 1960s. A new playing field was consequently opened for the designer. Olle Eksell's corporate identity programme for Mazetti (1956–1958) and Rune Monö's for ICA (1962–1964) are, as has been mentioned, among the pioneering works, but also Monö's work for SAS (from 1946 to the early 1960s), Bernadotte Design/AID's identity programme for Alfa-Laval (1969–1972) and Marabou (1966–1969) are worth highlighting. Design agencies gradually developed an ever-increasing graphical competence as the commissions expanded and became more interdisciplinary. 'It seemed natural that a product designer must be able to work equally well in commercial graphic design', writes Monö and continues:

> The SAS project became the beginning of a long chain of such work. Sometimes motivated by product commissions where the brand needed to be adapted to the new design, sometimes the graphic design commission came completely separately. (Monö 1997: 142)

The fastest and probably most accomplished launch of a new Swedish brand started in 1979 when a trial shipment of premium vodka from the brand Absolut Vodka left Vin & Sprit's factory in Åhus bound for New York. It was claimed that the vodka had a soft cereal quality and possessed a rare purity. Whether this was a distinguishing characteristic from the many similar and more famous brands on the market is debatable, but what definitely stood out was the unusual bottle of crystal-clear glass, which was developed with inspiration from old medicine bottles by the art director Hans Brindfors (b. 1947) and Gunnar Broman at the advertising agency Carlsson & Broman in Stockholm. The bottle was also named the year's best packaging by the American Art Directors Club the following year in a prestigious competition with 250 packages from around the world. In the hands of skilled marketers Absolut Vodka was developed into a veritable global success, which after many spectacular campaigns, two-word ads, artist collaborations and bottle launches was Sweden's most important food export in 2002 (Olsson 2004), and six years later in connection with the sale to Pernod Ricard was categorized as one of Sweden's absolutely strongest brands.

In recent decades, interest in protecting and developing corporate identities and brands has completely exploded. People have understood the importance of visual communication in order to be visible and get noticed in the information-rich society we live in. Although word and figure brands have been dominant, more and more companies have started using suggestive, so-called unconventional brands to stand out and capture consumers' interest. According to an EU directive from 1988, all communicable signs that can be perceived by the five human senses can, in principle, be registered as a trademark, but in reality it has primarily concerned colour brands, audio brands and distinctive packaging. Typical examples are the coffee brand Löfbergs Lila with its well-established colour, Hemglass with its famous theme tune and the austere, ice-blue bottle for Svenskt Brännvin, shaped by the designer Gunnel Sahlin with inspiration from eighteenth-century rectangular liquor bottles (Lunell 2007).

In the 1990s companies also began to realize that it was no longer just about selling a physical product, but also, like the example of Absolut Vodka, selling a symbol of a particular lifestyle. In this regard the strategic designer working in the long-term became an important partner. New design consultancies or design departments that had branched out from the big advertising agencies specialized in strategic brand building. Among the more successful were Ytterborn & Fuentes from 1996, where Stefan Ytterborn (b. 1963) after working with IKEA's PS range signed up, among others, Hackman Tools and Rörstrand as clients with his partner Oscar Fuentes (b. 1963). In Gothenburg, the big advertising agency Forsman & Bodenfors created a special design department the following year, headed by Anders Kornestedt (b. 1966). The department changed its name to Happy F&B in 2001 and soon won national and international awards, one after the other with their smart and consistent campaign work for the Röhsska Museum, Arkitekturmuseet (The Swedish Museum of Architecture) and Arctic Paper. Stockholm Design Lab was founded by Björn Kusoffsky (b. 1965) and Thomas Eriksson (b. 1959) in 1998, which among other things would renew SAS and Moderna Museet's identities and design a packaging concept for IKEA Food in the same simple spirit as KF's Blåvitt from the 1970s.

The strategically active design agencies could now offer complete solutions for companies' internal and external communications, products and services. They developed identity programmes that not only unified the graphic design and expression on everything from business cards to packaging and web solutions, but also ensured that the company's brand permeated the organization and management. They worked narratively, through something that in the business world usually goes by the term storytelling. Consumers often wanted to know more than the product itself, which possibly came from the other side of the world, could communicate. 'The unique story, rooted in the company's history, became an instrument in the abstract market to create a credibility and intimacy that the consumer could identify with', writes Cristina Zetterlund (2002). Further effectiveness and impact were achieved with the film media, communicated through television, the web and mobile phones. Sometimes famous directors, actors and models were hired, but more often they chose the shrewder path and worked with amateurs or created animations. Whatever the approach, the strategic design has resulted in the boundaries between design, advertising and marketing being erased, while the designer has become a key player at the highest level of management within the companies' organizations.

Central to visual communication is that the message hits the mark and that it is up to date and useful. The more it is encapsulated in symbols or in a slogan, the more powerful and exact it has to be. There are many Swedish companies with enduring slogans, such as 'Mmm … Marabou', Läkerol's 'Makes people talk' and IKEA's 'inte för de rika – men för de kloka (not for the rich – but for the wise)'. Ericsson had for a time the egocentric 'Making yourself heard', which worked well as long as phones were only used for talking and listening. When the company realized that modern telephony was as much about image and networking, they changed it to the more universal but ineffectual 'Taking you forward'. Nokia's 'Connecting people' has however proved to be far more durable over time. Skånska Cementgjuteriet, which in 1984 changed its name to the more internationally viable and internet-friendly Skanska, was forced a number of years later to also change the colours in their well-established logo. When the construction company was going to reach out globally, their black and yellow logo did not work, since the combination was for many people a warning colour that signalled potential harm. This argument is put forward by the colour psychologist Karl Ryberg, who also points out that several of the most dangerous poisonous snakes have these colours (Oppenheim 2008).

Logos have become increasingly advanced. When Sony Ericsson unveiled its logo for a new brand being developed in 2001, it was taken into a new era, at least by Swedish standards. An uppercase 'S' and a lowercase 'e' were merged into a sphere-like almost floating shape. Sony Ericsson's art director Takuya Kawagoi, who was responsible for the logo, claimed that it expressed the flexibility and organic movement within the company, but there is no doubt that it also reflected the new reality of the telephone. The mobile phone had developed into a so-called 'stand-alone object', which moves freely in 360 degrees and is not dependent on any position or specific foundation like the stationary phone. Other telephone companies, such as the British Vodafone and the American AT&T, had previously tried to create a three-dimensional logo but without managing to convey the same dynamism.

It is not only companies that have reviewed their logos and visual identities. Organizations, institutions and municipalities have also latched on to the trend and tried to rationalize and standardize their various entities as much as possible. It has taken place after a usually much-needed examination of how their communication has worked, both externally and internally. In the establishment of new operations, the creation of a logo is now included as a requirement. When the Umeå Institute of Design started in 1989 a great deal of work was devoted to giving the school a strong visual identity. The logo was changed several times before it got its final shape. The first proposals were characterized by an industrialist idiom in which a stylized screw together with a discordant, almost oriental moon shape created the letters ID. The final D combined with a half U resulted in a clearer and stronger link to Umeå University, while the overtly instrumental touch was toned down. This logo worked for a while before it too was discarded when Umeå University, like many other universities, banned the use of independent logos. All entities were to conform to a common visual identity, which in this case was based on a logo from the 1960s designed by Sigurd Persson.

Old logos are commonly modernized to better fit increasingly wide visual identity programmes with their more open forms of communication. In recent years, authorities and organizations with diffuse communication strategies have tightened their logos, with a view to achieving a greater uniformity and brand loyalty. The University of Gothenburg's logo was inspired by the old petroglyphs in Bohuslän and depicted a stylized male figure with a shield and ship encircled by the Latin phrase *Universitas Regia Gothoburgensis*.

The problem was that the complicated logo with difficult to read text was not adapted to modern communication requirements. There were discussions about investing in a brand new logo, but after a few attempts they decided instead to simplify and clarify the existing one, which would also be supplemented with regulations and applications in the form of a manual. The commission for the transformation was given to the graphic designer Eva Engstrand (b. 1951), later rector of HDK.

Brand building is distinguished by far-sightedness, although changes may of course sometimes be necessary. The Röhsska Museum's unique Ö-logo by H. C. Ericson from 1991 was an example of a necessary adjustment to the times. Since 1958 the museum had in various contexts used a very expressive emblem depicting a stylized Chinese Fu Lion, of the same type that flanks the museum's entrance. It suited the museums of the time which mainly focused on arts and crafts and East Asian material, but not really a Röhsska with pretensions to being Sweden's design museum; the logo gave the wrong signals and did not sum up its ambitions. With the letter logo Röhsska gained for the first time a consistent graphical platform for its brand building, which has been subsequently developed by Happy F&B in a creative and skilful manner.

KONSTSLÖJD

RÖHSSKA

MUSEET

GÖTEBORG

S. BOSTRÖM

MCMLVIII

Fig. 5.8 In 1958 the Röhsska Museum acquired a brand that was associated with the prestigious Chinese collections, but that did not fit as well a few decades later when the museum increasingly wanted to reflect the current design interest. The museum director at the time, the typographically interested Christian Axel-Nilsson, gave H. C. Ericson the task of designing a visual identity programme. The letter Ö became the core of this, as Röhsska and Göteborg (Gothenburg) have a characterful but odd letter at the end of the Swedish alphabet. As a starting point the 'ö' created plenty of opportunities for typographic exercises. See also Figs 5.9 and 5.10.

RÖhsska museet

Fig. 5.9 Example of Röhsska Museum branding exercise. See also Figs 5.8 and 5.10.

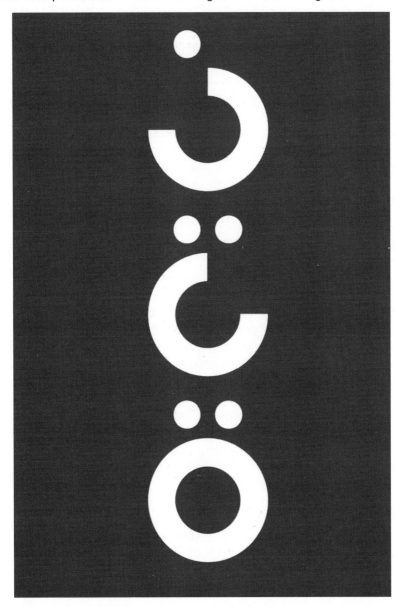

Fig. 5.10 Example of Röhsska Museum branding typography exercises. See also Figs 5.8 and 5.9.

Corporate culture is perhaps best reflected in buildings and environments. What, for example, Volvo's Kalmar factory from the early 1970s meant as a symbol of the Swedish work model or indeed what the new city hall in Kiruna, 'Kirunabornas vardagsrum (The people of Kiruna's living room)', meant for the self-esteem of its residents in the 1960s cannot be overemphasized. One of the Swedish companies that has most consistently and successfully influenced corporate culture with design-based management-thinking is the furniture company Materia in Tranås. It was founded in 1992 by the two interior designers Kersti Sandin Bülow (b. 1950) and Lars Bülow (b. 1952), but is since 2004 included in the Kinnarps group. The background was that the two designers wanted to materialize their own design ideas, not just design for other manufacturers. With their own furniture ideas, and those of an increasing number of younger co-workers, they demonstrated new, more effective ways to meet in public contexts and smarter storage solutions. It might be conference rooms without tables, chairs without backs, swivel armchairs, sound-damping furniture or billowing magazine racks and expandable wastepaper baskets. With their latest factory building from 2008, they went all out and made their whole company into a showroom notable for its transparency, participation and their own furniture groups. Here factory workers, office staff and visitors meet both physically and with the same dignity in an environment that is well thought-out in every detail.

Standards of Taste and the Gender Power Order Are Challenged

Despite the hype surrounding Swedish design, we have to understand that a large portion of the population had and continues to have problems with the bare, undecorated industrial design and this despite IKEA's rise, all the glossy interior design magazines and interior design programmes on television. Until the turn of the millennium, one seldom encountered the words beautiful or ugly in the design debate, at least after Gregor Paulsson's *Vackrare vardagsvara* (More beautiful everyday items). This is because the concepts are associated with taste; something that is taboo, according to the design critic Stephen Bayley (2000). He points out that the cause is a tradition of uncertainty. Our attitudes to sex and money can be discussed, but not taste, as it reveals our background in a more ruthless way. It was different in the nineteenth century, says Bayley, when taste was assumed to be something that every reasonable person could acquire. Then the big museum managers had no trouble at all morally convincing or aesthetically correcting their audience.

At the same time, the dichotomy beautiful–ugly is limited as it reduces the experience to mainly visual aspects. There was a clear awareness of this among Swedish designers in the latter half of the twentieth century. When something was very well designed, explained the design manager of the KF-owned Gustavsberg Stig Lindberg, then we talked about it being 'cleverly done'. The industrial designer Rune Monö argues in a similar way when he, in the book *Svensk industridesign* (Swedish Industrial Design) (Brunnström 1997: 280), points out that the term beautiful had a hard time winning favour with the production technicians. In addition, the reason why someone thought something was beautiful was not just related to a harmonious and interesting design. The word 'attractiveness' was better. It was less controversial and at the same time more comprehensive. To it you could add concepts such as nostalgia, status, sentimental value, group affiliation, self-fulfilment, etc. And, what was even more important for the manufacturer/marketer: trendiness, style …

The term '*ändamålsenlig design* (appropriate design)', or 'right design' which many people use today, is probably more common than both 'beautiful' and 'attractive' in the design context. That the 'appropriate' was the beautiful was established already in functionalism's infancy, but the concept very much remains central to the notion of how a high quality and competitive Swedish product should be designed. Even though it has rarely been debated, there has existed among the big, heavy design players, the Swedish Society of Crafts and Design, Nationalmuseum and the Röhsska Museum, a hidden taste agenda during the whole twentieth century. It has been, and perhaps still partly is, deeply rooted in these institutions and has not infrequently had an air of a 'we know best' mentality. That is why Mats Theselius's somewhat incomprehensible carrot stand (1996) and Per B. Sundberg's (b. 1964) kitsch radios (1997-) were met with surprise, and that is why there was an uproar when Zandra Ahl's (b. 1975) books *Fult & snyggt* (Ugly & beautiful) (1998) and *Svensk smak* (Swedish taste) (2001 with Emma Olsson) were released. 'Less is more is pathetic – a kind of "anorexia-aesthetics". How banal is it not to see all the white lilies, austere rooms and all the everyday glass. That, and nothing else is our time's great emptiness of style and tastelessness' she argued provocatively (1998: 10) and also lamented that there was only one function, the practical, which was approved according to official Swedish standards of taste. She did not know then how in tune with the times she was. A few years later Anders Emilson (2005) pointed out:

> To cultivate a culture, as in Sweden, where everyone must think along the same lines quickly leads to a dead end and that is where the Swedish design culture was at the end of the 20th century, when the scene was dominated by neomodernism and blonde simplicity.

Today the hypothesis 'one people, one state, one style' no longer applies; instead strongly function-driven Modernism is becoming a style among many others. The functional is interpreted in a broader context by today's budding young designers. The lavish is today just as correct as the simple and there is a predilection for mass effect, similar to the nineteenth-century galleries with paintings hanging from floor to ceiling. Pattern ornamentation has undergone a renaissance, perhaps because we live in a more multicultural society and in a society where a disproportionate emphasis is given to the self and the body. Even the reawakened interest in textile fashion pays attention to close-fitting and what can be exposed. The gym culture, spa, massage, fashion shows, piercing, tattoos, plastic surgery, plasticized corpses and focus on the body is everywhere and the surface is more important than ever. We encounter decorative, intricate, powerful surface patterns in both expected and unexpected places, not only on textiles and wallpapers, but on mobile phones, as LEDs in headlights and even as ornamentation on traditional appliances such as washing machines. Patterns attract the design-interested

Fig. 5.11 A few years into the twenty-first century there was still a continuing renaissance of pattern ornamentation in Sweden. It pervaded much of the student work at the design colleges, but also had an impact on the trend-sensitive industrial production. This washing machine from Electrolux is part of the series 'Inspired by White' but is really a patterned protest from 2006 against the traditional so-called white goods.

youth of today whose parents were brought up in a country with a fairly ascetic relation to decoration.

Patterns and textiles are traditionally female design areas representing soft and sensual values. Theresa Digerfeldt-Månsson (2009) demonstrates, supported by several scientists, our growing need for these values along with society's increased computerization and technologization: high-tech simply requires high touch. In recent years, a lot of experimenting and researching has been done in Sweden on broadened uses for textiles from both artistic and technical standpoints.

These interior textiles are in the form of, for example, tufted textiles as noise-reduction screens and free-standing sculptures, pleasant enveloping armchairs of pressed polyester felt; these technological textiles range from geotextiles for landscaping to textiles for toiletries, medical use and other so-called smart textiles; and this includes fashion and clothing, which according to some commentators is about to take over the world. Nevertheless, there are many neglected areas. The publication *Formgivning Normgivning* (Normative Design) (Jahnke 2006: 62) notes that practically all work clothes and personal protective equipment in heavy industry are suited for men's bodies:

> When women use them it becomes doubly wrong, partly because they fit poorly, which causes purely practical discomfort, but it is also emotionally unpleasant to wear ill fitting as well as male coded clothing.

That men have stood for the norm also applies to many other areas. Automotive safety designs, for example, are generally designed based on knowledge of how the male body reacts in accidents. Male dummies have been used for as long as crash tests have been performed, even though it is know that women are shorter, weigh less and sit differently. Not until 2006 were serious discussions conducted about developing a female crash test dummy, after it had been established that women are at far greater risk of debilitating neck injuries than men. Even office work can cause damage. In 2009 the versatile Monica Förster (b. 1966) therefore tailored a chair to specific ergonomic requirements for female postures (Plate 22).

Car design has always been a typically male department and, therefore, it caused a sensation when Volvo let a group of nine women have sole responsibility for developing a concept car; nothing like it had happened since Harley Earl had a group of female designers employed at GM's styling studio, mostly to spruce up the interiors in the 1950s. The idea was hatched in 2001 in connection with a seminar on the theme '*kvinnor som kunder* (women as customers)'. There were many (men) who had predicted that it would be a fiasco, but, on the contrary, the results far exceeded expectations. Volvo YCC, which was ready to be shown at the Geneva Motor Show in March of 2004, met with an overwhelmingly positive response, both there and at the subsequent New York Motor Show. It was presented as a sporty coupe with gull-wing doors and a number of practical details. With, in particular, a lowered hood the driver had full control of all the car's four corners from the driver's seat. Maintenance was simplified to a minimum by the hood not being openable except at a workshop, the paint being dirt-repellent and the washer fluid being filled from the outside. It had an automatic parking function and plenty of storage space, the headrests were split to create space for a ponytail and there was room for a handbag between the seats and an umbrella stand. Although YCC received numerous awards and became Volvo's most written about car up to that point, it never went into production. But as a kind of think tank for future Volvo models it is unsurpassed (Volvo YCC 2005).

Part of the concept of the Volvo YCC was that it would mainly attract potential female car buyers, but, as many people have claimed, just meeting women's expectations often results in also exceeding men's. In any case, there was every reason to target the female market since it accounted for 65 per cent and influenced

Fig. 5.12 Volvo Cars became the first car manufacturer ever in 2004 to show a concept car that was engineered and designed solely by a team of women. The nine women had not only ensured that YCC was appealing to the eye but also equipped it with a large number of practical details. For example, the coupe is equipped with a chain of lights that light up when the broad gull-wing doors open and a centre console with multiple storage compartments and a cooler. There is space in the car's sides for first aid kit, umbrella and flashlight. In order to facilitate a more comfortable driving experience, YCC is equipped with a system that automatically adjusts the seat, headrest, seat belt, steering wheel and pedals to the driver's size; this is linked to a hologram that shows when the driver has the best possible visibility.

85 per cent of all car purchases, according to Penny Sparke (Volvo YCC 2005). In other product categories market segmentation has been taken even further. Mobile phones have for years been produced targeting particular consumer groups with different lifestyles. Ericsson was a front runner at the end of the 1990s when it developed the first cross-country phones specially designed for professional outdoor work and rugged outdoor activities. There are now special mobiles for girls, mobiles for seniors, Disney mobiles for children, mobiles for football fans and even mobile phones that are specially designed for different religious groups. A considerably older version of segmentation is the product differentiation that aims to sell special solutions to separate individuals, to supply us with special utensils. This is particularly obvious in the leisure sector, for example with golf shoes or bike gloves, but is increasingly spreading into more expensive durable goods. In these contexts it is also a popular move to capitalize on established brands within different premium segments through so-called *cross-branding* or *co-branding*. On the PC side, producers have allied with various sports car brands, Acer with Ferrari and Asus with Lamborghini, while the Swedish Koenigsegg has formed a joint brand with Intel (Brunnström 2006).

Segmentation and product differentiation is associated with the production and service sectors gradually being adapted towards more individual, tailored solutions (mass customizing). Mass production, which had its definitive breakthrough with Ford's automotive factories, looks like it may become a parenthesis in human history. Aids in the form of advanced design software, computer controlled prototyping and flexible manufacturing mean that production can be tailored to individual needs in a completely different way than before. The ability to work with small batches, change material and quickly adjust production to an almost craft-like process creates the conditions for offering advanced solutions, both for specific professional needs as well as less complex consumer needs. The internet is functioning increasingly well as a sales channel for the most niche products; this new distribution phenomenon has been described by the best-selling authors Seth Godin (2006) and Chris Anderson (2006) in terms such as *Small is the New Big* and *Massclusivity* respectively.

Mass customizing enables *one-of-a-kind* solutions 'on demand' or 'just for you' as they say in the ads, which is fitting as we are in every respect living in the era of the accessory. Customized production has come the furthest with personal products such as clothes, shoes and glasses, but with the use of digital printing technology, also in areas such as books and wallpaper prints. It has also brought with it an upswing for and appreciation of previously marginalized professional groups.

Take for example the revolution in knife manufacturing. Suddenly not just the giants IKEA and Tupperware but even a small but expanding company like Hultafors in Bollebygd (the introducer of the carpenter's rule) have discovered the benefits of employing the skills of Sweden's biggest design consultancy, the Stockholm-based Veryday. They call it multifunctional 'craftman's knives' [*sic*], which means that for almost every kind of craftsman trade there should be a knife that is tailored to how the people in that specific trade actually work. They have developed a knife for plumbers with a file on the blade so that they can file off burrs on cut pipes, a knife for painters and decorators with a screwdriver for removing electrical boxes and opening paint cans and for carpenters a cut-off knife with a chisel and so on.

Sustainability Permeates the Design

Although segmentation satisfies more consumer groups and customized production minimizes surplus stock, continuously developing new products is problematic. It puts a strain on both the environment and natural resources. A growing number of designers today are reacting against this waste and engaging in a more ecologically sustainable design. In the wake of climate change and unbalanced ecosystems there exists in Sweden a widespread ecological awareness of a completely different depth than during the environmentalist movement's childhood in the 1960s and 1970s. The nerdy and holier-than-thou connotations are gone. To design, produce and consume organically has instead become trendy. Designers are joining networks such as Det naturliga steget (The natural step), O2, Faktor 10 and Vagga till vagga (Cradle to Cradle), where different principles are developed to imitate the natural cycles and conserve materials and natural resources. They also try to use storytelling to create a more emotional attachment to the product so that we want to keep it for longer, or simply try to change our thought patterns from the need to own to the need to share or rent products and services.

Several projects with a bearing on our energy consumption have been realized or are under development, where the concern is about both encouraging a transition from fossil fuels to electricity and reducing energy consumption. As the heating and operation of buildings is responsible for about 40 per cent of total energy consumption, systems that are built with new, energy-efficient solutions attract ever-increasing attention. Another radical solution is the well-insulated so-called passive house which is largely heated by the energy that already exists in the house, primarily from humans and domestic appliances. New approaches are also being taken in the case of electric vehicles, both in respect to cars and various kinds of rail transport. SkyCab is an example of a personal rapid transit system with electric vehicles on rubber wheels, which like the old monorail travel on a rail supported by pillars, which not only frees up the ground level but also gives off a minimal amount of emissions. In urban areas where rapid and convenient connections between home, work and services are needed, this could be a competitive complement to electric cars, alongside the bicycle.

At the Interactive Institute in Stockholm, designers, engineers and theorists have for many years worked on various projects to highlight electricity consumption in our homes. In the project Static from 2004–2005 they were able to present several interesting solutions by linking the entities of heat and light, such as the Power-Aware Cord, where the power consumption is indicated using a built-in light string in the cord and the completely self-sufficient curtain Energy Curtain, which stores energy in solar cells during the day and then when the sun goes down uses the energy to function as a light source using fibre optics and LEDs. Another example is the Flower Lamp, a flower-like moving lamp that is connected to the electricity meter and which rewards energy-saving behaviour by slowly unfurling its leaves; if on the other hand the consumption increases the leaves close (Ilstedt Hjelm 2007). The project Aware from 2006–2008 includes the light Puzzle Switch, which appeals to our sense of order to turn the light off after us; when the colours and patterns have been matched together the switch indicates that the power is off (www.tii.se). Within the textile sector, the group Smart Textiles at Textilhögskolan (Swedish School of Textiles) in Borås has been an important cooperative partner. It is a centre of cutting-edge expertise in the innovation, development, design and production of the next generation of textile products; their many projects include cooling clothes for over-heated firemen and textile mats that cool the laptop, thereby extending the battery life (www.smarttextiles.se).

Fig. 5.13 At the Interactive Institute in Stockholm a number of interesting projects have been implemented on encouraging energy-saving behaviour. Aware Puzzle Switch is a two-coloured rotary light switch that appeals to our sense of order: when the colour pattern has been matched the light is turned off. It was designed in 2007 by Loove Broms & Karin Ehrnberger.

In Sweden, there is a plentiful fresh water supply, which is relatively evenly distributed across the country and reaches consumers through sophisticated pipe systems. Electrolux achieved a both environmental and energy-saving synergy by being the first company to take advantage of this to offer consumers cold sparkling water directly out of their refrigerators through the water supply network; thereby reducing the need to carry home bottled water, which has possibly been transported a long distance, from the store. In Sweden there is also a long tradition of cooperating with nature. The light is important but also the snow. One way of utilizing natural resources based on local conditions has been developed in the Icehotel project in Jukkasjärvi. The hotel complex, which is situated by the Torne River outside Kiruna in the northernmost part of Sweden, is built in the late autumn out of snow and 4,000 tonnes of crystal-clear ice blocks, which have been sawn out of the frozen river. In the spring it all melts down again and the cycle is complete.

For more than twenty-five years, a viable industry has been created by offering exotic nights on reindeer skins in five degrees below zero conditions. The ice rooms, ice furniture, ice art, ice church, ice bar and the Ice Globe Theatre are designed in a new way every year by artists and designers from all over the world. The facility's goal is to be able to produce more energy than it uses and become carbon negative (www.icehotel.se).

On the material side, the use of wood has a long history in a forest-rich country like Sweden. It is a renewable resource that can occur in many forms. Wood also binds carbon dioxide and has significantly lower emissions than other comparable materials. The tradition of making houses and furniture out of wood is strong in Sweden and the interest in the material has recently grown even more since we have been able to demonstrate the benefits of also building high apartment buildings and bridges out of wood. Consequently, strong, solid laminated timber constructions and the industrial heat treatment of wood, which makes it stronger, more stable and more resistant to decay, are on the advance.

Composites, mainly consisting of wood fibres, are increasingly becoming a complement to regular wood. It can replace environmentally unfriendly pressure impregnation outdoors, be used for details, and cast, pressed and injection-moulded for all sorts of purposes in the furniture industry. In terms of packaging, cardboard and corrugated cardboard dominate – materials that from a lifecycle perspective are considerably more environmentally friendly than glass and plastic (Plate 23). Boxes made of solid corrugated cardboard have almost the same stability and rigidity as wooden boxes and are today recycled at a rate of around 90 per cent. The fact that weight is a significant factor in the sustainability context is proven by Ericsson, which has replaced its plywood transport packaging with considerably lighter corrugated cardboard and thereby significantly reduced carbon dioxide emissions (www.klimat-kompassen.se).

In addition to recycling, weight and size reductions, many young designers are interested in reusing in different forms. Clothing and furnishings are two areas that in this context have always attracted great interest.

Fig. 5.14 The timber company Södra has developed a super-strong and recyclable paper composite called DuraPulp, which consists of paper pulp and bioplastics made from cornstarch. The material offers hope of new exciting applications; for example, the architect office Claesson Koivisto Rune has used it for the paper pulp children's chair Parapu.

Among numerous completed projects are the network Creatables' noticeboards and newspaper baskets made of felt left over from the manufacturing of tennis courts, Ecoistics' hammocks made from leftover seat belts, Maria Westerberg's colourful cushions and folding walls of textile waste materials, the design studio Apokalyps Labotek's soaps made from discarded frying oil and Design Stories' pouffes made from lint in the charity Emmaus Björkås's bale press which is normally used in connection with their clothing drives.

Faced with the predicted climate changes, it is the ecological dimension of sustainability that many today see as the most important. At the same time one has to be aware that there are also social, economic and cultural dimensions to sustainability that may be difficult to reconcile. A combined business, environmental and humanitarian project that appears to have succeeded in this is the solar-powered reading light Sunnan, which was designed in 2008 by Nicolas Cortolezzis at IKEA in Älmhult. The project was initiated by Ingvar Kamprad, who was surely inspired by the American MIT project running concurrently, OLPC, One Laptop per Child, in which green-white mini-computers are sold cheaply or donated to developing countries. In a similar way, for each Sunnan sold IKEA will donate another to UNICEF for distribution to children in homes without electricity so they can do their homework after dark.

It seems as if the collective solidarity with low-priority groups in society that emerged during 1970s is to some extent being revived. There is also an understanding that a disability need not be a permanent condition but can be time-bound or situationally bound. The philosophy of universal design/Design för alla (Design for all) plays an important role in solving this design problem; products and services should be usable by and sold to all, they must be able to satisfy many different applications and be easy to understand without special knowledge. The products should communicate all necessary information, they must tolerate mishandling and be manageable with minimal effort. In addition, body size, position and mobility should be of no importance when interacting with them. If one assumes these principles the chances of products and services being accessible to all people with major or minor disabilities increases (Hansson 2006).

One way of moving the design focus away from the products themselves is the development of service design, which has expanded greatly in recent years. Here the customer or consumer is the focus and may concern developing systems for better customer relations and individualization of services at banks, hospitals and hotels, design of receptions at museums, municipal services or services over the internet. Businesses have long sought to tie up their clients with long-term service contracts. Now people using marketing speak are talking about 'the extended product' that includes both the core product and related services, and where the boundaries between them become ever more fluid (Johansson 2006). Total solutions and customization are the watchwords for industry as well. In the beginning of the twenty-first century, the chief of design for Volvo 3P, Aina Nilsson Ström (b. 1953), was working on designing packaging solutions for safe and secure truck transport on the roads, from the cab to the concept of accommodation. At the same time Ergonomidesign (Veryday) designed a timesaving express check-in for business passengers for SAS, where ticket vending machines were just a part of a much larger immaterial commission.

All design ideas do not necessarily have to be reproduced but may remain conceptual or virtual. These issues were brought to the fore in the exhibitions *Formbart* (Formable) at Liljevalchs konsthall in Stockholm and *Konceptdesign* (Conceptual Design) at Nationalmuseum, two of the many activities that took place in 2005 in connection with the government-proclaimed Designåret (Year of Design). In the exhibition catalogue for *Konceptdesign*, Cilla Robach (2005) reflects on the separation of art and design, and argues that the design world was moving towards the arts, while 'many artists were approaching the perceived "solid" disciplines design and architecture at a time when fact and fiction – the virtual and real – were increasingly merging. One of the aims was precisely to "differentiate the design from the product-oriented economically-driven realm"'.

Since 1993, the Dutch Droog Design has overturned our way of perceiving objects and shapes. In Sweden, the groups Uglycute (1999) and Front (2003) emerged as two exponents of the new conceptual wave, with spectacular exhibitions that resounded around the world. They represented a kind of anti-design where the ideas themselves and the design process were more important than more traditional design connotations such as style and finish (Plate 24). This socio-critical conceptual design should primarily seek to ask questions and stimulate debate. Robach (2005: 23) raises the question of whether they are examples of 'a new generation of consumers with different expectations on products than their parents. Consumers who have grown up in an age where the internet and mobile telephony have offered a global platform for continuous contact. Perhaps they find immaterial experiences, critical questioning and communicative values more attractive than material symbols?'

Design is today limitless and the flow of ideas is free. Design thinking and design methods are spreading to ever more sectors of society. What started as an alliance between art and technology, today tends to be about design as a tool for business development. It took over a century for the technicians to accept the designer as an equal party. It seems to be going considerably faster for the economists, although many researchers point out that the designer's more subjective methods based on intuition and feeling have been difficult to fuse with the economists' rational ideals (Svengren Holm and Johansson 2007 and Digerfeldt-Månsson 2009). Trends and concepts supersede one another, even if the content in many cases is remarkably similar, although framed in different packages. Of course seeing does not sate the eye and the ear is not full from listening; perhaps there are a few new things under the sun, to paraphrase somewhat liberally the words of wisdom in the first chapter of Ecclesiastes. However, the fundamental task, which once joined art and industry, remains the importance of utilizing the designer's sensitivity and tools to satisfy human needs. At the same time, we must not turn a blind eye to the environmental responsibility resting heavily on the designer's shoulders, or to quote the findings of the British design critic John Thackara:

> Eighty percent of the environmental impact of the products, services, and infra-structures around us is determined at the design stage. Design decisions shape the processes behind the products we use, the materials and energy required to make them, the ways we operate them on a daily basis, and what happens to them when we no longer need them. (Thackara 2005:1)

The Collections, Meeting Places, Archives, Awards

There is not the same range of museums, venues and archives within the field of design as in art and cultural history. That makes it at once both easy and difficult to write the history of Swedish design: easy because the knowledge is concentrated in a few places, difficult because much of it is still undocumented and unsystem-atized. A major source is, of course, the journal *Form*, which started in 1932 with its predecessor *SST* (*Svenska Slöjdföreningens Tidskrift* [Swedish Society of Crafts and Design's Journal]) from 1905. But despite a rich range of journalism over the years and several books that cover various parts of the discipline, the best surveys are in the form of exhibitions, mainly at the Röhsska Museum in Gothenburg and Nationalmuseum in Stockholm.

Both the Röhsska Museum and Nationalmuseum have entire floors devoted to educational exhibitions on the design and crafts history of recent centuries. A prob-lem with museums, however, is that the objects can only be experienced visually in their glass display cases. Even the most common everyday objects obtained fall within the museum's rules as soon as they are incorporated and registered in the collections.

A few other museums, which are in possession of major collections of interesting artefacts relating to design history, should also be mentioned; they have also signif-icantly increased their interest in the design field in recent years. Nordiska museet started its collecting activities with a focus on folk costumes, but now has a great breadth in its collections, which span, for example, furniture, textiles, wallpaper, packaging, toys and eating utensils. There is also a good deal on display in their thematic permanent exhibitions. Similar material can be found at Kulturen in Lund, which has even more objects, and at Göteborgs stadsmuseum (The Gothenburg City Museum). Tekniska museet (Technical Museum) in Stockholm has, in addition to the world's finest collection of Swedish and foreign telephones, an excellent collection of vacuum cleaners, workshop machinery and older industrial products. There are also large archival collections in all of these museums.

Design exhibitions are also shown at the Swedish Society of Crafts and Design's exhibition halls. In Malmö, the local association for Skåne has long had its own premises, known as Form/Design Center. In Stockholm, the Swedish Society of Crafts and Design has periodically pursued prolific exhibition activity, at various premises. The lack of a permanent venue and clear responsibilities has gradually developed into an almost national trauma, which gave rise to several government enquiries. In 2002 the Swedish Society of Crafts and Design was given a government mandate to act as a meeting place for form and design, that is to say function as an exhibition and knowledge centre and stimulate research and documentation in the field. As of 2010 this responsibility has been taken over by Arkitekturmuseet (The Swedish Museum of Architecture, since 2013 under the new name The Swedish Centre for Architecture and Design (ArkDes)). Meeting places became a fashionable concept in the 2000s. With the help of funding from the state KK-stiftelsen (The Knowledge Foundation) several cross-boundary meeting places were launched geared towards the experience industry. Among other things, the lively meeting place for design ADA (Association for Design and Advertising) was established in Gothenburg in connection with Designåret 2005 (Design year 2005).

To better understand the origins of the artefacts and the work processes behind them requires access to various forms of archival material. This concerns sketches, renderings, models and prototypes, but also written archival material in the form of correspondence, records, marketing materials and the like. This material is normally stored in the commissioning companies' archives or is in the possession of the design consultants. However, one consequence of mergers and transitions of ownership is that not all companies see their old documents as an important part of brand building but rather consider their historical archives as a burden on the expense account. In the case of the design consultants' own preserved documents, they are often at risk after the creator's death if there is little interest from the beneficiaries and estate. It is on these occasions that it is important to have an active and committed external archivist.

The Swedish Society of Crafts and Design's historic archives have long been a rich source to tap into and one that many have taken advantage of. Their project *Levande design* (Living design) constitutes important newly added material, consisting of filmed interviews with key people active in the design field. The project started in 2007 and samples are available on their website (www.svenskform.se). Older design historical material can be found in the country's regional state archives, city archives, social movement archives and Riksarkivet (National Archives); however, it rarely has its own avenue of inquiry and therefore tends to drown in the other public archival material. Many museums also have a long tradition of accepting certain design historical archival material, usually in connection with acquisitions or donations of objects for the collections.

As a result of the steadily increasing interest in design, there are now some specialized archives available much to the joy of both the industry and researchers. These archives have grown out of slightly different circumstances and complement rather than compete with each other. The oldest is located in Pukeberg on the outskirts of Nybro in Småland. Its name is simply Designarkivet (The Design Archive) (www.designarkivet.se) and started in 1978 as an ancillary activity for Kalmar konstmuseum

(Kalmar Art Museum). The model was the successful Skissernas museum (Museum of Sketches) in Lund and the idea was that the archive would primarily cover south-eastern Sweden. It started with donated sketches that reflected Arthur Percy's activity at Karlskrona porslinsfabrik (Karlskrona Porcelain Factory) but as new material was incorporated the boundaries had to be revised, both concerning material types and coverage. The textile materials quickly attained a prominent position and today the archive holds about 100,000 archived objects, of which there are about 25,000 rolled textiles. Designarkivet, originally called Arkiv för svensk formgivning (Archives of Swedish Design), moved from Kalmar to new, more modern premises near the glass-works in Pukeberg 2006–2008. Nybro Municipality invested in a multimillion effort to create a small design centre in the area.

In 2000, the Swedish Society of Crafts and Design initiated an internet-based research database (www.designarkiv.se) with a comprehensive amount of material from the society's archives, photo archives and library. The database was produced by Centrum för Näringslivshistoria (The Centre for Business History or CfN, formerly Stockholms företagsminnen [Stockholm's Business Memories]) and was launched in 2007. That same year, a major design effort took place at CfN when the Swedish Society of Crafts and Design's extensive and previously scattered archives were consolidated and moved there. A special exhibition department was also furnished with donated sketches, models and prototypes from different design companies, for example, A&E Design, Lars Lallerstedt and Innovator. CfN (www. naringslivshistoria. se) is a corporate and industrial history centre whose purpose is to preserve and present their history. It started in 1974 and is considered to have the world's largest collection of archival material and objects relating to business history. The collections come from more than 7,000 active and discontinued businesses and include material from the eighteenth century until today. Several large companies' collections of documents are deposited here, such as H&M, Electrolux and Ericsson, which means that it is also possible to find much that is of design historical interest in this content-rich material.

At the Centrum för Näringslivshistoria (The Centre for Business History), there is some graphic design material that primarily reflects Swedish advertising history, but in 2001 an archive with solely this focus was created. This is Sveriges arkiv för reklam och grafisk design (Sweden's archives for advertising and graphic design), or Rum för reklam (Space for advertising) as it also called, and is based in Landskrona Museum. The initiative for the archive had been taken by Sveriges Reklam & Designhistoriska förening (Swedish Advertising & Design Historical Association), which had formed in 1996. The archive moved with its 100,000 objects in 2008 to its own premises at the top of the large and centrally located museum building. Here poster collections coexist with sketches, advertisements, books, clips, movies, pictures, correspondence and some objects. New donations are received continuously, but several of the big Swedish names are already represented, some with extensive material.

Encouraging and rewarding creative efforts through scholarships or prestigious awards has a long tradition. During the nineteenth century a government scholarship from Konstakademien (Royal Academy of Fine Arts) or Kommerskollegium (The National Board of Trade) was perhaps the only opportunity for a talented artist, architect or engineer to study classical art first-hand or visit the major international exhibitions. In the same tradition but somewhat more modest are the grants that are today still awarded to talented graduating students at for example Konstfack and Högskolan för design och konsthantverk (School of Design and Crafts or HDK). The first large specialized design prize was the Nordic Lunning Prize. It was awarded during the period 1951–1970 to a total of forty-four Scandinavian designers and craftsmen, of which fourteen were Swedish. The prize, which was named after the Danish-American businessman Frederik Lunning, amounted to US$15,000.

The prestigious Lunning Prize gained a Swedish successor through Torsten and Wanja Söderberg's Prize in 1994. It was created by Torsten och Ragnar Söderbergs stiftelser (The Torsten and Ragnar Söderberg Foundations), which is one of the largest financiers of Swedish research. Torsten Söderberg was the head of the family business Söderberg & Haak's operations in Gothenburg and was also the chairman of the Röhsska Konstslöjdmuseets vänner (The Friends of the Röhsska Museum) for over ten years. He shared his design interest with his wife Wanja. In connection with the centenary of the husband's birth the Söderberg Foundations therefore decided to create a Nordic design and craft prize in the name of Torsten and Wanja. The prize is awarded annually and the prize money has been gradually increased and in 2015 amounted to one million kronor, making it one of the world's largest design prizes. The prize is administered by the Röhsska Museum, which also organizes a large solo exhibition with the winner in connection with the award ceremony. Mats Theselius became the first Swede to win Torsten and Wanja Söderberg's Prize (1997) and the others are Kerstin Wickman (joint critics award-winner, 1999), Björn Dahlström (2001), H. C. Ericson (2002), and the nine female car designers responsible for the project Volvo YCC (2005), Front (2010) and Ann-Sofie Back (2014).

In addition to this large and wide-ranging prize, every design and business area has its own prizes and awards. Bruno Mathssonpriset (Bruno Mathsson Prize) was established in 1983 by Bruno Mathsson and his wife Karin. In 2009 the prize money totalled 200,000 kronor. Several female furniture designers are among the winners of the last few years, for example, Gunilla Allard (2000), Anna von Schewen (2003) and Anna Kraitz (2008). The Guldknappen (Gold Button) award is presented every year by the magazine *Damernas Värld* to a fashion designer who has distinguished themselves through their collections. Since 2008, the creations from all the Guldknappen winning collections are included in Nordiska museet's (Nordic Museum) collections. Another closely related and noted prize, The Nordic Award in Textiles, was founded in 2000 by the foundation Fokus in Borås, a town known for its textile production. The prize, which is the largest of its kind in the Nordic region, amounts to 250,000 kronor and also includes a solo exhibition at Textilmuseet (Museum of Textile History) in Borås.

In the graphical field there are a number of awards with Guldägget (Golden egg) being the most famous. Guldägget was established in 1961 by SAFFT

(Swedish Association of Commercial Artists) to reward those advertisers who helped create advertising of high artistic quality. For a number of years the winners have been presented in a lavish advertising art book. Among the most decorated Guldägg winners over the years are Forsman & Bodenfors in Gothenburg, while the most durable entry has to be the general goods company ICA's multiple Guldägg winning series of commercials for television; after hundreds of episodes since its inception in 2001 and still in production in 2015, the agency King has demonstrated the importance of storytelling in visual communication. All material related to Guldägget is archived in Rum för Reklam (Space for advertising) at the Landskrona Museum. Svensk Bokkonst (Swedish Book Art), which every year honours and exhibits twenty-five exemplarily produced books, was started in 1933 to inspire better quality in Swedish book production. Berlingpriset (Berling Award) is an annual, typographically oriented design award that is addressed to eminent Swedish graphic designers. It was founded by Karl-Erik Forsberg, the creator of the Berling Roman typeface, and began being awarded in 1991. It is primarily the royalties from the font that finance the prize, which in 2014, when Björn Kusoffsky won, amounted to 15,000 kronor. The organization Svenska Tecknare (The Association of Swedish Illustrators) has organized the jury competition Kolla! (Look!) since 2005, which rewards graphic design and illustration as well as motion media and web design. Since 2005, there is also Svenska Designpriset (Swedish Design Award), which was launched by the company Batteri Kommunikation together with the magazine *Cap & Design* and is an annual competition for all who work in graphic communications.

An international equivalent to the aforementioned Utmärkt Svensk Form (Excellent Swedish Design), now Design S, is the honorary Red Dot Award, which is annually awarded by Design Zentrum Nordrhein Westfalen in Essen, Germany. It began in 1955 as a collection of excellent industrial products for a permanent exhibition, through among other things the establishment of a contest for best product design. Since then, Red Dot Award has evolved into the world's premier design award with several competition categories: Design team of the year (since 1991), Communication design (since 1993) and Design concept (since 2005); a development that aptly reflects the design field's changes and focus. The fact that in 2008 more than 11,000 entries from 61 different countries were submitted might serve as an example to understand the full extent of the competition. Even though the awards are fairly numerous, there is also room for an exclusive group of winners with exquisite design under the title of Best of the Best. Veryday is the only Swedish company that has been named the Design Team of the Year (2014), which is a 'Hall of Fame' of international design. However, a number of Swedish products have been awarded Best of the Best. In the context of Germany's reconstruction of the 1950s another prestigious international honorary award was started, iF (International Design Forum) Design Award with slightly fewer entries but with more prize categories.

Two main contributors should be mentioned for their award of scholarships in support of research and educational purposes within the field of design: Estrid Ericsons stiftelse (Estrid Ericson Foundation) www.estrid-ericsons-stiftelse.nu and Torsten och Ragnar Söderbergs stiftelser (Torsten and Ragnar Söderberg Foundations) www.soderbergsstiftelser.se. For support for larger design historical projects one turns primarily to Vetenskapsrådet (Swedish Research Council) www.vr.se or Riksbankens Jubileumsfond (Bank of Sweden Tercentenary Foundation) www.rj.se.

Bibliography

60 år Svensk Bokkonst (1995), Utställningskatalog nr 581, Stockholm: Nationalmuseum.

A:son Palmqvist, Lena (1988), 'Sjuhäradsbygdens bondefabrikörer', in *Bebyggelsehistorisk tidskrift nr 16*, Stockholm: Föreningen Bebyggelsehistorisk tidskrift.

acceptera (1931), Stockholm: Tiden.

Adelswärd, Gösta (1963), *Varaktigare än kopparn. Åtvidaberg 1413–1963*, Stockholm: AB Åtvidabergs Industrier.

AGA 50 år 1904–1954, Stockholm: Svenska AB Gasaccumulator.

AGA-journalen (1928), Stockholm: Gasaccumulator.

Åhrén, Uno (1925), *Breaks*, Stockholm: Svenska Slöjdföreningens årsbok.

Åkerman, Brita et al. (1984), *Kunskap för vår vardag. Utbildning och forskning för hemmen*, Stockholm: Förlaget Akademilitteratur AB.

American Engineering Council (1921), *Waste in Industry*, New York: McGraw-Hill.

Anderson, Chris (2006), *The Long Tail: Why the Future of Business is Selling Less of More*, New York: Hyperion.

Arnshav, Marina (1997), *Monteringsfärdiga trähus under andra hälften av 1800-talet. En studie av tre snickerifabriker i Stockholm*, Seminarieuppsats i konstvetenskap, Stockholms universitet.

Arström, Folke (1953), 'Aktuella riktlinjer inom amerikansk formgivning', in *Hantverk och kultur 1951–1952*, Stockholm: Statens hantverksinstitut.

Artéus, Margareta (ed.) (1992), *Kosta 250: 1742–1992 250 Years of Craftsmanship*, translated by Alan Imber and Kim C. Bastin, photographs by Jörgen Reimer, Kosta: Kosta Boda.

Artéus Thor, Margareta (2006), *Gemlas värld. En lekfull industri i skönhetens tjänst*, Fagerhult: Frommens förlag.

Arwidson, Bertil (2006), *100 år med svenska möbler. Från snickeri till möbelindustri*, Stockholm: Svensk Byggtjänst.

Bark, Jane (2001), *Jane Barks bilder. Från femtiotalet till idag*, Stockholm: Bark Design Förlag.

Bayley, Stephen (2000), *Taste*, Köpenhamn: Danish Design Center.

Beckman, Ulf and Gunilla Widengren (ed.) (1994), *Konstfack 150 år, Tanken och handen*, Stockholm: Page One Publishing.

Bedoire, Fredric (1981), 'Den stora arbetsplatsen', in *S:t Eriks årsbok*, Stockholm.

Bergenblad, Harry and Walter Hallerstig (1989), *300 år med sikte framåt – En bok om Husqvarna*, Husqvarna AB.

Bergengren, Kurt (1963), 'Förpackningarna – maskörjobb eller samhällsfråga?', *Form* nr 10. Stockholm: Svenska slöjdföreningen.

Berglund, Erik (1997), *Tala om kvalitet. Om möbelmarknaden och brukarorienterad produktutveckling*, Västerljung: Bokförlaget Axplock.

Bernadotte, Sigvard (1997), *Design Sigvard Bernadotte*, Stockholm: Nationalmuseum.

Birch, Stuart (2000), 'Global Viewpoints, Design Roots', *Automotive Engineering International* (April).

Birde, Marie (2007), 'Tidlösa trasor', *Dagens Nyheter* (10 September 2007).

Biström, Lars and Bo Sundin (1997), 'Utombordsmotorer. Design och innovativa värden', in Lasse Brunnström (ed.), *Svensk industridesign. En 1900-talshistoria*, Stockholm: Norstedts.

Björkman, Ivar (1998), 'Sven Duchamp – expert på auraproduktion: om entreprenörskap, visioner, konst och företag', Diss., Stockholms universitet.

Böhn-Jullander, Ingrid (1992), *Bruno Mathsson: möbelkonstnären, glashusarkitekten, människan*. Lund: Bokförlaget Signum.

Boman, Monica (ed.) (1991), *Svenska möbler 1890–1990*, Lund: Bokförlaget Signum.

Boman, Monica (ed.) ([1989] 2000), *Estrid Ericson. Orkidé i vinterlandet*, Stockholm: Carlssons.

Bowallius, Marie-Louise (1999), 'The Origin and Professionalisation of Swedish Graphic Design 1930–1965', MA thesis, Design History Course, V&A/RCA.

Brunius, Jan and Niels-Henry Mörck (ed.) (1998), *HDK 150 år, jubileumsskrift 1848–1998*, Göteborg.

Brunnström, Lasse (ed.) ([1997] 2004), *Svensk industridesign. En 1900-talshistoria*, Stockholm: Norstedts (Prisma).

Brunnström, Lasse (2006), *Telefonen, en designhistoria*, Stockholm: Bokförlaget Atlantis.

Brunnström, Lasse and Karin Wagner (ed.) (2015), *Den (o)hållbara förpackningen* (with a short English summary), Stockholm: Balkong förlag.

Brunnström, Lasse, Bengt Norling, and Bengt Spade (2002), *Juvelkvarnen i Göteborg. En hörnpelare i svensk livsmedelsförsörjning*, Göteborg: Göteborgs Stadsmuseum.

Brunnström, Lisa (1990), *Den rationella fabriken. Om funktionalismens rötter*, Diss Umeå: Dokuma förlag.

Brunnström, Lisa (2004), *Det svenska folkhemsbygget. Om Kooperativa Förbundets arkitektkontor*, Stockholm: Arkitektur förlag.

Bush, Donald J. (1975), *The Streamlined Decade*, New York: George Braziller.

Carson, Rachel ([1962] 1963), *Tyst vår*, Stockholm: Tiden.

Childs, Marquis W. (1936), *Sweden the Middle Way*, London: Faber.

Conradson, Birgitta (1977), *Sillburkar och tvålkartonger, om våra förpackningar och deras historia*, Stockholm: Nordiska museet.

Co-op reklam i Sverige under ett kvarts sekel (1955), Stockholm: Kooperativa förbundet.

Cornell, Elias (1952), 'De stora utställningarnas arkitekturhistoria', Diss., Bokförlaget Natur och kultur, Stockholm.

Cornell, Elias (1967), 'Bruno Mathsson och tiden', in *Arkitektur nr 3*. Stockholm: Bokförlaget Natur och kultur.

Dahlbäck Lutteman, Helena (1991), 'Storhetstid med världsrykte, 1917 – andra världskriget', in *Svenskt glas*, Stockholm: Wahlström & Widstrand.

Danielson, Sofia (1991), *Den goda smaken och samhällsnyttan*, Stockholm: Nordiska museet.

Design Sigvard Bernadotte (1997), Nationalmuseums utställningskatalog, Stockholm: Nationalmuseum.

Digerfeldt-Månsson, Theresa (2009), 'Formernas liv i designföretaget – om design och design management som konst', Diss., Stockholms universitet, inst. för företagsekonomi, Stockholm.

Dormer, Peter ([1993] 1995), *Design since 1945*, London: Thames & Hudson.

Dreyfuss, Henry (1959–1960), *The Measure of Man: Human Factors in Design*, New York: Whitney Library of Design.

du Rietz, Peter (ed.) (2002), *Dammsugare – städning och Electrolux*, Stockholm: Tekniska museet.

Eklund Nyström, Sigrid (1992), 'Möbelarkitekt på 1930-talet: om inredningsfirman Futurum och hur en ny yrkesgrupp etablerar sig', Diss., Nordiska museet, Stockholm.

Eksell, Olle ([1964] 1999), *Design = ekonomi*, Malmö: Bokförlaget Arena.

Eksell, Olle (1999), *Mina ögonblick*, Malmö: Bokförlaget Arena.

Emilson, Anders (2005), *Design = Förändring. Konceptdesign*, Stockholm: Nationalmuseum.

Engman, Hans (ed.) (1999), *Årsringar 1899–1999*, Edsbyn: Bilder av Edsbyverken från hantverk till modern industri.

Ericson, Estrid (1968), *Josef Frank*, Stockholm: Nationalmuseum.

Ericson, Sigfrid (1948), *Slöjdföreningens skola 1848–1948. Skolans historia genom hundra år*, Göteborg.

Ericsson, Anne-Marie (2005), *M/S Kungsholms inredning: mästerverk i svensk art deco*, Lund: Signum.

Fallan, Kjetil (2017), *Designing Modern Norway: A History of Design Discourse*, London and New York: Routledge.

Form (1958), Articles by Tomàso Maldonado and Gunnar Jonsson, Form. Svenska Slöjdföreningens tidskrift.

Frank, Josef (1934), *Form* nr 30, Stockholm: Svenska slojdföreningen.

Frayling, Christopher (1993), 'Research in Art and Design', *Royal College of Art Research Papers 1*, nr 1, London.

Frick, Gunilla (1986), *Konstnär i industrin*, Stockholm: Nordiska museet.

Gårdlund, Torsten (1941), 'Om den tidiga svenska träförädlingsindustrin,' *Ekonomisk tidskrift*, Uppsala.

Gårdlund, Torsten (1942), *Industrialismens samhälle*, Stockholm: Tiden.

Garnert, Jan (1993), *Anden i lampan. Etnologiska perspektiv på ljus och mörker*, Stockholm: Carlssons.

Glambek, Ingeborg (1997), *Det nordiske i arkitektur og design sett utenfra*, Oslo.

Glambek, Ingeborg (2003), 'Kunstindustrimuseer. Opprettelse og opprinnelig formål', in Arne Bugge Amundsen, Bjarne Rogan and Margrethe C. Stang (ed.), *Museer i fortid og nåtid*, Oslo: Novus.

Godin, Seth (2006), *Small is the New Big*, London: Penguin Books.

Göransdotter, Maria (2005), 'God smak som fostran eller folkbildning? – Om kurser i heminredning på 1940-talet', in *Årsbok för folkbildning 2004*, Stockholm: Föreningen för folkbildningsforskning.

Gordan, Dan ([2002] 2005), *Svenska stolar och deras formgivare 1899–2001*, Stockholm: Byggförlaget.

Gram, Magdalena (1994), 'Bokkonstnären Akke Kumlien: tradition och modernitet, konstnärsidentitet och konstnärsroll', Diss., Norstedts, Stockholm.

Gram, Magdalena (2006), 'När typografin blev "modern": om modernismens genombrott i svensk typografi', *Biblis* nr 34, s. 51–63, Stockholm: KB.

H&M Annual report (2008). Stockholm: H&M.

Hagströmer, Denise (2001), *Swedish Design*, Stockholm: Svenska Institutets förlag.

Hald, Arthur (1947), 'Hemutställningen 1917 och dess upptakt. Intervju med Elsa Gullberg', in *Form nr 10*, Stockholm.

Hald, Arthur (1985), *Design*, Stockholm: Design Center.

Hald, Arthur (1989), 'Elsa Gullberg – chef för Slöjdföreningens förmedlingsbyrå', in *Elsa Gullberg – textil pionjär*, Stockholm: Nationalmuseum, utställningskatalog nr 523.

Hald, Arthur (1991), *Gustavsberg, verktyg för en idé. Hjalmar Olssons skildring av 60 års arbete*, Stockholm: Bokförlaget Atlantis.

Hansson, Jonas (2002), 'Den industriella världen', in *Konsten 1915–1950*, Lund: Signums svenska konsthistoria.

Hansson, Lena (2006), 'Universal Design a Marketable or Utopian Concept', Diss., Centrum för konsumentvetenskap, Göteborg.

Haug, Wolfgang Fritz ([1971] 1975), *Kritik av varuestetiken*, Stockholm: Pan/Norstedt.

Hedqvist, Hedvig (1995), '50-åriga Form/Design Center', in Kerstin Wickman (ed.), *Formens rörelse*, Stockholm: Carlssons.

Hedqvist, Hedvig (2002), *1900–2002: Svensk form – internationell design*, Stockholm: DN.

Herlitz-Gezelius, Ann Marie (1992), *Åren som gått. Nordiska kompaniet*, Lund: Signum.

Hogdal, Lis (1995), 'Demokratisk design och andra möbler', in *Arkitektur nr 4*, Stockholm: Arkitektur förlag.

Houltz, Anders (2003), *Teknikens tempel. Modernitet och industriarv på Göteborgsutställningen 1923*, Hedemora & Göteborg: Gidlunds förlag & Göteborgs Stadsmuseum.

Houltz, Anders (2005), *Snillen, kullager och Volvobilar*. Available online: http://www2.hist. uu.se/historikermote05/program/idehist/Anders%20Houltz%20paper.pdf (15 July 2009).

Huldt, Åke H. (1953), 'Ingrid Dessau – Signe Persson på Galerie Moderne', *Form*, Stockholm: Svenska Slöjdföreningens tidskrift.

Hult, Jan (1992), 'The Itera Plastic Bicycle', *Social Studies of Science*, 22: 2.

Husqvarna, *Husqvarna. Kokspisar och kaminer 1897–1952*, Gamleby: PM-Bokförlag i samarbete med Husqvarna Fabriksmuseum.

IKEA (1995), *Demokratisk design: En bok om de tre dimensionerna form, funktion, och pris på IKEA*, Älmhult: IKEA.

Ilstedt Hjelm, Sara (2007), 'Energi som syns', in *Under ytan: en antologi om designforskning*, Stockholm: Raster förlag & SVID.

Isacson, Maths (1988), 'Proto-industrins och fabriksindustrins regionala utveckling i Norden – en översikt', in *Bebyggelsehistorisk tidskrift nr 16*, Stockholm: Ekonomisk-historiska institutionen.

Isacson, Maths (2007), *Industrisamhället Sverige. Arbete, ideal och kulturarv*, Lund: Studentlitteratur.

Ivanov, Gunnela (2004), 'Vackrare vardagsvara – design för alla? Gregor Paulsson och Svenska Slöjdsföreningen 1915–1925', Diss., Umeå: Institutionen för historiska studier.

James, Tim (2002), *The Story of a Kitchen Classic*, Bath: Absolute Press.

Jahnke, Marcus (ed.) (2006), *Formgivning Normgivning*, Göteborg: Centrum för konsumtionsvetenskap.

Johannesson, Lena (1995), *Gerd Miller – illustratör eller Hon som ritade 50-talet*, Stockholm: Carlssons.

Johansson, Claes (1997), *Tretti knyck. Mopeden i Sverige*, Stockholm: Byggförlaget.

Johansson, Gotthard (1945), 'Hur bor vårt folk? Bostadsvanorna utforskas', *Form* nr 1, Stockholm: Svenska slöjdföreningen.

Johansson, Gotthard (1952), 'Josef Frank och Svenskt Tenn', in *Josef Frank. Tjugo år i Svenskt Tenn. Nationalmusei utställningskatalog nr 188*, Stockholm: Nationalmuseum.

Johansson, Ulla (2006), *Design som utvecklingskraft. En utvärdering av regeringens designsatsning 2003–2005*, Växjö: Växjö universitet.

Josef Frank 1968, Stockholm: Nationalmuseum.

Kåberg, Helena (ed.) (2007), *Förfärligt härligt*, Stockholm: Nationalmuseum, utställningskatalog.

Kåberg, Helena (2003), 'Rationell arkitektur. Företagskontor för massproduktion och masskommunikation', Diss., Uppsala universitet, Uppsala.

Kåberg, Helena (2006), 'Affischpojken Stig Lindberg', in *Stig Lindberg. Nationalmusei utställningskatalog nr 649*, Stockholm: Nationalmuseum.

Kalha, Harri (2003), '"Just one of those things" – The Design in Scandinavia Exhibition 1954–57', in Halén and Wickman (ed.), *Scandinavian Design beyond the Myth*, Stockholm: Arvinius Förlag/Form Förlag.

Kallin, Sten (2007), Från matematikmaskin till IT. Intervju av Anna Orrghen 10 September 2007. Available online: www.tekniskamuseet.se/upload/Dokochforskning/7_Sten_Kallin.pdf

Key, Ellen (1899), *Skönhet för alla: fyra uppsatser*, Stockholm: Verdandi.

Kicherer, Sibylle (1990), *Olivetti: A Study of the Corporate Management of Design*, London: Trefoil.

Kolmodin, Anne and Aurora Pelli (2005), *Design för innovation och tillväxt – en framtida konkurrensmöjlighet*, Östersund: Institutet för tillväxtpolitiska studier.

Konstfack 150 år. Tanken och handen (1994), Stockholm: Page One Publishing AB.

Kooperativa Förbundets arkitektkontor 1925–1949, del 2. (1949), Stockholm: Kooperativa Förbundets bokförlag.

Korvenmaa, Pekka (2009), *Finnish Design: A Concise History*, Helsinki: University of Art and Design Helsinki.

Krantz, Knut, Ryberg, Gunnar et al. (1955), *Co-op reklam i Sverige under ett kvarts sekel*, Stockholm: KF: s bokförlag.

Kristoffersson, Sara (2003), 'Memphis och den italienska antidesignrörelsen', Diss., Acta Universitatis Gothoburgensis, Göteborg.

Kristoffersson, Sara (2014), *Design by IKEA: A Cultural History*, London: Bloomsbury Academic.

Lagerquist, Marshall (1943), *Pinnstolar: ett bidrag till Nässjö stolfabriks historia*, Nässjö: Nässjö stolfabrik.

Lagerström, Hugo (1928), 'Elementärtypografi', in *Nordisk Boktryckarekonst*, Stockholm: Bröderna Lagerström Boktryckare.

Lange, Rustan (1953), 'Industriell formgivning inom bilindustrien', in *Chalmeristernas tidning Tofsen*, Göteborg: Chalmers studentkår.

Larsen, Lars Bang (2007), 'Undergroundtidningen Puss', *Hjärnstorm nr 92–93*.

Larsson, Lena (1945), 'På visit hos 100 familjer', *Form* nr 1, Stockholm: Svenska slöjdföreningen.

Larsson, Lena (1960), 'Köp, slit, släng. Några funderingar kring ett slitstarkt ämne', *Form* nr 7–8. Stockholm: Svenska slöjdföreningen.

Larsson, Lena (1991), *Varje människa är ett skåp*, Stockholm: Bokförlaget Trevi & Bra Böcker.

Lennermo, Jonas (2007), *Puss kysser ingen*. Available online: www.tidskrift.nu (05 June 2009).

Lidman, Sara (1966), *Samtal i Hanoi*, Stockholm: Bonnier.

Lidman, Sara (1968), *Gruva*, Stockholm: Bonnier.

Lindberg, Sten G. (1987), *Karl-Erik Forsbergs bokstavskonst*, Västerås: Tryckcentra AB.

Lindberg, Sten G. (1994), *Karl-Erik Forsberg – the Swedish Designer of the Berling Roman*, Stockholm: Nationalmuseum.

Lindblad, Thomas (2004), *Bruksföremål av plast*, Lund: Bokförlaget Signum.

Lindh, Björn-Eric (1992), *Scania fordonshistoria 1891–1991*, Stockholm: Streiffert & Co.

Lindqvist, Sven (1957), *Reklamen är livsfarlig*, Stockholm: Bonnier.

Lindström, Hugo (1997), 'Min tid med Ralph Lysell och Alvar Lenning', in Lasse Brunnström (ed.), *Svensk industridesign. En 1900-talshistoria*, Stockholm: Norstedts.

Lindström, Hugo and Knut Ljungh (1958), 'Den moderna postlådan – av plast, naturligtvis', *Plastvärlden*, nr 10. Svensk inköpstidning AB.

Linn, Björn (1997), 'Svenska fordon – svensk form', in Lasse Brunnström (ed.), *Svensk industridesign. En 1900-talshistoria*, Stockholm: Norstedts.

Linn, Björn (2002), 'Att ge tingen form', in *Konsten 1915–1950*, Lund: Signums svenska konsthistoria.

Livstedt, Åke (1994), 'Metallkonsthantverk', in *Tanken och handen. Konstfack 150 år*, Stockholm: Page One Publishing.

Löndahl, Göran (1996), 'Kyla och livsmedel, igår och idag', in *Kyla på gott och ont (red. Ingvar Holmér). Arbete och hälsa, nr 5*, Stockholm: Arbetslivsinstitutet.

Lundqvist, Pia (2008), 'Marknad på väg. Den västgötska gårdfarihandeln 1790–1864', Diss., Historiska institutionen, Göteborgs universitet, Göteborg.

Lunell, Erika (2007), 'Okonventionella varumärken – form, färg, doft, ljud', Diss., Norstedts Juridik AB, Stockholm.

Maddock, Peter (1996), *Designing Sweden. En personlig betraktelse om den svenska designvärlden från femtiotalets mitt till nittiotalet*, Unpublished manuscript.

Magnusson, Lars and Maths Isacson (1988), 'Proto-industrialisering – en förusättning för den industriella revolutionen? Inledning', in *Bebyggelsehistorisk tidskrift nr 16*, Stockholm: Ekonomisk-historiska institutionen Uppsala universitet.

Mandal, A. C. ([1974] 1982), *Den sittande människan*, Stockholm: Liber Förlag.

Martinius, Birgitta (2012), *Stolar från Lindome: 1740 till 1850*, Mölndals stadsmuseum.

Marx, Karl ([1867] 1969), *Kapitalet I*. Lund: Cavefors/Clarté.

Maufe, Edward (1931), Contemporary Swedish Architecture. *The Architectural Review*. London: Architectural P.

Meggs, Philip B. and Alston W. Purvis ([1983] 2006), *Meggs' History of Graphic Design*, Hoboken, NJ: John Wiley & Sons.

Mollerup, Per (2002), 'Varumärkets historia', in *Identitet: om varumärken, tecken och symboler*, Nationalmusei utställningskatalog.

Monö, Rune (1997), 'Fem decennier som designkonsult', in Lasse Brunnström (ed.), *Svensk industridesign. En 1900- talshistoria*, Stockholm: Norstedts.

Munthe, Gustaf (1926), 'Röhsska Konstslöjdmuseet I Göteborg', in *Studiekamraten*, Stockholm.

Munthe, Gustaf (1945), 'Hundra år – och sedan', in *Vår bostad 1945*, Göteborg: Röhsska Konstslöjdmuseet.

Mötesplats för form och design. Delbetänkande från Form- och designutredningen (1999), Stockholm: SOU, 123.

Nader, Ralph ([1965] 1967), *Den livsfarliga bilen*, Stockholm: Rabén & Sjögren.

Näslund, Iwan (1988), 'Möbelmannen', in Elisabet Stavenow-Hidemark (ed.), *Inspiration och förnyelse: Carl Malmsten 100 år*, Höganäs: Wiken.

Official Descriptive and Illustrated Catalogue of the Great Exhibition 1851, Volume III, *Foreign States*, London.

Nordgren, Sune (2007), *Personakt Sven Lundh*, Malmö: Bokförlaget Arena.

Nyström, Bengt and Jan Brunius (2007), *Rörstrand under 280 år: med fajans, flintgods, porslin & stengods*, Västerås: Ica Bokförlag.

Ohrlander, Gunnar (2003), 'De kallar mig en förlegad blytyp. Gunnar Ohrlander samtalar med Carl Fredrik Hultenheim', *Biblis*, nr 21. Stockholm: Biblis.

Olsson, Christer (1987), *Volvo. Lastbilarna under sextio år*, Malmö: Förlagshuset Norden AB.

Olsson, Kenth (2004), *Från vikingar til vodka*, Kristianstad: Accent Förlag.

Oppenheim, Florence (2008), Rött eller blått? *DIK Forum nr 09*. Stockholm: DIK-förbundet.

Ortmark, Åke (1963), *Sveket mot konsumenterna*, Stockholm: Rabén & Sjögren

Pagold, Susanne (2006), *Function rules. En bok om Ergonomidesign*, Stockholm: Arvinius Förlag.

Papanek, Victor (1970), *Miljön och miljonerna. Design som tjänst eller förtjänst?* Stockholm: Bonnier.

Partington, Angela (1996), 'Perfume: Pleasure, Packaging and Postmodernity', in Pat Kirkham (ed.), *The Gendered Object*, Manchester: Manchester University Press.

Paulsson, Gregor (1915), 'Anarki eller tidsstil', in *Svenska Slöjdföreningens Tidskrift*, Stockholm: Svenska slöjdföreningen.

Paulsson, Gregor (1919), *Vackrare vardagsvara*, Stockholm: Svenska Slöjdföreningen.

Paulsson, Gregor ([1950] 1973), *Svensk stad del 1. Liv och stil i svenska städer under 1800–talet*, Lund: Studentlitteratur.

Paulsson, Gregor and Eva Rudberg (ed.) (1994), *Hakon Ahlberg: arkitekt och humanist*, Stockholm: Statens råd för byggnadsforskning.

Perers, Maria (2003), 'G. A. Berg – Swedish Modernist Designer and Propagandist', Master's thesis, The Bard Graduate Center for Studies in the Decorative Arts, Design and Culture, Bard College, New York.

Petroski, Henry (2006), *Success Through Failure: The Paradox of Design*, Princeton, NJ: Princeton University Press.

Pettersson, Bo ([2001] 2003), *Handelsmännen H&M*, Stockholm: Ekerlids Förlag.

Pulos, Arthur J.*The American Design Adventure*, Cambridge, MA: MIT Press.

Puranen, Britt-Inger (1984), 'Tuberkulos, En sjukdoms förekomst och dess orsaker, Sverige 1750–1980'. Diss., Umeå: Umeå Studies in Economic History.

Råberg, Per G. ([1970] 1972), *Funktionalistiskt genombrott. Radikal miljö och miljödebatt I Sverige 1925–1931*, Stockholm: Norstedts.

Robach, Cilla (1995), 'Designens status skulle höjas', in Kerstin Wickman (ed.), *Formens rörelse. Svensk Form genom 150 år*, Stockholm: Carlssons.

Robach, Cilla (2005), (red.) *Konceptdesign*, Stockholm: Nationalmuseum.

Rörstrand 280 år: med fajans, flintgods, porslin, och stengods (2007), /Bengt Nyström & Jan Brunius/, Västerås: Ica.

Rosell, Gustaf (1997), 'Sekelskiftets ingenjör – uppfinnare och estet', in Lasse Brunnström (ed.), *Svensk industridesign. En 1900-talshistoria*, Stockholm: Norstedts.

Rudberg, Eva (1999), *Stockholmsutställningen 1930. Modernismens genombrott i svensk arkitektur*, Stockholm: Stockholmia förlag.

Rudberg, Eva (2000), 'Vardagens utopi', in *Utopi & verklighet. Svensk modernism 1900–1960*, Stockholm: Moderna museet & Norstedts.

Rudberg, Eva och Eva Paulsson (ed.) (1994), *Hakon Ahlberg: arkitekt & humanist*, Statens råd för byggnadsforskning.

Sampe, Astrid (1984), *svensk industritextil: Swedish Industrial Textiles*, Stockholm: Nationalmuseum.

Sandberg, Klas (2000), *Den kreativa revolutionen – Den svenska reklambranschen 1960–1980*, D-uppsats i Media och kommunikationsvetenskap, Uppsala universitet.

Sandin Bülow, Kersti (2007), 'Design = Kvalitet?', in Lars Strannegård (ed.), *Den omätbara kvaliteten*, Stockholm: Norstedts akademiska förlag.

Schönbäck, Hedvig (1997). 'Volvos bildesign', in Lasse Brunnström (ed.), *Svensk industridesign – en 1900-talshistoria*, Stockholm: Norstedts.

Segerblom, Mats (1983), *Algots. En teko-koncerns uppgång och fall*, Stockholm: Liber förlag.

Selkurt, Claire (2003), 'Design for a Democracy – Scandinavian Design in Postwar America', in *Scandinavian Design beyond the Myth* (ed. Halén and Wickman), Stockholm: Arvinius Förlag/Form Förlag.

Shand, Morton (1930), *Stockholm 1930. The Architectural Review*, August (special number). London: Architectural P.

Simon Thomas, Mienke (2008), *Dutch Design: A History*, London: Reaktion Books.

Sköld, Björn-Åke (1997), 'Sixten Sason: designlegend och förebild', in Lasse Brunnström (ed.), *Svensk industridesign, En 1900-talshistoria*, Stockholm: Norstedts.

Söderholm, Carolina (2008), *Svenska formrebeller1960- och 70-tal*, Lund: Historiska media.

Sparke, Penny (1983), *Consultant Design: The History and Practice of the Designer in Industry*, London: Pembridge Press.

Stahre, Ulrika (2006), Så blev hon en bil. *Expressen*, 5 September 2006. Stockholm: Bonnier AB.

Stavenow, Åke (ed.) (1939), *Swedish Arts and Crafts. Swedish Modern – A Movement Towards Sanity in Design*, Stockholm: The Royal Swedish Commission, New York World's Fair.

Stavenow-Hidemark, Elisabet (2000), 'Möbelkonst och inredningar', in *Konsten 1845–1890*, Lund: Bokförlaget Signum.

Steinwall, Carin and Åsa Crona (1989), *Moderouletten*, Stockholm: Bonnier.

Stubelius, Torsten (1914), *Teknisk tidskrift*, veckoupplagan, Stockholm: Svenska Teknologföreningen.

Sund, Bill (1993), *The Safety Movement. En historisk analys av den svenska modellens amerikanska rötter*, Stockholm: Arbetarskyddsnämnden.

Sundvall, Peggy (2006), *Parkering i Göteborg genom ett halvt sekel*, Göteborg: Gatubolaget.

Svengren Holm, Lisbeth (1995), 'Industriell design som strategisk resurs. En studie av designprocessens metoder och synsätt som del i företags strategiska utveckling', Diss., Lund.

Svengren Holm, Lisbeth and Ulla Johansson (2007), 'Design Management', in Sara Ilstedt Hjelm (ed.), *Under ytan*, Stockholm: Raster förlag.

Tärby, Gunnar (1977), *Lindome. Västsvenskt möbelsnickeri under 300 år*, Stockholm: Liljevalchs.

Tempelman, Emmy C. (1943), 'Kristallpalatset och Londonutställningen', in *Konstvärldens julbok*, Stockholm: Otto G. Carlsund.

Thackara, John (2005), *In the Bubble: Designing in a Complex World*, Cambridge, MA: MIT Press.

Thue, Anniken (1998), 'The Role of a Decorative Arts Museum. Mirror of Society or Independent "Oasis"', *Scandinavian Journal of Design History*, 8. Danish Museum of Decorative Art.

Torekull, Bertil (1998), *Historien om IKEA. Ingvar Kamprad berättar*, Stockholm: W&W.

Tunberg, Anders (1997), 'Saabs bildesign', in Lasse Brunnström (ed.), *Svensk industridesign. En 1900-talshistoria*, Stockholm: Norstedts.

Typografi Vidar Forsberg (1982), Utställningskatalog nr 89, Stockholm: Kungliga Biblioteket.

Vår bostad 1937. Röhsska Konstslöjdmuseets permanenta utställning av modern svensk konstindustri, Göteborg.

Volvo YCC (2005), Röhsska museets katalog för Torsten och Wanja Söderbergs pris nr 12, Göteborg: Röhsska museet.

Waldén, Katja (1995), 'Röster från nittio år', in *Form nr 3*. Stockholm: Föreningen Svensk Form.

Walker, John A. (1989), *Design History and the History of Design*, London: Pluto Press.

Werner, Jeff (2008), *Medelvägens estetik. Sverigebilder i USA, del I & II*, Hedemora/Möklinta: Gidlunds förlag.

Wickman, Kerstin (1991), 'Byggbart, utbytbart, flyttbart', in Monica Boman (ed.), *Svenska möbler 1890–1990*, Lund: Bokförlaget Signum.

Wickman, Kerstin (1994), 'Industridesign', in *Konstfack 150 år. Tanken och handen*, Stockholm: Page One Publishing AB.

Wickman, Kerstin (ed.) (1995), *Formens rörelse: Svensk Form genom 150 år*, Stockholm: Carlssons.

Wickman, Kerstin (1997), *Signe Persson-Melin: Keramiker och formgivare*. T & M förlag.

Wickman, Kerstin (2003), 'Design Olympics – the Milan Triennals', in *Scandinavian Design beyond the Myth* (ed. Halén and Wickman), Stockholm: Arvinius Förlag/Form Förlag.

Wickman, Kerstin (2005), 'Contact with Ulm', *Scandinavian Journal of Design History*.

Wickman, Kerstin (2007), 'En katt bland hermelinerna', in *Under ytan. En antologi om designforskning*, Stockholm: Raster förlag/SVID.

Widenheim, Cecilia (2000), 'Utopi och verklighet. Aspekter på modernismen i svensk bildkonst', in *Utopi & verklighet. Svensk modernism 1900–1960*, Stockholm: Moderna museet & Norstedts.

Widman, Dag (1963), 'Försummad vardagsvara', *Form* nr 7. Svensk slöjdföreningen.

Widman, Dag (1975), *Konsthantverk, konstindustri, design 1895–1975. Konsten i Sverige*, Stockholm: Almqvist & Wiksell.

Widman, Dag (1998), 'Pionjärår, genombrott, triumf. Ett halvt sekel av konstnärlig expansion', in Kerstin Wickman (ed.), *Orrefors. Etthundra år av svensk glaskonst*, Stockholm: Byggförlaget

Wigstrand, Hans (1999), *50 år med svensk reklam – en resumé*, Stockholm: Resumé.

Wiwen, Nilsson (1975), *Silver från 1920–30-talen*. Malmö museum, utställningskatalog.

Wollin, Nils G. (1951), *Från ritskola till konstfackskola. Konstindustriell undervisning under ett sekel*, Stockholm.

Woodham, Jonathan (1997), *Twentieth Century Design*, Oxford: Oxford University Press.

Wulff, Thorild (1966), *Resa till Kina år 1912. Dagboksanteckningar m.m. utgivna av Göran Axel-Nilsson*, Göteborg: Wettergren & Kerbers förlag.

Yasuko Suga (2004), 'Designing the Morality of Consumption: "Chamber of Horrors" at the Museum of Ornamental Art 1852–1853', *Design Issues* nr 4. Chicago: University of Illinois.

Zetterlund, Christina (2002), *Design i informationsåldern. Om strategisk design historia och praktik*, Diss., Stockholm: Raster Förlag.

Zetterlund, Christina (2005), 'Design: 1995–2005', in Kerstin Wickman (ed.), *Design: Stockholm*, Stockholm: Stockholms stadsmuseum.

Internet Addresses (2016)

www.clasohlson.se

www.babybjorn.com

www.smarttextiles.se

www.icehotel.se

www.klimatkompassen.se

www.svenskform.se

www.designarkivet.se

www.designarkiv.se

www.naringslivshistoria.se

www.landskrona.se/se-gora/kultur-noje/museerochkonsthall/museum/arkivochsamlingar/rumforreklam/

www.estrid-ericsons-stiftelse.nu

www.soderbergsstiftelser.se

www.vr.se

www.rj.se

List of Permissions

Plates

Figures

Index